Indianization

of

Rights & Duties

Indianization of Rights & Duties

Dr. Gokulesh Sharma

LL.D.

Judge,

Civil Court, Kanpur

Manas Publications

New Delhi-110 002 (INDIA)

MANAS PUBLICATIONS
(Publishers, Distributors, Importers & Exporters)
4858, Prahlad Street,
24, Ansari Road, Darya Ganj,
New Delhi - 110 002 (INDIA)
Ph.: 23260783, 23265523
Fax: 011 - 23272766
E-mail: manaspublications@vsnl.com

First Published 2003

ISBN 81-7049-164-9

Typeset at
Manas Publications

Printed in India at
SHRI BALA JI PRINT ART
and Published by Mrs Suman Lata for
Manas Publications, 4858, Prahlad Street,
Mathur Lane, 24, Ansari Road, Darya Ganj,
New Delhi - 110 002 (INDIA)

PREFACE

This temporal world is of no use without life on earth. The life is quite hopeless and cumbersome without the right to fundamental needs of society and individual. Society and individual are complementary to each other. There are certain basic and inherent right of society as well as of Individual without which no society and individual can live smoothly and the existence of both shall come under danger.

There is one gospel truth about these rights that these are universal in application throughout world. There applicationlity and enforcement is not at the wishes merely of Individuals or Government or King. Sometimes riders may be imposed but these riders on rights are not of permanent in character and they can never be so. These basic and Fundamental Rights are available to all without barrier to the boundaries of states and, cut marks of religion and various facets of languages in the world.

There are various types of governmental systems in the world. There is democracy as opposed to dictatorship. There is communism as opposed to capitalism. There are still traces of kingship and autocracy. Whatever kind of the governmental system may be for any country or state there is a direct or indirect guarantee of these basic and Fundamental Rights to the people. No state can boast even for sake of argument that their citizens are without Fundamental Rights.

Here I do admit that there are rarely exceptional states in the world, whose number cannot exceed more than two or three, where we can say that people or inhabitants of that state are not enjoying these basic and Fundamental Rights. At present the Hill and Tiny state of Afghanistan in South East Asia is an unfortunate example of it where it can be said that people are enjoying no rights at all. The life is under danger there. Peoples are leaving nation and taking shelter in neighboring countries. The government of Taliban is not recognized by states of the world.

Leaving one or two exceptions of like nature every nation has guaranteed basic and Fundamental Rights to citizens as well as to inhabitants.

I have attempted to draw a list of these basic and Fundamental Rights at world level. I have studied in detail the legal and constitutional status of at least 35 nations to reach a fair conclusion. I have collected the law of basic and Fundamental Right of these 35 nations, in a comparative table under the specific heading of Fundamental Rights as per Indian Constitution. I have also collected the position of charter of basic and Fundamental Rights at international field. Whatever is the position of these rights under U.N.O. or its agencies has also been considered in detail.

Due weight and regards have been given to the duties of Individuals and society to each other. It has been said that rights and duties are co-relative. They are complementary to each other. There are express and direct provision of fundamental duties in some nations in their constitution or otherwise. In some nations there are implied and in direct provision of these kinds of duties in the constitution or otherwise. There are few exceptional nations, which do not provide about fundamental duties directly or indirectly. I have to add here that no state or nation can exclude the role of natural law in the application to the legal provision of that nation. It is the natural law or duty of every Individual or nation to abide by the law and to keep the running of the nation smooth as per law. It, by itself provides full observance of fundamental and as well as legal duties of individual and society. The present book has dealt with Fundamental Rights and duties of individual and society in details. Full discussion in this regard has been given in due places.

The book has been divided among six chapters. The first chapter deals with the introduction of Fundamental Rights and duties among constitutions of different foreign nations at international level.

Second chapter deals with the comparative study of Fundamental Rights only at world level among different constitutions of various foreign nations. I have attempted to affix the Fundamental Rights of different foreign nations in comparison to Fundamental Rights under Indian constitution. In short the study of Fundamental Rights under Indian constitution vis-a-vis other constitutions of different foreign nations has taken place. It will show the clear-cut picture of comparison of Fundamental Rights along with these rights of different foreign nations.

Third chapter alike second one deals with the constitutional study of fundamental duties and Directive Principles at world level among different constitutions of various foreign nations. I have attempted to appeal to the readers of the book about comparison of Indian fundamental duties and Directive Principle vis-à-vis constitutions of different foreign nations. In short the complete discussion and comparative study of Indian constitution along with other foreign constitutions has been move.

Chapter four describes special situation of South East Asian countries. The complete charter of Fundamental Rights and duties of Pakistan, Nepal, China, Russia and Bangladesh has gathered momentum. I have explained provision of Fundamental Rights and duties of these South East Asian countries in details.

Fifth chapter discloses about the status of Fundamental Rights and duties under international law. Universal declaration of human rights and its several covenants have been considered minutely. Full details of these provisions have been given in brief, I can say that complete details about Fundamental Rights and duties at international level has been taken up for study here.

Lastly the conclusion has been drawn up about the book. It has been said that Fundamental Rights and duties are complimentary to each other. Certainly in Indian precept, a duty occupies more important role rather than Fundamental Rights. The conferment of human rights provisions through protection of Human Rights Act is a bold slip in this regard. The Act is very good and it covers within its ambit every kind of Fundamental Rights as well as legal rights. But I am afraid to say that the protection of Human Rights Act does not say anywhere that it is also the fundamental right of individual to carry out their work as per law. In other words the act does not direct about the enforcement of duties.

It is hereby suggested that when all kinds of human rights have been protected by the provision of the human rights of the provision under Constitution of India. Like wise the observance of duties by the individual as well as by the society should be made mandatory and compulsory. Hence it can be concluded that every individual as well as society is duty bound to comply with duties sincerely as well as to claim fundamental and legal rights in guaranteed execution. The compliance of both is essential. They are inseparable. Both rights and duties require execution in free sense.

I have tried to apprise the readers of the book about the present Fundamental Rights as well as fundamental duties in Indian precept as well as comparatively at world level. What kinds of Fundamental Rights and duties & Directive Principle are available in different nations of the world have been collected & shown in the book. The book has shown a clear-cut picture of Fundamental Rights & duties along with Directive Principal at world level at micro-base Level. It is a concise & steady study.

I have also reviewed the views of various jurists and case law of superior courts of U.K, U.S.A & other foreign nations along with the decision of Indian Supreme Court.

All issues relating to Fundamental Rights and duties have been considered in depth. All issues have been analyzed concisely and if any mistake is discovered or any other kind of omission of any provision is brought to my knowledge then I render the apologies for the same in advance. I call for suggestions from reader for further improvement of the text.

The work is dedicated to my elder brother Late Pandit Sundar Lal Sharma, whose high directives and his love to observe duties. First then to claim for rights, inspired me & persuaded me to carry out the task of completion of this book. I am highly indebted to my wife Smt. Neeta Sharma whose high co-operation to me in all fields made my way clear and I am thankful to other friends who helped me a lot and enlighten me properly to carry out this work.

Finally I am highly grateful to Mr. V.K. Garg of Manas publication who has published this book within no time in foolproof manner.

I think the book shall be greatly useful and deeply helpful for those who have due regards to the study of Fundamental Rights & duties. The book shall serve useful purpose if it is respected by public at large and considered by Judges, professors, advocates & other social workers as well as to those engaged in the field of political science. I shall highly thankful for all concerned in this regard.

Dr. Gokulesh Sharma

Judge LL.D.

Civil Court, Kanpur

CONTENTS

CONTENTS

CHAPTER 1
Introduction to Fundamental Rights and Duties under World Constitutions

The evolution of thought on Fundamental Rights has been vividly portrayed by Sapru, J. In Motilal V. Uttar Pradesh Government[1] thus:

"The history of the evolution of thought on the rights of man takes up back into the seventeenth century or even earlier from the time of Tom Paine's rights of Man, Jefferson's Declaration of rights, U.S.S.R. and the French Revolution, schools of thought have exited down to H.G. Wells and the U.N. Discussion of human right which assert that man has certain natural or inalienable rights and that it is the function of a state, in order that human liberty might be preserved and human personality developed, to give recognition and free play to those rights. Fundamental Rights were to be found in practically every constitution that comes into existence after World War I. After World War II as a result of Human Rights, they have become even more visibly important in most constitution formed after that war."

Now we should consider the real state of affairs of Fundamental Rights in various countries. Let us first start from British Empire.

1. Rights in England or English Theory

In the older constitution such as the unwritten one of England, such constitution guarantees are not specifically stated. Their availability to citizens at any time depends upon the prevailing laws, which are framed according to the exigencies of the political situation. Old constitutionalists believed that to state in writing such rights was to limit them or entrench them with reservations. They thought it was best hot to disturb the citizens' minds and hopes, which could not be fulfilled. It is safe to secure for these very rights under the ordinary law of the country. In Liversidge V. Anderson, [2] Lord Wright observed:

> "In the constitution of this country (Great Britain) there are no guarantee or absolute rights. The safeguard of British liberty is in the good sense of the people and in the system of representative government".

In the words of profession G.M. Trevelyan, "The essence of the English constitution is law, respected and enforced".

Professor Dicey had put it "In England the right to individual freedom is part of the constitution because it is inherent in the ordinary law of land; there is one which can hardly be destroyed without the thorough revolution in the institutions and manner of the nation". The rights and liberties of English men are guaranteed by their tradition and law-mostly judge made law. Though the rights of Englishmen are neither defined nor guaranteed, they do exist. There is no grant." [The law and the constitution]

The advantage in this is that these can be no suspension of such rights in England because suspension implies grant. The rights are inherent in the ordinary law of the land. National emergencies call in their aid the supremacy of parliament, which has all the power to suspend the exercise of the full liberty enjoyed by the Englishmen.

Individual liberty in England is secured by judicial decisions by resorting to "writ" or "remedies". But while courts are supreme, parliament can alter any law. No Fundamental Rights limit the power of parliament. Court is the bulwark of individual liberty against all executive excesses, but parliament is omnipotent. The right in the charters like the Magna Carta, the Bill of Rights, etc. merely declared the existing common law. These charters bound only the executive but not parliament.

In England we have:

1. The right of personal freedom secured by *habeass Corpus Acts.*
2. The right to property protected by legal remedies.
3. The right to freedom of speech or discussion so as not to infringe the law of libel, slander and defamation etc.
4. The right of public meeting short of committing nuisance or trespass upon other's property.
5. The right of association, e.g., under the Companies Act and the Trade Union Act, etc.
6. The right to trial in accordance with principles of natural justice such as the right to be heard, a reasonable opportunity to state one's case, and a man not be a judge in his own case.
7. The right to strike or to withhold his labour so there is no breach of contract, tort or crime.

In England, the check is on executive tyranny and hence all maxims of liberty and justice are to be applied against high handedness of the executive. In America, the check is both on the executive and the legislature in the matter of curtailing individual liberties. The executive in England is not subject to any body except to do in accordance with Law of parliament. Lord Atkin declared thus-

> "In accordance with British jurisprudence no member of the executive can interfere with the liberty of the, or property of a British subject except on the condition that he can support the legality of his action before a court of justice. And it is the tradition of British justice that Judges should not shrink from deciding such issues against the face of the executive".

Lord Show observed:

> "Parliament is supreme and courts have to carry out the edicts of parliament and cannot question their competence at all. The only corrective to parliament is parliament itself.
>
> "Acted upon by a fresh wave of public duty, a higher sense of duty, a wider range of experience or a broader perspective in the regions of applied justice". (American Law Review April 1911 Volume 45 page 275)

2. American Fundamental Rights : –

The sacrosanct nature of Fundamental Rights has always been preserved in America. Thus justice Miller observed in U.S.A.: -

> "There are such rights in every free government beyond the control of the state. A Govt. which recognized no such rights, which held the lives, the liberty and property of its citizens subject at all times to the absolute disposition and unlimited control of even the most democratic of power, is after all but a state despotism. It is true it is despotism of the many of the majority if you chose to call it so, but it is nonetheless a despotism." [2]

In America, Fundamental Rights are regarded as the basic human right judged by the yardstick of the "due process" clause. In this context as laid down in Meyer Vs. Nebraska [4] "Liberty" is a term of wide connotation which includes not only freedom from bodily restraint but also the right of the individual to contract. To engage in any of the common pursuits of life, to acquire useful knowledge, to marry establish a home and bring up children to worship God according to the dictates of one's conscience, and generally to enjoy those privileges long recognized as common law as essential to the orderly pursuit of happiness by free men.

In Maxwell V. Dow-[5] these Fundamental Rights are comprehensively classed as-

"Protection by the Government, the enjoyment of life and liberty with right to acquire and possess property of every kind, and to pursue and obtain happiness and safety, subject, nevertheless, to such restraints as the government may prescribe for the general good of the whole".

The language of section 2 arts IV and the 14th and 5th amendments in the U.S. constitution bring out the same idea of basic fundamental right of American citizens.

3. Other Countries

CANADA

Among the British Common Wealth countries, Canada has written constitution enabling judicial review of legislative acts. But the British North American Act does not contain many constitutional guarantees. Some provisions there are to protect the rights of the Roman Catholic and the French in Canada as also English Protestants in Quebec. Sectarian minorities are protected as also the French and English languages. But the citizen as such is not assured of specific rights, just as in English he had to seek the aid of common law and ordinary statute law.

But there are trends in Canada, which show that an intolerant majority in the legislature or the cabinet can play havoc with minority rights. These instances are the padlock law of Quebec, 1937 against communism the press bill of Alberta, the "Spyhunt" incidents of 1946,deportation of Canadian citizens of Japanese descent, etc. The remedy for these is only political action agitation and throwing out the government. If constitution guarantees had been out, resort to court could have yielded remedies.

AUSTRALIA

Australia follows the pattern of Canada, though; there are no serious minority problems as the people are all imbued with British tradition. The common Law affords all the protection. The only protective provision in the common Wealth Act of 1900 (Section 116) prohibits the Common wealth from making any law for establishing religion, or for improving any religious observance, or for prohibiting the free exercise of any religion; and it provides that no religious test shall be required as a qualification for any official or public trust under the common wealth. The move to assure further rights by the constitutional alteration (post war Reconstruction and Democratic rights) Act, 1944, did not succeed for want of approval by the electorate in a referendum.

SWITZERLAND

Switzerland is the oldest and most stable federl union. The Swiss constitution is clear about its guarantees. Article 54 assures a wife on marriage the citizenship of the commune of her husband. Article 44 prohibits expulsion of the citizen from his canton of origin. Article 55 assures liberty of the press. Necessary safeguards to prevent abuses. Freedom of association (Article 562) assurance of trial in the ordinary court of the land, abolition of ecclesiastical jurisdiction (Article 58) abolition of capital punishment (Article 45), freedom of trade, economic rights and benefits such as old age and sickness insurance (Article 48), the right to petition etc. (Article 59), the liberty of conscience and creed (Article 50), etc. are all guaranteed to the swiss citizen, whose political rights can be taken away only by federal legislation within the prescribed limits (Article 66).

EIRE

Ireland provides all the safeguards for her citizens. There is a guarantee of liberty to the citizen subject only to public order and morality. Freedom of speech, right to form association are all guarantee subject only to public order and morality. No discrimination on the score to political creed, religion or class is countenanced as per-section 40. Sex is no bar to citizenship (Section 9). Equality before law is assured (Section 40). Private ownership is recognized (Section 43). The institution is protected and no law can be passed for grant of dissolution of marriage (Section 41). There are also directive principles of social policy set up (Section 45).

Trial by jury is assured (section 38). Personal liberty cannot be taken away except in accordance with law (section 40). The dwelling of citizen is inviolable.

SOVIET RUSSIA

Chapter VI (33 to 38) and VII (39 to 69) of the constitution of U.S.S.R 1977 as amended up-to-date, prescribes equality of citizens rights and basic rights, freedoms and duties of citizens of U.S.S.R in brief-

Soviet Russia presents a single union citizens are afforded asylum when they seek protection from prosecution for defending the interests of the working class or for their scientific activities or their struggle for national liberation (Article 38). The people's assessors participate in all court except where it is otherwise prescribed by law (Article 52). There is always a public trial and the right to be defended by counsel except where prohibited by law (Article 51). The citizen is assured freedom of speech, freedom of press, freedom of assembly and freedom of procession and demonstrations but these should be in conformity with the interests of the working people (Article 39 and 50). Inviolability of person is assured and there can be no arrest except by decision of court or with the sanction of a procurator (Article 54). The inviolability of the home and privacy in correspondence is guaranteed (Article 44 and 56) women have equal rights and all benefits appertaining their needs and sex (Article 53). Article 36 assures equality of rights to citizens irrespective of their nationality or race in all spheres of economic, state, cultural and political life. The rights to vote for all persons above 18 years are clear (Article 95).

The economic structure of the state is built by the socialist system of owning instruments of production by the republic private property is however, allowed within a limit (Art. 54 and 57) capitalism is buried while labour is encouraged. Inheritance to private property is protected (Art. 57). The principle is "He who does not work, neither shall he Eat" It is socialism from each according to his ability, to each according to his work (Art. 40) employment is guaranteed and also payment according to quantity and quality (Art. 118). Right to leisure, maintenance in old age, and also when sick or incapacitated for work, are all recognized (Arts. 41,42 and 43). Freedom to worship and freedom to do anti religious propaganda are both assured (Art., 52). Right to education (Art. 45) is assured. Military service for defense of the fatherland is compulsory (Article 62 and 63).

Like the constitution of U.S.S.R. these rights have been adopted with out any reservation by the constitution of People's Republic of China. Chapter III enumerates these rights entitled as "Fundamental Rights and duties of citizens. The social and economic rights are enumerated in art. 86(2), 91, 92, 93 and 96. The constitution of Spanish Republic, Philippines and Ireland had included economic as well as social rights of the citizens as a whole.

NOTES

1. AIR 1954 All 257.
2. Eshugbaryi V. Govt. of Nigeria, A.I.R. 1931 P.C. 248.
3. Savings and Loans Association V. Jopeka (1875) 22 Law Ed. 455 (461).
4. (1923) 262 US 390.
5. (1900) 44 Law Fil. 597.

CHAPTER 2

Comparative Study of Fundamental Rights Under World Constitutions

Generally all democratic countries have a written or un-written Constitution with a special guarantee to people about Fundamental Rights. Even non-democratic countries guarantee Fundamental Rights to people just to show society at large that they have regard and respect for the Fundamental Rights of human beings. Today's position is that roughly all modern Constitutions of countries who are Members of UNO have a provision of Fundamental Rights, either directly or indirectly.

Let us now consider a comparative table of Indian Fundamental Rights along with a complete study of Fundamental Rights and analogous provisions of Constitutions of foreign countries.

I am placing an Article-wise study of Fundamental Rights of the Indian Constitution along with a study of corresponding Fundamental Rights under Foreign Constitutions as follows:

Article 14

1. *Equality before law:* The State shall not deny to any person equality before the law or the equal protection of the laws within the territory of India.

Foreign Constitutions

USA: Section 1 of the 14th Amendment. "No state shall... deny to any person within its jurisdiction the equal protection of the Laws."

Eire: Section 40 (1): "All citizens shall, as human persons, be held equal before law."

This does not mean that the State shall not in its enactments have due regard to differences of capacity — physical and moral and social function.

Burma: Section 13: "All citizens irrespective of birth, religion, sex or race are equal before law; that is to say, there shall not be any arbitrary discrimination between one citizen or class of citizens and another."

Argentina: Article 16 prohibits the prerogative of blood or of birth, personal privileges and titles of nobility. All inhabitants are equal before the law and if they satisfy the requirements of fitness they are all equally admissible for employment. Taxation is equal as also public burdens.

Chile, Article 10: All inhabitants of the Republic are assured equality before the law and also practice of all beliefs, liberty and conscience and the free exercise of all religious that may not be contrary to morality, good usage or to public order. No privileged class is recognized nor any form of slavery. Any alien who does slave traffic cannot live in Chile nor be naturalized in the republic.

Nicaragua: Article 106 treats all Nicaraguans as equal before the law except in regard to women on account of the differences inherent in their nature or where the good of the family is concerned. Article 107 denies all privileges by reason of birth, nobility, race or social status.

Uruguay: Article 8 guarantees that all persons are equal before the law, no other difference being recognized among them other than that of talent or virtue.

Australia: In Australia the Constitution does not, like that of USA, attempt any comprehensive guarantee of individual rights or liberty. Most of its prohibitions and restrictions relate to distribution of power between the commonwealth and the states, (e.g., Sections 90,114,115) or to the maintenance of the federal structure (e.g. Sections 92,99,114,117), though individuals may benefit from the operation of these sections. Some kinds of rights can be read through Sections 51 (XXXI), 80 and 116. Section 51 (XXXI) provides for laws regarding acquisition of property on just terms. Free exercise of religion is guaranteed under section 116, which prohibits any law antagonistic to such free exercise. Under the doctrine of implied immunity of instrumentalities the commonwealth was prohibited from discriminating against States. It could not interfere with banking inside a State under colour of the Commonwealth Banking Act, 1945.

The Law of Non-Discrimination

Article 15

Prohibition of discrimination on grounds of religion, race, caste, sex or place of birth:

1. The State shall not discriminate against any citizen on any rounds listed above.
2. No citizen shall, on grounds only of religion, race, caste, sex, place of birth or any of those above, be subject to any disability, liability restriction or condition with regard to:
   (a) Access to shops, public restaurants, hotels and places of public entertainment.
   (b) The use of wells, tanks, bathing ghats, roads, and places of public resort maintained wholly or partly out of State Funds or dedicated to the use of the general public.
3. Nothing in this Article shall prevent the state from making any special provision for women and children.
4. Nothing in this Article or in clause (2) of Article 29 shall prevent the state from making any special provision for educationally backward classes of citizens or for the Scheduled Castes and the Scheduled Tribes.

Foreign Constitutions

USA: The 15th Amendment (1870), Section 1, runs:

"The right of the citizens of the united States to vote shall not be denied or abridged by the United States or by any state on account of race, colour or previous condition."

"The right of citizens of the United States to vote shall not be denied or abridged by the United States or by any state on account of sex."

Australia: Section 117 of the Constitution Act postulates:

"A subject of the queen, a resident in any state shall not be subject in any other State to any disability or discrimination which may not be applicable to him if he were a subject of the queen resident in such other State."

Switzerland: Article 60 of the Constitution states:

> "Every canton is bound to accord to the citizens of the other confederated States the same treatment as to its own citizens in regard to legislation and judicial proceedings."

Equality is further assured by Article 4, which says:

> "In Switzerland there are no subjects; nor any privileges of rank, birth, person or family."

Japan: Non-discrimination and equality in the eyes of law is assured by Article 14 which states:

> "...There shall be no discrimination in political economic, or social relations because of race, creed, sex, social status or family origin."

Equality of opportunity in matters of public employment

Article 16

1. There shall be equality of opportunity for all citizens in matters relating to employment or appointment to any office under the State.
2. No citizen shall, on grounds only of religion, race, caste, sex, descent, or place of birth be discriminated against in respect of any employment or office under the State.
3. Nothing in this Article shall prevent parliament from making any law prescribing, in regard to a class or classes of employment or appointment to an office under the government of, or any local or other authority within, a state or union territory prior to such employment or appointment.
4. Nothing in this Article shall prevent the state from making any provisions for the reservation of appointments or posts in favour of any backward class of citizens, which, in the opinion of the state, is not adequately represented in the services under the state.

4-A: Nothing in this article shall prevent the state from making any provision for reservation in matters of promotion to any class or classes of posts in the services under the State in favour of the Scheduled Castes and see P. 26 in the services under the State.]

4-B: Nothing in this article shall prevent the state from considering any unfilled vacancies of a year which are reserved for being filled up in that year in accordance with any provision for reservation made under clause (4) or clause (4-A) as a separate class of vacancies to be filled up in any succeeding year or years and such class of vacancies shall not be considered together with the vacancies of the year in which they are being filled up for determining the ceiling of fifty percent reservation on total number of vacancies of that year. Constitutional Amendment 85th 2002, has multified the effect of Supreme Court Judgement of 17.6.95 by which the court had prohibited reservation in matter of promotion in government jobs.

5. Nothing in this Article shall affect the operation of any law which provides that the incumbent of an office in connection with the affairs of any religious or denominational institution or any member of the governing body thereof shall be a person professing a particular religion or belonging to a particular denomination.

Foreign Constitutions

United States of America: Article VI, Section 3, of the U.S. Constitution runs:

"...No religious test shall be required as a qualification to any office or public trust under the United States.

Australia: Section 116 of the Australian Constitution Runs:

"...No religious test shall be required as a qualification for any office or public trust under the commonwealth."

Burma: Section 14 of the Burmese Constitution States:

"...There shall be equality of opportunity for all citizens in matters of public employment and in the exercise of carrying on any occupation, trade, business or profession."

Government of India Act, 1935:

Section 275 says, "A person shall not be disqualified by sex, for being appointed to any occupation or be ineligible for office under the crown in India."

Article 17

Abolition of untouchability: - Untouchability is abolished and its practice in any form is forbidden. The enforcement of any disability arising out of untouchability shall be an offence punishable in accordance with Law. There is no parallel to this in any other Constitution unless one draws the analogy of the Negroes of South Africa.

Article 18

Abolition of Titles:

1. No titles, not being a Military or Academic distinction shall be conferred by the state.
2. No citizen of India shall accept any titles from any foreign State.
3. No person who is not a citizen of India shall, while he holds any office of profits or trust under the state, accept, without the consent of the president, any title from any foreign state.
4. No person holding any office of profit or trust under the State shall, without the consent of the president, accept any present, emoluments, or office of any kind from or under any foreign state.

Foreign Constitutions

United States of America: Article 1 Section 9—No title of nobility shall be granted by the United States. And no person holding any office of profit or trust shall, without consent of the congress, accept any present emoluments, office or title of any kind whatever, from any king, prince, or foreign State.

Japan: Article 14 — Peers and peered shall not be recognized. No privilege shall accompany any award of whichever decoration, or any other restriction nor shall any such award be valid beyond the lifetime of individuals who hold it and hereafter may receive it.

Eire Land: Section 40 (2) — Titles of nobility shall not be conferred by the state. No title of nobility or however may be accepted by any citizen except with the prior approval of the government.

Article 19

Protection of certain rights regarding freedom of speech, etc.:

1. All citizens shall have the right:
   a. To freedom of speech and expression;
   b. To assemble peaceably and without arms;
   c. To form associations or unions;
   d. To move freely throughout the territory of India;
   e. To reside and settle in any part of the territory of India;
   f. To practice any profession, or to carry on any occupation, trade or business.

2. Nothing in sub-clause 9(a) of clause (i) shall affect the operation of any existing law, or prevent the state from making any law, in so far as such a law impose reasonable restrictions on the exercise of the right conferred by the said sub-clause in the interests of (the sovereignty/integrity of India) the security of the state, friendly relations with foreign states, public order, decency or morality or in relation to contempt to court, defamation or incitement to an offence).
3. Nothing in sub-clause (b) of the said clause shall affect the operation of any existing law in so far as it imposes, or prevents the state from making any law imposing, in the interests of the sovereignty and integrity of India or public order, reasonable restrictions on the exercise of the right conferred by the said sub-clause.
4. Nothing in sub-clause (c) of the said clause shall affect the operation of any existing law in so far as it imposes or prevents the state from making any law imposing, in the interests of (the sovereignty and integrity of India or) public order or morality, reasonable restriction on the exercise of the right conferred by the said sub-clause.
5. Nothing in sub-clause (d) and (d) of the said clause shall affect the operation of any existing law in so far as it imposes or prevents the state from making any law imposing reasonable restriction on the exercise of any of the rights conferred by the said sub-clause either in the interests of any scheduled tribe.
6. Nothing in sub-clause (g) of the said clause shall affect the operation of any existing law in so far as it imposes, or prevents the state from making any law (i) imposing, in the interests of the general public, reasonable restrictions on the exercise of the right conferred by the said sub-clause, and in particular, (nothing in the said sub-clause shall affect the operation of any existing law in so far as it relates to, or prevents the state from making any law relating to (i) the professional or technical qualification necessary for practicing any profession or carrying on any occupation, trade or business, or (ii) carrying on by the state or by a corporation owned or controlled by the state, of any trade, business, industry or service, whether to the exclusion, complete or partial, of citizens or otherwise).

   Article 19 has following corresponding provision of Foreign Constitutions:

The Seven Freedoms and their Limitations

Freedom of speech and expression and restrictions thereon:

(a) *Clause 1 and 2 of Article 19, Corresponding provision of Foreign Constitutions*

United Nations: Article 17 of the United Nations Declarations of Human Rights postulates:

> "Every one has the right to freedom of opinion and expression, this right includes the freedom to hold opinion without interference and to seek, receive and import information and ideas, through any media and regardless of frontiers."

USA: The first amendment to the Constitution (1791) states:

> "The congress shall make no laws abridging the freedom of speech or of the press."

Germany: Article 188 of the Weimar Constitution 1919 postulated:

> "Every German has the right within the limits of general laws to express his opinion freely by word of mouth, writing, printed matter or picture, or in any conditions of his work or appointment and no one is permitted to injure him on account of his making use of such rights."
>
> "No censorship shall be enforced, but restrictive regulations may be introduced by law in reference to cinematographic entertainments. Legal measures are also admissible for the purpose of combating bad and obscene literature as well as for the protection of youth in public exhibitions and performances."

Eire: Section 40 (6) (1) of the Constitution of Eire-States:

> "The state guarantees liberty for the exercise of the following rights subject to public order and morality"

The right of the citizens to express freely their convictions and opinions..."

The education of public opinion being, however, a matter of such grave "import to the common good, the state shall endeavour that organs of public opinions such as the radio, the press, the cinema, while preserving their rightful liberty of expression, including criticism of governmental policy, shall not be used to undermine public order or morality or the authority of the state. the publication or utterance of blasphemous seditious or indecent matter is an offence which shall be punishable in accordance with law."

France: The preamble to the Constitution of the Fourth France Republic (1789) declares:

> "No one should be disturbed on account of his opinions, even religious, provided their manifestation does not derange the public order established by law."

> "The free communication of ideas and opinion is one of the most precious of the rights of men. Every citizen, then, can freely speak, write and print, subject to responsibility for the abuse of this freedom in cases determined by law."

Burma: In Article 17(j) of the Constitution of the Union of Burma (1918) we have:

There shall be liberty for the exercise of the following rights, subject to law, public order and morality:

(1) The right of the citizens to express freely their convictions and opinions.

Japan: Article XXI of the Japanese Constitution declares:

> "Freedom of assemblies association, speech and press and all other forms of expression are guaranteed. No censorship shall be maintained nor shall the secrecy of any means of communication be violated."

Federation of Nigeria: Section 25 promulgated on 1.10.1963 guarantees freedom of expression thus:

1. Every person shall be entitled to freedom of expression including freedom to hold opinions and to receive and impart ideas and information without interference.
2. Nothing in this section shall invalidate any law that is reasonably justifiable in a democratic society:
   (a) In the interests of defence, public safety public order, public morality or public health.
   (b) For the purpose of protecting the rights, reputations and freedom of other persons, preventing the disclosure of information received in confidence, maintaining the authority and independence of the courts or regulating telephone, wireless broad-casting, television, or the exhibition of cinematographic films or;
   (c) Imposing restrictions upon persons holding office under the state, members of the armed forces of the Federation or members of a police Force."

Australia: The freedom of speech protected by section 92 of the Constitution of Australia as laid down in James VX, does not mean free speech. It means speech hedged in by all the laws against defamation, blasphemy, citizen and so forth.

Some common rights guaranteed by other Constitutions. They may be catalogued thus:

(a) Privacy of correspondence:

i. Federal Republic of Germany (Article 10)
ii. Nicaragua (Article 110)
iii. Costa Rica (Article 24)
iv. Rumania (Article 33)
v. Czechoslovakia (Article 6)
vi. Korea (Article 4).

(b) Right of petitioning to public authorities

i. Germany (Article 17)
ii. Luxemburg (Article 27)
iii. Korea (Article 21)
iv. Costa Rica (Article 31)
v. Rumania (Article 35)
vi. Czechoslovakia (Article 23)

(c) Sanctuary offered for victims of political persecution:

i. Costa Rica (Article 31)
ii. Rumania (Article 35).

(d) Extradition of nationals to a foreign power prohibited:

i. Nicaragua (Article 50)

(e) Right to work:

i. Rumania (Article 19)
ii. Korea (Article 17).
iii. Luxemburg (Article 10)
iv. Czechoslovakia (Article 26).

(f) Right to leisure:

i. Rumania (Article 22)
ii. Czechoslovakia (Article 12).
iii. Germany (Article 16)

(g) Right to education:

i. Rumania (Article 22)

ii. Czechoslovakia (Article 12).

(h) Miscellaneous rights:

i. Asylum to debtors—Norway (Article 103)
ii. Usury prohibited—Nicaragua (Article 80)
iii. No person imprisoned for debt—Costa Rica (Article 38)
iv. One and the same judge shall not act as such for various stages of proceedings for decision of one and the same point—Costa Rica (Article 42).
v. Right to receive just remuneration for work done—Czechoslovakia (Article 27).

Other Countries

1. It may be pointed out that the Costa Rica Constitution Article 28 prohibits the carrying on of political propaganda by making use of religious beliefs while Article 30 guaranteed free assets to administrative departments for the purpose of obtaining information on matters of public interest. The Rumanian Constitution in Article 31 guarantees freedom to hold processions and demonstration while Article 17 postulates that propagation of racial or national hatred is punishable by law. Article 100 of the Norwegian Constitution enjoins the liberty of the press. It cannot be used where the person exercising the right intentionally or clearly shows or incites others to show disobedience to the laws, contempt of religion or morality or of the Constitutional authorities or resistance to their orders or has made false accusations against any person. An interesting provision is found in Article 24 of the Luxemburg Constitution that no security shall be exacted from authors, publishers, or printers and that they shall not be prosecuted if the author is a Luxemburg national and domiciles there.
2. ***China:*** In the Republic of China, no publication shall carry speeches or propaganda calculated to undermine or violate the three peoples' principles or overthrow the National Government or damage the interest of the Chinese Republic or disturb the public order. Discussion of a court case which is pending, is prohibited.

3. ***Norway:*** There is liberty of press. No person will be punished for any writing, whatever its contents may be, which he has caused to be printed for published unless he wilfully and manifestly has either himself shown contempt of religion or morality or the Constitutional powers or resistance to their orders or has advanced false and defamatory accusations against other persons.
4. ***Sweden:*** Publication which contains abusive, offensive or provocative pronouncements, regarding contemporary Nations or States with which Sweden is in friendly relations, their sovereign Government or higher officials etc. is also liable to confiscation and is also punishable.

Freedom of Assembly and Restrictions thereon

(b) Article 19 (1) (b) and Clause (3) Corresponding provision of Foreign Constitutions

USA: The first Amendment states:

"The Congress shall make no law…abridging…the right of people peaceably to assemble." The 14th Amendment guarantees to protect the above right. "No state shall make or enforce any law which shall abridge the privileges or immunities of the citizen of the United States, nor shall any State deprive any person of life, liberty, or property without due process of law nor deny to any person within its jurisdiction the equal protection of laws.

Eire: Section 40 (6) (1) of the Constitution postulates that the State guarantees liberty for the exercise of the right of the citizen to assemble peaceably and without arms.

Provision may be made by law to prevent or control meetings which are determined in accordance with law to be calculated to cause breach of the peace or to be in danger or nuisance to the vicinity of either house of the parliament.

Burma: Section 17 (11) of its Constitution states: "There shall be liberty in the exercise of the right to assemble, subject to law, public order and morality.

Japan: Article XXI postulates that the rights of assembly … are guaranteed.

Germany: Article 8 lays down that in case of open-air meetings the right to assemble may be limited by legislation.

Czechoslovakia: Article 24 states that the right of assembly cannot be exercised so as to endanger the popular democratic system of public peace and order.

Rumania: Article 21 states that freedom of press, of speech, of assembly and freedom to hold meetings, processions and demonstrations are guaranteed.

(c) Freedom of association and unions—Restrictions thereon. Article 19, Clause 1 (c) and clause 4 have following corresponding provision of Foreign Constitutions

USA: No specific guarantee in the Constitution but law prohibiting them is one of judicial growth.

Eire: Article 46 (6) extends the guarantee subject to public order and morality.

> "The right of citizens to form associations and unions is guaranteed. Laws however, may be enacted for the regulation and control in public interest of the exercise of the right but it shall not contain political religious or class distinction.

Burma : Article 17 (3)—Subject to law, public order and morality, the right of the citizens to form associations and unions. Any association or organization whose object or activity is intended or likely to undermine the Constitution is forbidden.

Germany: Article 9—All Germans have the right to form unions, societies, and associations, not contrary to the notions of international understanding and forbidden by Law.

Costa Rica: Article 25 postulates that no one may be forced to join any association.

Rumania: Article 32 prohibits the associations of a fascist or anti-democratic nature. Otherwise the right of associations and organizations is guaranteed to citizens.

Luxemburg: Article 26 states that the founding of religious corporations may be authorized by law.

Korea: Article 18 entitles workers to share in profits.

Czechoslovakia: Article 24 postulates the right of assembly and association are guaranteed in so far as they do not endanger the popular democratic system or public peace and order. The exercise of such rights may be governed by law. Article 25 states that for the protection of their rights, employees may associate in the United Trade Union and are entitled to defend their interest through it. The United Trade Unions are assured of extensive participations in the control of the National Economy. The interest of the persons employed in individual work and offices are represented by the United Trade Union Organization.

***Hungary*:** Article 56 states the guarantee of the right of associations for the purposes of developing the social, economic, and cultural activities of the workers.

Pakistan: Fundamental Right No. 7 reads:

> "Every person shall have the right to form association or unions subject to any reasonable restriction imposed by law in the interest of morality or public order."

(d) Freedom of Movement and residence and restrictions thereon—Article 19 Clause 1 (d) and (e) and clause 5. Corresponding provision of Foreign Constitutions.

USA: No specific guarantee. It is covered by Section 1, 14th Amendment of the Constitution.

Czechoslovakia: Section 7 enunciates:

1. Every citizen may reside or sojourn in any place within the Czechoslovak Republic. The right may only be limited in the public interest in virtue of the law.
2. The right to emigrate abroad only may be limited in the virtue of the Law.

Germany: Article 11 states:

1. All Germans enjoy freedom of movement throughout the federal territory.
2. This right shall only be restricted by legislation, where lack of adequate means of existence would involve a special burden on the community or where it is necessary for the protection of youth against neglect, for combating the risk of epidemic or for the prevention of punishable acts.

Article III of the German Reich is worded thus:

> "All Germans enjoy the right of exchange of domicile within the whole Reich. Every one has the right to stay in any part of the realm that he chooses, to settle there, acquire landed property and pursue any means of livelihood."

Switzerland: Article 45 provides:

> "Every Swiss citizen has the right to settle in any part of Switzerland, subject to the production of a certificate of origin or similar document. The right of settlement may, by way of exception, be refused to or withdrawn from persons who have been deprived of their civic rights as the result of a penal conviction. The right of Settlement may also be withdrawn from persons who have been repeatedly sentenced for grave misdemeanours and from persons who become a permanent burden upon public charity, and whose commune or canton of origin refuses to provide adequate assistance for them after having been officially requested to provide it. In cantons in which domiciliary relief is provided, permission for settlement may be made conditional, in case of citizens of the canton, upon the person being capable of work and not having a permanent charge upon public charity in their former domicile in the canton of origin. The canton in which a Swiss citizen settles may not require from him any security or impose any special charge upon him in respect of each settlement. Similarly, communes may not impose on Swiss citizens domiciled within their area any charges other than those imposed upon their own citizens."

Dazing: Article 75 provides:

> "All nationals shall enjoy freedom of movement within the free city and shall have the right to stay and to settle at any place they may choose, to acquire real property and to earn their living in any way. The right shall not be curtailed without legal sanctions."

Japan: Article XXII states:

> "Every person shall have freedom to choose and change his residence and to choose his occupation to the extent that it does not interfere with the public welfare."

Yugoslavia: It is provided that:

> "No citizen may be expelled from one part of the country to another nor obliged to reside in a specified place save in such cases as may be expressly determined by law, No person may in any circumstances be expelled from his domicile without sentence by a court."

Burma: Article 17 (IV) provides:

> "Subject to law, public order and morality, the right of every citizen to reside and settle in any part of the Union is guaranteed."

Rumania: Article 28:

> "The individual liberty of the citizen is guaranteed."

The freedom of movement and residence is deemed to be included in the guarantee of the individual liberty of the citizen unless there is a lawful prohibition relating to movement or residence.

Nicaragua: Article 55 guarantees

> "The right to move in any country. There is both the right to emigrate and immigrate."

Korea: Article 10 states:

> "All citizens shall be free from 'limit residence', restrictions on domicile or restrictions on change of domicile."

Freedom of property and acquisition—holding and disposition, and restrictions thereon

Article 19 (1) (f) and (5). This freedom has been deleted from the list of Fundamental Rights. Now it is a simple legal right under Article 300-A of the Constitution. But corresponding provisions of Foreign Constitutions are as follows.

USA: The 14th Amendment states, "...Nor shall any state deprive any person of life liberty or property without due process of law." The 5th Amendment states:

> "No person shall be...deprived of life, liberty or property without due proceed of law, nor shall private property be taken for public use without just compensations."

Eire: Article 43 postulates:

i. The State acknowledges that man in virtue of his rational being, has the natural right, antecedent to positive law, to the private ownership of external goods.

   The State accordingly guarantees to pass no law attempting to abolish the right of private ownership or the general right to transfer, bequeath and inherit property.

ii. a) The State recognizes however that the exercise of the rights mentioned in the foregoing provisions of the Article ought, in civil society, to be regulated by the principles of social justice.

b) The State accordingly may, as occasion arises, delimit by law the exercise of the said rights with a view to reconciling their exercise with the exigencies of the common good."

Burma: Article 17 (iv) guarantees to every citizen the right to acquire property subject to law, public order and morality."

The Government of India Act (1935) Section 298 of the Act postulated:

1. "No subject of his majesty domiciled in India shall on grounds only of religion, place of birth, descent, colour or any of them...be prohibited on any such grounds from acquiring, holding or disposing of property or carrying on any occupation, trade, business or profession in India."
2. "Nothing in this section shall affect the operation of any law which prohibits, either absolutely or subject to exceptions, the sale or mortgage of agricultural land situated in any particular area and owned by a person belonging to some class of persons engaged in or connected with agriculture in that area, to any person not belonging to that class."

Virginia: Article 1 postulates:

"That all men are by nature equally free and independent and have certain inherent rights of which, when they enter into a state of society, they cannot by any compact, deprive or divest their posterity, namely the enjoyment of life and liberty with the means of acquiring and possessing property and obtaining happiness and safety."

France: Article XVII states:

"The right to property being inviolable and sacred, no one ought to be deprived of it, except in cases of evident public necessity, legally ascertained and on condition of a previous just indemnity."

Rumania: Article 7 postulates:

The common property of the people constitutes the material basis of the economic progress and national independence of the Rumanian People's Republic. It is the duty of all citizens to protect and develop the common property of the people. Article 8—Private property and the right to inherent property are recognized and guaranteed by law. Private property acquired by work and thrift enjoys special protection.

Article 9

The land belongs to those who till. The state protects property based on peasant's work. It encourages and assists village cooperation.

In order to stimulate agricultural progress, the state may create agricultural undertakings owned by the state.

Article 10

Expropriations for reasons of public utility may be made in virtue of a law, on payment of just compensation determined by the judiciary.

Czechoslovakia:

Section 8

Subject to the general provisions of law, every citizen may acquire fixed and other property in any place in the Czechoslovakia Republic and carry on a gainful occupation there.

Section 9

1. Private ownership may only be restricted by law.
2. Expropriation may only take place in virtue of the law and on payment of compensation, unless it is laid down by law that compensation shall not be payable.
3. No person shall misuse the right of property to the detriment of the community.

Federal Republic of Germany (old): Basic law for the Federal Republic, dated 23 May, 1949.

Section 14 states:

1. "Property and the right of inheritance are guaranteed. The scope and limits shall be determined by the laws".
2. "Property involves responsibilities. It must be used so as to serve the general good at the same time."
3. "Expropriation is only permissible for the good of the community. It can only be affected by legislation, or in virtue of a law, prescribing the nature and amount of compensation...."

Hungary: *Section 8.*

1. The Constitution recognizes and protects all property acquired by work.
2. Private property and private enterprise must not be harmful to the public interest.
3. The Constitution guarantees the right of inheritance.

Germany: *Section 22.*

1. Property is guaranteed by the Constitution. The scope and limitations of ownership are determined by the laws and social obligations towards the community.
2. The right of inheritance as regulated by civil law is guaranteed. The share of the State in the inheritance is prescribed by law.

Section 23.

Property restrictions and expropriations can only be imposed for the good of the community and in virtue of a law. They shall be accompanied by suitable compensation unless the law otherwise determines.

Costa Rica: Article 44 states: Property shall be inviolable; no one shall be deprived of the property save in the public interest lawfully proved and with prior compensation in conformity with the law. In case of war or internal disorder, it is not necessary that compensation should precede, provided the payment must be made within two years after the end of the emergency.

The Legislative Assembly may, for reasons of public necessity, by a vote of two thirds of its members, impose limitations on property in the social interest.

VI The freedom of profession, trade, etc. and restrictions thereon: Article 19 (1) (g), 19 (6)

Corresponding Foreign Constitutions

Burma: Article 17 (iv) holds:

> "Subject to law, public order and morality, the right to follow any occupation, trade, business or profession"

Switzerland: Article 31 guarantees "freedom of trade and industry throughout the confederation," but reserves the following to the state, viz., salt and gunpowder monopolies, federal duties, import duties of wine and other alcoholic beverages.

Germany: Article 12 States:

"All Germans have the right of free choice of occupation, place of employment and place of training. The pursuit of an occupation may be regulated by legislation. No one shall be forced to do a particular job except in virtue of an established general obligation to perform a public service lying equally upon all."

Nicaragua: Article 82 of the 1948 Constitution extends a guarantee to citizens the right to freely adopt any profession industry or trade not contrary to morality, public health or security.

Rumania: Article 19 postulates:

"All citizens have the right to work. The state gradually secures the full exercise of this right by the planned organization and development of the national economy."

Czechoslovakia: Article 26 declares:

1. All citizens have the right to work.
2. His work is secured in particular by organization of work directed by the state in accordance with a planned economy.

Article 27 states:

1. All working members of the population possess the right to just remuneration for the work done.
2. This right is secured by the state wages policy, which is administered with the United Trade Union Organization and directed towards the constant raising of standards of living of the working population.
3. Remuneration shall be governed by the quality and quantity of the work and by the benefit which it brings to the community.
4. In equal conditions, men and women are entitled to equal remuneration for equal work.

Hungary: Article 9 States:

1. In the Hungarian People's Republic, labour is the foundation of the social order.
2. Every able-bodied citizen has the right and the duty to work to the best of his ability, and is bound in honour to do so.
3. By their labour, by participation in work competitions, by strengthening labour discipline and improving working methods, the workers serve the cause of building up socialism.
4. The Hungarian People's Republic strives to apply in practice the socialist principle: "From each according to his ability, to each according to his work."

Costa Rica: Article 56 postulates:

> "Work is the right of the individual and an obligation towards society. The state must ensure that all have an honest and useful occupation which is properly paid and must prevent such occupation from giving rise to conditions which in any way impair the liberty or dignity of the individual or reduce labour to the level of a mere commodity. The state guarantees the right to a free choice of employment."

USA: There is no specific provision in the Constitution of the United States guaranteeing the right of freedom of profession or freedom of trade, occupation, etc. The 14th Amendment assuring the citizens that no state shall deprive any person of life, liberty or property without due process of any contains the guarantee to the individual freedom to practice any profession or trade he chooses.

Protection in respect of conviction for offences

Article 20

1. No person shall be convicted of any offence except for a violation of a law in force at the time of the commission of the act charged as an offence, nor be subjected to a penalty greater than that which might have been inflicted under the law in force at the time of the commission of the offence.
2. No person shall be prosecuted and punished for the same offence more than once.
3. No person accused of any offence shall be compelled to be a witness against himself.

Foreign Constitutions

USA: Article 9 (3) postulates:

> "No ex post facto law shall be passed."
>
> "No person shall be...subject for the same offence to be twice put in jeopardy of life or limb...No person shall be compelled in any criminal case to be a witness against himself."

Eire: Article 15 (5) says:

> "The Oireachtas shall not declare acts to be infringements of the law which were not so at the date of their commission."

Burma: Article 24 states:

> "No person shall be convicted of crime except for violation of a law in force at the time of commission of the act charged as an offence nor shall he be subject to a penalty greater than that applicable at the time of the commission of the offence."

Japan: Article 39 says:

> "No person shall be held criminally liable for an act which was lawful at the time it was committed."
>
> "No person shall be held criminally liable for an act... of which he has acquitted nor shall be in any way be placed in double jeopardy."
>
> "No person shall be compelled to testify against himself."

Czechoslovakia: Article 35 says:

> "Penalties may only be provided or imposed in virtue of the law."

Costa Rica: Article 34 reads—"No law shall be given retrospective effect to the prejudice of any person or of his vested property rights or of any judicial situation."

Article 36—"In Criminal matters, no one shall be compelled to be a witness against himself, or against his spouse, parents, children or collateral relatives of blood or marriage up to the third degree."

Article 42—One and the same judge shall be not act as such at different stages of proceedings for the decision of one and the same point. No one shall be tried more than once for the same offence."

Government of India Act, 1935!

1. No provision existed prohibiting ex post facto laws.
2. No Provision existed regarding autrefois convict or autrefois acquit. But Section 403 of the Criminal Procedure Code, embodied the principle of autrefois convict or autrefois acquit.

The legislature was competent to pass ex post facto laws under the act of 1935. But courts were loath to lean in favour of retrospective operation. United Nations—Article 11 (2) postulates:

> "No one shall be held guilty of any penal offence on account of any act or omission which did not constitute a penal offence, under national or international law at the time when it was committed. Nor shall a heavier penalty be imposed than one that was applicable at the time the penal offence was committed."

Article 21

Protection of life and personal liberty—No person shall be deprived of his life or personal liberty except according to procedure established by law.

Corresponding Foreign Constitutions:

USA: The 5th Amendment to the 1791 Constitution of USA says:

"No personal shall be... deprived of his life, liberty or property without due process of law" (with reference to federal power).

The 14th Amendment (with reference to states)

"Nor shall any state deprive any person of life.

Japan: Article XXXI says:

> "No person shall be deprived of his personal liberty nor shall any other criminal penalty be imposed, except according to procedure established by law."

Eire: Article 40 (4) reads:

> "No citizen shall be deprived of his personal liberty save in accordance with law."

Burma: Article 16 states:

> "No citizen shall be deprived of his personal liberty, nor his dwelling entered nor his property confiscated save in accordance with law."

Rumania: Article 28 provides:

> "The individual liberty of the citizens is guaranteed. No person shall be arrested and detained for more than 48 hours without a warrant from the department of prosecutions from the examining authorities appointed by law or an authorization from the courts in conformity with the provisions of the law."

Article 29 states:

> "The home is inviolable. No person shall enter a citizen's home or residence without his consent save in his presence and in virtue of a written order from the competent authority or if the citizen is caught in the act of committing an offence."

Article 30 states:

"No person shall be condemned and suffer any penalty save in virtue of a judicial decision pronounced in conformity with the law."

Czechoslovakia: Article 2 says (1): "personal freedom is guaranteed. It may be limited or withdrawn only in virtue of the law."

Article 3 states:

1. No person shall be tried except in the cases laid down by the law and then only by a court or authority competent under the manner prescribed by law.
2. Unless caught in the act of committing an offence no person shall be arrested except on the written order of a judge, reason therefore. The order shall be delivered at the time of arrest or if this is not possible within 18 hours there after.
3. No person shall be taken into custody by a public official except in the cases prescribed by law; he must then be either released within 48 hours or brought before a court or authority which is competent to proceed with the case from the view of its nature."

The Federal Republic of Germany (old): Section 2 provides:

1. Every one has the right to develop his personality freely in so far as does not violate the rights of others or offend against the Constitutional order or moral law.
2. Every one has the right of personal security of life and limb. Personal liberty is inviolable. These rights can only be curtailed by virtue of a law.

Hungary: Article 57 states

"The Hungarian People's Republic safeguards the freedom and inviolability of the person and the privacy of the home and correspondence of its citizens."

Germany: Section 8 states:

"Personal liberty, inviolability of the home, secrecy of postal communications and the right to settle in any place desired are guaranteed. The state can only take away these freedoms in pursuance of the laws applying to all citizens."

Costa Rica: Section 20 of the Republic Constitution states:

"Every man is free in the Republic. No one who is under the protection of its laws shall be a slave."

Section 23 states:

"The home and all other private premises of persons living in the republic shall be inviolable—provided that they may be entered on written order of a competent judicial officer or to prevent offence from being committed or left unpunished or to avoid grave injury to persons or property subject to what is prescribed by law."

United Nations: Article 3 and 7 of the Draft Declaration of Human Rights read:

"Every one has the right to life, liberty and security of person." "No one shall be subjected to arbitrary arrest or detention."

Danzig: Article 74 states:

"The liberty of the person has been declared inviolable and no limitation or deprivation of personal liberty may be imposed by public authority except by virtue of a law."

Korea: The 1948 July Constitution states: No citizen shall be arrested etc. unless according to law.

Article 22

Protection against arrest and detention in certain cases:

1. No person who is arrested shall be detained in custody without being informed, as soon as may be, of the grounds for such arrest nor shall he be denied the right to consult and to be defended by a legal practitioner of his choice.
2. Every person who is arrested and detained in custody shall be produced before the nearest Magistrate within a period of twenty four hours of such arrest excluding the time necessary for the journey from the place of arrest to the court of the Magistrate and no such person shall be detained in custody beyond the said period without the authority of a Magistrate.
3. Nothing in Clause (1) and (2) shall apply:
   a. To any person who for the time being is an enemy alien; or
   b. To any person who is arrested or detained under any law providing for preventive detention.

4 No law providing for preventive detention shall authorise the detention of a person for a longer period than three months unless—

a an Advisory Board consisting of persons who are, or have been, or are qualified to be appointed as, Judges of a High Court has reported before the expiration of the said period of three months that there is in its opinion sufficient cause for such detention:

Provided that nothing in this sub-clause shall authorise the detention of any person beyond the maximum period prescribed by any law made by Parliament under sub-clause (b) of clause (7); or

b such person is detained in accordance with the provision of any law made by Parliament under sub-clause (a) and (b) of clause (7).

[To come into effect on enforcement of Section 3 of Constitution (Forty-fourth Amendment) Act, 1978]

18 [(4) No law providing for preventive detention shall authorise the detension of a person for a longer period than two months unless an Advisory Board constituted in accordance with the recommendations of the Chief Justice of the appropriate High Court has reported before the expiration of the said period of two months that there is in its opinion sufficient cause for such detention:

Provided that an Advisory Board shall consist of a Chairman and not less than two other members, and the Chairman shall be serving or retired Judges of any High Court:

Provided further that nothing in this clause shall authorise the detention of any person beyond the maximum period prescribed by any law made by Parliament under sub-clause (a) of clause (7).

Explanation. — In this clause. " appropriate High Court" means,—

(i) in the case of the detention of a person in pursuance of an order of detention made by the Government of India or an officer or authority subordinate to that Government, the High Court for the Union territory of Delhi;

(ii) in the case of the detention of a person in pursuance of an order of detention made by the Government of any State (other than a Union Territory), the High Court of that State; and

(iii) in the case of the detention of a person in pursuance of an order of detention made by the administrator of a Union territory or an officer or authority subordinate to such administrator, such High Court as may be specified by or under any law made by Parliament in this behalf.]

5 When any person is detained in pursuance of an order made under any law providing for preventive detention, the authority making the order shall, as soon as may be, communicate to such person the grounds on which the order has been made and shall afford him the earliest opportunity of making a representation against the order.

6 Nothing in clause (5) shall require the authority making any such order as is referred to in that clause to disclose facts which such authority considers to be against the public interest to disclose.

7 Parliament may by law prescribe —

a the circumstances under which, and the class or classes of cases in which, a person may be detained for a period longer than three months under any law providing for preventive detention without obtaining the opinion of an Advisory Board in accordance with the provisions of sub-clause (a) of clause (4);

b the maximum period for which any person may in any class or classes of cases be detained under any law providing for preventive detention; and

c the procedure to be followed by an Advisory Board in an inquiry under sub-clause (a) of clause (4).

[To come into effect on enforcement of section 3 of Constitution (Forty-Fourth Amendment) Act. 1978]

7 Parliament may by law prescribe—

19 [(a)] the maximum period for which any person may in any class or classes of cases be detained under any law providing for preventive detention; and

19 [(b)] the procedure to be followed by an Advisory Board in an inquiry under [20][clause (4)].

Foreign Constitutions

America (USA): The 6th Amendment runs as under:

"In all criminal prosecutions the accused shall enjoy the right to a speedy and pubic trial, and to be informed of the nature and cause of the accusations, to be confronted with the witness against him; to have compulsory process for obtaining witnesses in his favour, and to have the assistance of counsel for his defence."

Japan: Article XXXIV states:

"No person shall be arrested or detained without being at once informed of the charges against him or without adequate cause; and upon court in his presence and the presence of his counsel."

Article 23

Prohibition of Traffic in Human Beings and Forced Labour:

1. Traffic in human beings and beggars and other similar forms of forced labour are prohibited and any contravention of this provision shall be an offence punishable in accordance with law.
2. Nothing in this Article shall prevent the State from imposing compulsory service. The state shall not make any discrimination on grounds only of religion, race, caste or class or any of them.

Corresponding Foreign Constitutions

USA: 13th Amendment declares:

Section 1:

"Neither slavery nor involuntary servitude except as punishment for crime where of the party shall have been duly convicted, shall exist within the United States, or any place subject to their jurisdiction.

Section 2:

"The congress shall have power to enforce this Article by appropriate Legislation."

Burma: Article 19 states:

1. Traffic in human beings and
2. Forced labour in any form, involuntary servitude except as a punishment for crime where of the party shall have been duly convicted, shall be prohibited.

Explanation: "Nothing in this section shall prevent the state from imposing compulsory service for public purposes without any discrimination on grounds of birth, race, religion or class."

Japan: Article XVIII of the Japanese Constitution of 1946 states:

"No person shall be held in bondage of any kind; involuntary servitude, except as punishment for crime, is prohibited."

United Nations: Article 4 states:

"No one shall be held in slavery or servitude; slavery and the slave trade shall be prohibited in all their forms.

Federal Republic of Germany (old): Article 12 enunciates:

1. "All Germans have the right of free choice of occupation, place and employment and place of training. The pursuit of occupation may be regulated by legislation.

2. No one shall be forced to do a particular job except in virtue of an establishment, general obligation to perform a public service lying equally upon all.
3. Forced labour is only permissible where a sentence of imprisonment is ordered by a court."

Article 24

Prohibition of employment of children in factories etc. No child below the age of fourteen years shall be employed to work in any factory or mine or engaged in any other hazardous employment.

Corresponding Foreign Constitutions

Czechoslovakia: Article 11 of the Constitution reads:

> The states guarantees to children special care and protection and in particular, takes systematic measures to increase the population of the nation.

Article 29 states:

1. Every person possesses the right to public health. All citizens possess the right to medical care and to provisions in old age and also during incapacity for work and when unable to maintain themselves.
2. Women are entitled to special care during pregnancy and maternity, and children and young persons are entitled to all facilities for full physical and mental development."

Germany: Article 18 of the German Democratic Republic states:

> "Youth is protected against exploitation and guarded against moral, physical, and spiritual neglect. Child labour is prohibited."

Costa Rica: Section 51 states:

> "The family, as a natural element and foundation of society, shall be entitled to the special protection of the state. Mothers, children, the aged and helpless invalids shall likewise be entitled to this protection."

Article 25

Freedom of conscience and free profession, practice and propagation of religion:

1. Subject to public order, morality and health and to other provisions of this part, all persons are equally entitled to freedom of conscience and the right freely to profess, practice and propagate religion.
2. Nothing in this Article shall affect the operation of any existing law or prevent the state from making any law
   a. Regulating or restricting any economic financial, political or other secular activity, which may be associated with religious practice;
   b. Providing for social welfare and reforms or the throwing open of Hindu religious institutions of a public character to all classes and section of Hindus. The wearing and carrying of Kirpans shall be deemed to be included in the profession of the Sikh religion. Hindus shall include Sikh, Jain or Buddhist Religions.

Corresponding Foreign Constitutions

USA: The First Amendment states:

Congress shall make no law respecting an establishment of religion or prohibiting the free exercise thereof.

Australia: Section 116 reads:

"The commonwealth shall not make any law for establishment of religion or for imposing any religious observance or for prohibiting the free exercise of any religion and no religious tests shall be required as a qualification for any office or public trust under the commonwealth."

Japan: Article 20 says:

"Freedom of religion is guaranteed to all... no person shall be compelled to take part in any religious act, celebration, rite or practice.

Burma: Article 20 declares:

"All persons are equally entitled to freedom of conscience and the right freely to profess and practice religion subject to public order, morality or health and to the other provisions of this Chapter. But it shall not include any economic, financial, political or other secular activities that may be associated with religious practice. It shall not debar the state from enacting laws for the purpose of social welfare and reform.

Article 21 :(3):

"The state shall not impose any disabilities or make any discrimination on the ground of religious faith or belief. (4): The abuse of religion for political purposes is forbidden and any act which is intended or likely to promote feelings of hatred, enmity or discord between racial or religious communities or sects is contrary to this Constitution and may be made punishable by law."

China: Article 36 states:

"The people shall have the freedom of religious belief."

Yugoslavia: Article 12 states:

Liberty of religion and of conscience shall be guaranteed. All recognized religions shall be equal before law and may be practiced in public.

Switzerland: Article 49 lays down:

Liberty of conscience and creed is inviolable. No person may be compelled to became a member of any religious instruction, perform any act of religion, or incur any penalties, of any kind what so ever by reason of his religious opinions.... The exercise of civil or political requirement or conditions of any kind what so ever." Article 50 says that the free exercise of religion is guaranteed within limits compatible with public order and morality.

Eire: Article 44 (2) states:

"Freedom of conscience and the free profession and practice of religion are subject to public order and morality guaranteed to every citizen.

1. The State guarantees not to endow any religion.
2. The state shall not impose any disabilities or make any discrimination on the ground of religious profession belief or status.

France: Clause (1) of Preamble:

"No one ought to be disturbed on account of his opinion, even religious, provided their manifestation does not derange the public order established by law."

Ceylon(Srilanka): Section 29 (2) of the Ceylon (Constitution) order provides:

"No such law shall"

b. Prohibit or restrict free exercise of any religion or

c. Make a person of any community or religion liable to disabilities or restrictions to which persons of other communities or religions are not made liable.

d. Confer on any persons of any community or religion any privilege or advantage which is not conferred on persons of other communities or religions.

Rumania: Section 27 says:

> "Freedom of conscience and religion are guaranteed by the state. The different religions may be freely organized and practiced if their ritual and practices are not contrary to the Constitution, public, safety or good morals. And religious denominations shall be regulated by law.

Czechoslovakia: Article 15—freedom of conscience is guaranteed.

20: No person shall suffer prejudice by reason of his view of the world, faith or conviction Article 16

i. Every person has the right to profess in private and in public any religious creed or to be without religious persuasion.

ii. All religious persuasions and persons of no religious persuasion are equal before the law.

Article 17 (1) every person is free to perform the acts connected with any religious persuasion or the absence of religious persuasion. No persons shall be constrained by direct or indirect means to take part in such acts.

Germany: Section 4:

Freedom of faith and conscience and freedom of religious and ideological profession are inviolable.

3. The undisturbed practice of religion is guaranteed.
4. No one shall be forced to serve in war as a combatant against his conscience. The detailed rules shall be prescribed by federal legislation.

Hungary: Section 54 states:

People have the liberty of conscience of all citizens and freedom of religious worship. In order to ensure liberty of conscience the Hungarian People's Republic separates the church from the state.

Costa Rica: Section 76:

Roman Catholic Apostolic Religion is the religion of the state, which contributes to its maintenance without impeding the free exercise in the Republic of other forms of worship not contrary to universal morality and good behaviour.

United Nations: Article 19 of UN Declarations of Human Rights postulates:

Every one has the right to freedom of thought, conscience, and religion. This right includes freedom to change his religion or belief and freedom, either alone or in community with others and in public or private, to manifest his religion or belief in teaching, practice, worship and observation."

Article 26

Subject to public order, morality and health, every religious denomination or any section thereof shall have the right. (a) To establish and maintain institutions for religious and charitable purposes; (b) to manage its own affairs in matters of religion (c) to own and acquire movable and immovable property and (d) to administer such property in accordance with law.

Corresponding Foreign Constitutions

Freedom to manage religious affairs:

USA: The First Amendment says:

"Congress shall make no law respecting an establishment of religion."

Eire: Article 44 (2) states:

"Every religious denomination shall have the right to manage its own affairs, own, acquire and administer movable and immovable, and maintain institutions for religious or charitable purposes.

"The property of any religious denomination or any educational institution shall not be diverted save for necessary works of public utility and on payment of compensation."

Sri Lanka (Ceylon): Section 29 (2) reads:

"No such law shall alter the Constitution of any religious body except with the consent of the governing authority of that body; provided that, in any case where the religious body is incorporated by law, no such alteration shall be made except at the request of the governing authority of that body."

Rumania: Section 27 states:

"...The organization and functioning of the different religious denominations shall be regulated by law."

Germany: Section 41 (2) says:

"Institutions belonging to religious societies, religious acts and religious instruction shall not be misused for unconstitutional objects or in the interests of a political party."

Section 43 states:

i. "Every religious society shall order and administer its own affairs subject to the law applying to all.
ii. "The religious societies shall continue to be corporations in public law in so far as they were so hitherto. Other religious societies shall receive like right on application."

Section 45 states:

i. The forms of public support given to the religious societies in virtue of law, contract of special legal title, shall be commuted by law.
ii. The property and other rights of the religious societies and unions in their establishment, foundations and other property for purpose of public worship, instruction and charity are guaranteed."

Article 27

Freedom as to payment of taxes for promotion of any particular religion. No person shall be compelled to pay any taxes, the proceeds of which are specifically appropriated in payment of expenses for the promotion of maintenance of any particular religion or religious denomination.

Corresponding Foreign Constitutions

USA: The First Amendment (1791) sets down:

"The Congress shall make no law respecting establishment of religion."

Japan: Article 22 states:

"No religious organization shall receive any privileges from the states, nor exercise any political authority."

Switzerland: Article 40 reads:

"...No person may be compelled to pay taxes the proceeds of which are specially appropriated in payment of the purely religious expenses of any religious community of which he is not a member."

Rumania: Section 27 states:

"The different religions may be freely organized and practiced.

Germany: The Section 4 states:

i. Freedom of faith and conscience and freedom of religions and ideological profession are inviolable.
ii. The undisturbed practice of religion is guaranteed.
iii. No one shall be forced to serve in wartime as a combatant against his conscience. The detailed rules shall be prescribed by federal legislation.

Section 43 (4) says:

The religious societies in public law shall be entitled to levy taxes from their members on the basis of state taxation lists, subject to general provisions.

Section 45 (1) states:

"The forms of public support given to the religious societies in virtue of law, contract or special legal title shall be commuted by law."

Article 28

Freedom as to attendance at religious institution or instruction or religious worship in certain educational institutions:

1. No religious instruction shall be provided in any educational institution wholly maintained out of state funds.
2. Nothing in clause shall apply to any educational institution, which is administered by the state but has been established under any endowment or trust, which requires that religious instruction shall be imparted in such institutions.
3. No person attending any educational institution recognized by the state or receiving aid out of state funds shall be required to take part in any religious instruction that may be imparted in such institution or to attend any religious worship that may be conducted in such institution or in any premises attached there to unless such person or if such person is a minor his guardian, has given his consent thereto.

Corresponding Foreign Constitutions

Germany: Section 7 (2) provides:

1. The person responsible for bringing up children shall have the right to decide whether the child shall attend religious instruction.

2. Religious instruction shall be part of the curriculum in all public schools other than nondenominational schools. Religious instruction shall, subject to state supervision, be given in accordance with the principles of religious societies. No teacher shall be required against his will to give religious instruction.

Japan: Article XX says:

"Legislation providing state aid for schools shall not...be such as to affect prejudicially the right of any child to attend a school receiving public money without attending religious instruction in that school."

Rumania: Section 17 states:

1. Every person is free to perform the acts connected with any religious persuasions. This right shall not, however, be exercised in a manner contrary to public order and morality. It shall not be permitted to be misused for non-religious ends.
2. No person shall be constrained by direct or indirect means to take part in such acts.

Germany: Section 44 says:

The right of the church to give religious instruction in school premises is guaranteed. The religious instruction shall be given by persons chosen by the church. No one shall be forced to give or prevented from giving religious instruction. The person responsible for the child's upbringing shall decide whether it shall attend religious instruction or not.

Section 46 (1) states:

In so far as there is need for divine services and spiritual ministrations in hospitals, prisons and other public establishments, the religious societies shall be allowed to perform acts of religion. No one shall be compelled to participate in such acts.

Article 29

Protection of interests of Minorities.

1. Any section of the citizens residing in the territory of India or any part thereof having a distinct language, script or culture of its own shall have the right to conserve the same.
2. No citizen shall be denied admission into any educational institution maintained by the state or receiving aid out of state funds on grounds only of religion, race, caste, language or any of them.

Corresponding Foreign Constitutions

Burma: Article 22 provides:

"No minority, religious, racial or linguistic, shall be discriminated against in regard to admission into state educational institutions."

Rumania: Section 22 states:

In the Rumania People's Republic all citizens have the right to education. The state provides for the exercise of this right by organizing and developing compulsory free primary education by granting state scholarships to meritorious pupils and students, and by organizing and developing vocational and technical education.

Section 23 states:

The states encourages and supports the development of science and art, and organizes research institutes, libraries, publishing houses, theatres, museums and musical academies.

Czechoslovakia: Section 12 says:

1. All citizens have the right to education.
2. The state takes care to ensure that every person receives education and training in accordance with his abilities and having regards to the needs of the community.

Section 13:

1. All schools are state schools.
2. Elementary education is uniform, compulsory and free.

Section 14:

All education and instruction shall be so arranged as to be in harmony with the results of scientific research and compatible with the democratic order.

Section 19:

1. Freedom to engage in creative mental activity is guaranteed. Scientific research and publication of its results and likewise art and its expressions are free in so far as they do not violate the penal law.
2. Cultural assets are under the protection of the state. The state ensures that they are accessible to all and supports science and art in the interests of the cultural development of the nation, progress and the general welfare. In particular it takes care that creative workers are assured of favourable conditions for their work.

Germany: Section 5 (3) enunciates:

Art and science, research and teaching are unrestricted. The freedom to teach does not release the teacher from his duty to be loyal to the Constitution.

Section 7:

1. The whole educational system shall be under the supervision of the state.
2. The right to establish private schools is guaranteed.

Costa Rica: Section 77 states:

Public education shall be organized as a complete process in which the various levels are correlated, from the pre-school stage to the University.

Section 78:

Primary education is compulsory; primary, preschool and secondary education is free and is provided at national expense. The state shall facilitate the higher studies of persons who lack the necessary funds.

Section 79:

Freedom of education is guaranteed provided that every private teaching shall be subject to state inspection.

Section 80:

Private initiative in educational matters shall receive state encouragement in the manner prescribed by law.

Section 87:

Freedom of teaching is a fundamental principle of university education.

Section 89:

The cultural aims of the Republic include the protection of natural beauty, the preservation and extension of the historic and artistic inheritance of the nation and support of private initiative for scientific and artistic progress.

Article 30

Right of minorities to establish and administer educational institutions.

1. All minorities, whether based on religion or language, shall have the right to establish and administer educational institutions of their choice.
   a In making any law provinding for compulsory aquision of any properly of an educational institution established and administered by a minority, referred to in clause (i), the state shall ensure that the amount fixed or determined under any law for the aquisition of such property is such as would not restrict or abrogate the right Guaranteed under that clause

2. The State shall not in granting aid to educational institutions, discriminate against any educational institution on the ground that it is under the management of a minority, whether based on religion or language.

Corresponding Foreign Constitutions

Eire: Article 42 (3) of the 1937 Constitution provides:

The state shall not oblige parents in violation of their conscience and lawful preference to send their children to schools established by the state or to any particular type of school designated by the state."

Article 44 (4) states:

"Legislation providing state aid for schools shall not discriminate between schools under the management of different religious denominations."

Rumania: Section 24 states:

In the Rumanian Constitution people's right of using their native language and of organizing education at all levels in the said language is guaranteed to the other nationalities living side by side with the Rumanian people.

Canada

In the Canadian Constitution, it is stated in section 93, that in and for each province, the legislature may exclusively make in relation to education, subject to and according to the following provisions:

1. Nothing in any such law shall prejudicially affect any right or privilege with respect to denominational schools which any class of persons have by law in the province or the Union.
2. All the powers, privileges and duties at the Union by law conferred and imposed in upper Canada on the separate schools and schools trustees of the Queen's Roman Catholic subjects shall be and the same are hereby extended to the dissentient schools of the Queen's Protestant and Roman Catholic subjects in Quebec.

(Article 31) Compulsory acquisition of property:

This fundamental right of property has been omitted from list of Fundamental Rights. It is simply legal right under Article 300A. The corresponding Foreign Constitutions provisions are as follows.

USA: The Fifth Amendment says:

"Nor shall any person be deprived of...property without due process of law."

Eire: Article 43 postulates:

1. i. The State acknowledges that man, in virtue of his rational being, has the natural right antecedent to positive law, to the private ownership of external goods.
2. (ii) The State accordingly guarantees to pass no law attempting to abolish the right of private ownership or the general right to transfer, bequeath and inherit property."
3. (iii) The state recognizes, however, that the exercise of the rights mentioned in the foregoing provisions of this Article ought in civil society, to be regulated by the principles of social justice.
4. (iv) The State, accordingly may, as occasion requires delimit by law the exercise of the said rights with a view to reconciling their exercise with the exigencies of the common good."

Japan: Article 29 states:

"The right to own property is inviolable but property right shall be defined by law in conformity with the public welfare."

Article 30 says:

"The people are liable to taxation as fixed by law."

Burma: Clauses 1-3 of Article 23 States:

1. "Subject to the provisions of this section, the state guarantees the right of private initiative in economic sphere.
2. "No person shall be permitted to use the right of private property to the detriment of the general public.
3. "Private monopolist organizations such as cartels, syndicates and trusts formed for the purpose of dictating prices of or for monopolizing the market or otherwise calculated to injure the interests of the national economy are forbidden."

France: The preamble of the Constitution of the Fourth French Republic of 1946 postulates:

"Property being a sacred and inviolable right, no one can be deprived of it unless a legally established public necessity demands it, and on condition of just and prior indemnity."

Rumania: Section 9 says:

The land belongs to those who till it. The State protects property based on the peasant's work. It encourages and assists village co-operation.

Korea: Article 15 states:

Expropriation of private property shall be accompanied by payment of due compensation.

Nicaragua: Article 8 postulates

"None may be deprived of his property save by judgment of a court or after fair compensation to be determined by judicial authority or for reason of public utility or social interest in accordance with the law. In case of national war, internal disturbance or public calamity, the competent authorities may make use of property in so far as the public good so requires but the right to subsequent compensation shall be reserved."

Czechoslovakia: Section 8 says

"Subject to the general provision of law, every citizen may acquire fixed other property in any place in the Czechoslovak Republic and on a gainful occupation there."

Section 9:

Private ownership may only be restricted by law.

No person shall misuse the right of property to the detriment of the community.

Germany: Section 14 says:

1. Property and the right of inheritance are guaranteed. The scope and limits shall be determined by law.
2. Property involves responsibilities. It must be used so as to serve the good at the same time.

Hungary: Section 8 says:

1. The Constitution recognizes and protects all property acquired by work.
2. Private property and private enterprise must not be harmful to the public interest.
3. The Constitution guarantees the right of inheritance.

Costa Rica: Section 45 states:

Property shall be inviolable...

The legislative assembly may, for reasons of public necessity, by a vote of two-thirds of its members, impose limitations on property in the social interest.

Government of India Act, 1935:

The provision corresponding in Article 31 in the Government of India Act, 1935, is section 299, which states:

1. "No person shall be deprived of his property in British India save by authority of law."

2. "Neither the Federal nor a provincial Legislature shall have power to make any law authorizing the compulsory acquisition for public purposes of any land or any commercial industrial, undertaking, or any interest in or in any company owning any commercial or industrial undertaking, unless the law provides for the payment of compensation or specifies the principles on which and the manner in which it is to be determined."

31-A saving of laws providing for acquisition of estates, etc.

Not withstanding anything contained in Article 13, no law providing for:

(a) The acquisition by the states of any estate or any rights therein or the extinguishments or modification of any such rights, or

(b) The taking over of the management of any property by the state for a limited period either in the public interest or in order to secure the proper management of the property, or

(c) The amalgamation of two or more corporations either in the public interest or in order to secure the proper management of any of the corporations, or

(d) The extinguishments or modification of any rights of managing agents, secretaries and treasurers, managing directors, directors or management of corporations, or of any voting rights of shareholders thereof, or

(e) The extinguishments or modification of any rights accruing by virtue of any agreement, lease or license for the purpose of searching for, or winning, any mineral or mineral oil, or the premature termination or cancellation of any such agreement, lease or license, shall be deemed to be void on the ground that it is inconsistent with, or takes away or abridge any of the rights conferred by Article 14, 19.

Provided that where such law is made by the legislature of a state, the provisions of this Article shall not apply there to unless such law, having been reserved for the consideration of the president, has received his assent.

Provided further that where any law makes any provision for the acquisition by the state of any estate and where any land comprised therein is held by a person under his personal cultivation, it shall not be lawful for the state to acquire any portion of such land as is within the ceiling limits applicable to him under any law for the time being in force or any building or structure standing thereon or appurtenant there to, unless the law relating to the acquisition of such land, building or structure, provides for payment of compensation at rate which shall not be less than the market value thereof.

(a) The expression "estate" shall, in relation to any local area, have the same meaning as that expression or its local equivalent has in the existing law relating to land tenures in force in that area and shall also include:

i. Any Jagir, Inam or Muafi or other similar grant and in the state of Tamilnadu and Kerala, any German right;
ii. Any land held under ryotwari settlement;
iii. Any land held or let for purposes of agriculture or for purposes ancillary thereto, including waste land, forest land, land for pasture or sites of buildings and other structures occupied by cultivations of land, agricultural labours and village artisans;

(b) The expression "right", in relation to an estate, shall include any rights vesting in a proprietor, sub-proprietor, under-proprietor, tenure-holder, raiyat, under raiyat or other intermediary and any rights or privileges in respect of land revenue.

31-B validation of certain acts and regulations

Without prejudice to the generality of the provisions contained in Article 31-A, none of the Acts and Regulations specified in the Ninth Schedule nor any of them have become void, on the ground that such Act, regulation or provision is inconsistent with, or takes away or abridges any of the rights conferred by, any provisions of this part, and notwith-standing any judgment, decree or order of any court or tribunal to the contrary, each of the any competent legislations shall, subject to the power of any competent legislature to repeat or amend it, continue in force.

31-C saving of laws giving effect to certain directive principles

Notwithstanding anything contained in Article 13, no law giving effect to the policy of the state towards securing all or any of the principles laid down in part IV shall be deemed to be void on the ground that is inconsistent with, or takes away or abridges any of the rights conferred by Article 14 or 19 and no law containing a declaration that it is for giving effect to such policy shall be called in question in any court on the ground that it does not give effect to such policy.

Provided that where such law is made by the legislature of a state, the provisions of this Article shall not apply there to unless such law, having been reserved for the consideration of the president, has received his assent.

Corresponding Foreign Constitutions

(31-A-B-C-No Corresponding Provision)

Article 32

1. The right to move the Supreme Court by appropriate proceedings for the enforcement of the right conferred by this part is guaranteed.
2. The Supreme Court shall have power to issue directions or orders or with including writs in the nature of *habeas corpus*, *mandamus*, prohibition, *quo warranto* and *certiorari*, whichever may be appropriate, for the enforcement of any of the rights conferred by this Article
3. Without prejudice to the powers conferred on the Supreme Court by clause (1) parliament may by law empower any other court to exercise with in the local limits of its jurisdiction all or any of the power exercisable by the Supreme Court under clause (2).
4. The right guaranteed under this Article shall not be suspended except as otherwise provided for by this Constitution.

Corresponding Foreign Constitutions :

Burma: Article 15 (1) of the Burmese Constitution is a replica of Article 32 (1) of the Constitution of India. Article 25, clause (2) states (i.e. Article 32, clause (2) and (3) of Indian Constitution):

> "Without prejudice to the powers that may be vested in this behalf in other courts, the Supreme Court shall have power to issue direction in the nature of *habeas corpus*, *mandamus*, prohibition, *quo warranto* and *certiorari* appropriate to the rights guaranteed in this chapter."

Article 25(3) of the Burmese Constitution compares with clause (4) of Article 32 as hereunder: -

> "The right to enforce these remedies shall not be suspended unless, in times of war, invasion, rebellion, insurrection or grave emergency, the public safety may so require."

Article 27 states:

"Except in times of invasion, rebellion, insurrection or grave emergency, no citizen be denied redress by due process of law for any actionable wrong done to or suffered by him."

USA: Article 1 section 9 (2) postulates:

"The privilege of the writ of *habeas corpus* shall not be suspended unless when in cases of rebellion or invasion the public safety may require it."

Eire: Article 28 (3) posits:

Nothing in this Constitution shall be invoked to invalidate any law enacted by the Oireachtas which is expressed to be for the purpose of securing the public safety and the preservation of the state in times of war or armed rebellion or to nullify any act done or purporting to be done in pursuance of such law.

"In this sub-section, 'time of war' includes a time when there is taking place an armed conflict in which the state is not a participant but in respect of which each of the House of the Oireachtas shall be resolved that arising out of such armed conflict a national emergency exists affecting the vital interests of the State (first Amendment of the Constitution Act, (1939).

"Times of war shall also include such time after termination of the said armed conflict as may elapse until each of the Houses of Oireachtas shall have resolved that the said national emergency occasioned by such armed conflict has ceased to exist. (Second Amendment of the Constitution Act, 1941).

Germany: Article 48 postulates:

"Where public security and order are seriously disturbed or endangered within the Reich, the president of the Reich may take the measures necessary for their restoration intervening in case of need with the help of armed forces. For this purpose he is permitted for the time being to abrogate either wholly or partially the Fundamental Rights laid down in Articles 114, 115, 117, 118, 123, 124 and 153.

"The president of the Reich must, without delay, inform the Reichstag of any measures taken in accordance with paragraph 1 or 2 of this Article. Such measures shall be abrogated upon the demand of Reichstag.

"Where there is danger in delay, the State Government may take provisional measures of the kind indicated in paragraph 2, for its own territory. Such measures shall be abrogated upon the demand of the president of the Reich or the Reichstag."

Article 33

Power to parliament to modify the rights conferred by this part in their application to force:

Parliament may by law determine to what extent any of the rights conferred by this part shall, in their application to:

(a) The members of the Armed Forces, or

(b) The members of the Force charged with the maintenance of public order; or

(c) Persons employed in any bureau or other organization established by the state for purpose of intelligence or counter intelligence; or

(d) Persons employed in, or in connection with, the telecommunication system set up for the purpose of any Force, bureau or organization referred to in clause (a) to (c),

Be restricted or abrogated so as to ensure the proper discharge of their duties and the maintenance of discipline among them.

Corresponding Foreign Constitutions

Burma: Article 28 of the Burmese Constitution is on the same lines as Article 33 of India.

Eire: Article 38 (4) and (6) postulates:

1. "Military Tribunals may be established for the trial of offences against military law alleged to have been committed by persons while subject to military law and also to deal with a state of war or armed rebellion.
2. "A member of the defence forced not on active service shall not be tried by any court martial or other military tribunal for an offence cognisable by the civil courts unless such offence is within the jurisdiction of any court martial or other military tribunal under any law for the enforcement of military discipline.

"The provisions of Articles 34 and 35 of the Constitution shall not apply to any court or tribunal set-up under Section (3) or Section (4) of this Article."

Article 34

Restriction on rights conferred by this part while martial law is enforced in any area:

Now withstanding anything in the foregoing provisions of this part, parliament may by law indemnify any person in the service of the union or of a state or any other person in respect of any act done by him in connection with the maintenance or restoration of order in any area within the territory of India where martial law was in force or validate any sentence passed, punishment inflicted, for feature ordered or other act done under martial law in such area.

Note: No analogous provision anywhere else.

Article 35

Legislation to give effect to the provisions of this part:

Not withstanding anything in this Constitution:

(a) Parliament shall have, and the legislature of state not have, power to make laws

  (1) With respect to any of the matters which under clause (3) of Article 16, clause (3) of Article 32, Article 33 and Article may be provided for by law made by parliament; and

  (2) For prescribing punishment for those acts which are declared to be offence under this part; and parliament shall, as soon as may be after the commencement of this Constitution, make laws for prescribing punishment for the acts referred to in sub-clause (ii);

(b) Any law in force immediately before the commence-ment of this Constitution in the territory of India with respect to any of matters referred to in sub-clause

  (i) Of clause (a) or providing for punishment for any act referred to in sub-clause (iii) of that clause shall, subject to the terms thereof and to any adaptations and modifications that may be made therein under Article 372, continue in force until altered or repealed or amended by parliament.

Explanation: In this Article, the expression "Law in force" has the same meaning as in Article 372.

Corresponding Foreign Constitution

Burma: Article 39 posits:

"The parliament shall make laws to give effect to those provision of this chapter which require such legislation and to prescribe punishment for those acts which are declared to be offences in this chapter and not already punishable."

CHAPTER 3
Comparative Study of Directive Principles Under World Constitutions

Let us now consider various provisions of directive principles found under various world constitutions corresponding to the provisions of directive principles under Chapter 3 of the Constitution of India. These provisions are as follows:

Article 36

Definition: In this part, unless the context otherwise requires, "The state" has the same meaning as in part III.

- No corresponding provisions anywhere.

Article 37

Application of the Principles contained in this part:

The provisions contained in the part shall not be enforceable by any court, but the principles therein laid down are nevertheless fundamental in the governance of the country and it shall be the duty of the state to apply these principles in making laws.

Analogic provisions of Article 37

Burma: Article 32 postulates:

> "The principles set forth in this chapter are intended for the general guidance of the State. The application of these principles in legislation and administration shall be the care of the State but shall not be enforceable in any court of law."

Eire: Article 45 posits:

> "The principles of social policy set forth in this Article are intended for the general guidance of the Oireachtas. The application of these

principles in the making of laws shall be the care of the Oireachtas, and shall not be cognisable by any court under any of the provisions of the Constitution."

Article 38

The State to secure a social order for the promotion of welfare of the people.

1. The state shall strive to promote the welfare of the people by securing and protecting as effectively as it may a social order in which justice, social, economic and political, shall inform all the institutions of the national life.
2. The state shall, in particular, strive to minimize the inequalities in income, and endeavour to eliminate inequalities in status, facilities and opportunities, not only amongst individual but also amongst groups of people residing in different areas or engaged in different vocations.

Analogic provisions of Article 38:

Eire : Article 45, clause (1) posits:

"The State shall strive to promote the welfare of the whole people by securing and protecting as effectively as it may a social order in which justice and charity shall inform all the institutions of the national life."

Article 39

Certain principles of policy to be followed by the state:

The state shall in particular, direct its policy towards securing–

(a) That the citizens, men and women equally, have the right to an adequate means of livelihood;

(b) That the ownership and control of the material resources of the community are so distributed as best to subscribe to the common good;

(c) That the operation of the economic system does not result in the concentration of wealth and means of production to the common detriment;

(d) That there is equal pay for equal work for both men and women;

(e) That the health and strength of workers, men and women, and the tender age of children are not abused and that citizens are not forced by economic necessity to enter avocations unsuited to their age or strength;

(f) That children are given opportunities and facilities to develop in a healthy manner and in conditions of freedom and dignity and that childhood and youth are protected against exploitation and against moral and material abandonment.

Analogic Provisions of Article 39

Article 118 *posits:*

"Citizens of USSR have the right to work. That is the right to guaranteed employment and payment for their work in accordance with its quantity and quality. The right to work is ensured by the socialist organization of the national economy, the steady growth of the productive forces of Soviet society, the elimination of the possibility of economic crises, and the abolition of unemployment."

Article 120 *provides:*

"Citizens of the USSR have the right to maintenance in old age and also in case of sickness or disability.

This right is ensured by the extensive development of social insurance of factory and office workers at State expense, free medical service for the working people and the provision of a wide network of health resorts for the use of the working people."

Burma : Article (1) provides:

"The state shall ensure that the strength and health of workers and the tender age of children shall not be abused and that they shall not be forced by economic necessity to take up occupations unsuited to their sex, age and strength."

Eire : Article 45, clauses (2) (4) of the 1937 Constitution posits:

1. "The state shall, in particular, direct its policy toward securing
   - (a) That the citizens (all of whom, men and women equally, have the right to an adequate means of livelihood) may through their occupations find the means of making reasonable provision for their domestic needs;
   - (b) That the ownership and control of the material resources of the community may be so distributed amongst private individuals and the various classes as best to sub serve the common good;
   - (c) That especially the operation of free competition shall not be allowed so to develop as to result in the concentration of the

ownership or control of essential commodities in a few individuals, to the common detriment;

2. The state shall favour and, where necessary, supplement private initiative in industry and commerce.
3. The state shall endeavour to secure that private enterprise shall be so conducted as to ensure reasonable efficiency in the production and distribution of goods and as to protect the public against unjust exploitation.
4. The state shall endeavour to secure that the strength, health of workers, men and women and tender age of children shall not be abused and that citizen shall not be forced by economic necessity to enter avocations unsuited to their sex, age of strength."

Rumania : Section 19 states:

"All citizens have the right to work. The state gradually secures the exercise of this right by the planned organization and development of national economy."

Section 25 posits:

"Women have equal rights with men in all domains of state, economic, social, cultural and political life and in private law."

For equal work, women are entitled to remuneration equal to that of men.

Section 25 states:

"The state safeguards public health by establishing and developing health services and by encouraging and assisting public training."

Section 26 says:

The mother and children up to the age of 18 years shall enjoy special protection, prescribed by law.

Czechoslovakia : Section 1 (2) states:

"Men and women have equal status in the family and in the community and equal access to education and to all callings, offices and dignities."

Section 26:

1. All citizens possess the right to work.
2. This right is secured, in particular by the organization of work directed by the state in accordance with a planned economy.
3. Women are entitled in respect of pregnancy; maternity and child care to special treatment as regards their conditions of employment.

4. The Law shall prescribe special conditions of employment as regards young persons, having regards to the requirements of their physical and mental development.

Section 27:

1. All working members of the population possess the right to just remuneration for the work done.
2. In equal conditions men and women are entitled to equal remuneration for equal work.

Section 146:

The means of production are either national property of the property of the popular co-operative or in the private ownership of individual produce.

Section 162:

By means of a unified economic plan, the state directs all economic activities (in particular production, trade and transportation) so as to ensure an adequate level of national consumption, to increase the quantity, quality and flow of production and gradually raise the standard of living on the population.

Costa Rica : Section 50 posits:

The state shall endeavour to procure the greatest well being of all the inhabitants of the country, by appropriate distribution of wealth.

Section 51:

Mothers, children, the aged and helpless invalids shall likewise be entitled to this protection.

Section 56:

Work is the right of the individual and an obligation towards society. The state must ensure that all have an honest and useful occupation which is properly paid, and must prevent such occupation from giving rise to conditions which in any way impair the liberty or dignity of the individual or reduce labour to the level of a mere commodity.

UNO:

Article 21 (2) of the United Nations declaration of human rights postulates "Every one has right to equal pay for equal work."

France

The preamble to Constitution of 1946 postulates:

"The Law guarantees to women equal rights with men in all dominions."

Article 39 A

Equal justice and free legal aid.

The state shall secure that the operation of the legal system promotes justice, and shall, in particular, provide free legal aid, by suitable legislation or schemes or in any other way, to ensure that opportunities for securing justice are not denied to any citizen by reason of economic or other disabilities.

Article 40

Organization of village panchayats:

The state shall take steps to organize village panchayats and endow them with such powers and authority as may be necessary to enable them to function as units of self-government.

No corresponding provision anywhere

Article 41

Right to work, to education and to public assistance in certain cases

The state shall, within the limits of its economic capacity and development, make effective provision for securing the right to work, to education and to public assistance in cases of unemployment, old age, sickness and disablement, and in other cases of undeserved want.

There is no corresponding provision of Article 40 analogic provisions of Article 41:

Article 42 & 43 of USSR (Russia):

"Citizens of the USSR have the right to maintenance in old age and also in case of sickness or loss of capacity to work. This right is ensured by the expensive development of social insurance of workers and employees at state expense, free medical service for the working people and the provision of a wide network of health resorts for the use of the working people."

Article 45:

Citizens of the USSR have the right to education.

This right is ensured by universal compulsory elementary education including higher education, being free of charge; by the system of state stipends for the overwhelming majority of students in the universities and colleges, by instruction in schools being conducted in the native language and by the organization in the factories, state farms, machine and tractor stations and collective farms of free vocational, technical and agronomic training for the working people.

Burma : Article 33 stipulates:

1 The State shall direct its policy towards securing to each citizen the right to work;

2. The right to maintenance in old age and sickness or loss of capacity to work;

3. The right to rest and leisure, and

4. The right to education.

Article 40 further states :

The State shall ensure disabled ex-servicemen a decent living and free occupational training. The children of fallen solders and children orphaned by war shall be under the special care of the state.

France

"Every one has the duty to work and the right to obtain employment. Every human being who because of his age, his physical or mental condition or because of the economic situation, finds himself unable to work, has the right to obtain from the community the means to lead a decent existence... The nation guarantees equal access of children and adults to education professional training and culture."

Article 42

The state shall make provision for just and human conditions of work and maternity relief.

Corresponding Provisions

Burma: Article 37 states:

"The state shall specially direct its policy towards protecting the interests of nursing mothers and infants by establishing maternity and infant welfare centres, children's homes and day nurseries and towards securing to mothers in employment the right to leave with pay before and after child birth.

Article 43

Living wage, etc, for workers:

The state shall endeavour to secure, by suitable legislation or economic organisation or in any other way, to all workers, agricultural, industrial or otherwise, a living wages conditions of work ensuring a decent standard to life and full enjoyment of leisure and social and cultural opportunities and, in particular, the state shall endeavour to promote cottage industries on an individual or co-operative basis in rural areas.

Article 43 A

Participation of workers in management of industries:

The State shall take steps, by suitable legislation or in any other way; to secure the participation of worker in the management of undertaking, establishments or other organizations engaged in any industry.

Foreign corresponding provisions

Burma : Article 41 & 42 postulates:

Article 41:

The economic life of the union shall be planned with the aim of increasing the public wealth, of improving the material conditions of the people and raising their cultural level, of consolidating the independence of the union and strengthening the defensive capacity.

Article 42:

The state shall direct its policy towards giving material assistance to economic organizations not working for private profit. Preference shall be given to co-operative and similar co-operative organizations.

France

"The nation ensures to the individual and the development. It guarantees to all and notably to the child, the mother and the aged worker, protection of health, material, security and leisure."

Rumania

Section 12 says:

Work is the fundamental factor in the economic life of the state. It is an obligation lying upon every citizen. The state assists all working people, to protect them from exploitation and raise their standard of living.

Section 20 states:

All citizens have the right to leisure. The right to leisure is secured by regulation of the hours of work, by means of holidays with pay in accordance with the law, by the provision of rest houses, sanatoria, clubs, parks, sports grounds and institutions specially arranged for the purpose.

Czechoslovakia : Section 26:

(1) All citizens possess the right to work.

(2) This right is secured in particular by the organization of work directed by the state in accordance with a system of planned economy.

(3) Women are entitled in respect of pregnancy, maternity and childcare, to special treatment as regards their conditions of employment.

(4) The Law shall prescribe special conditions of employment as regards young persons having regard to the requirements of their physical and mental development.

Section 24:

1. All working members of the population possess the right to just remuneration for the work done.
2. The right is secured by the state wages policy, which is administered in agreement with the united union organization and directed towards the constant rising of the standard of living of the working population.

3. Remuneration shall be governed by the quality and quantity of the work and by the benefit which it brings to the community.
4. In equal conditions, men and women are entitled to equal remuneration for equal work.

Section 28:

(1) All working members of the population possess the right to leisure.
(2) This right is secured by statutory regulation of hours of work by means of holidays with pay and by provision of recreational facilities for the working population.

Section 29:

The protection of life and health at work is secured in particular by state supervision and regulations for safety precautions in work places.

***Germany** : Section 15:*

1. Labour is protected by the state.
2. The right to work is guaranteed. The state secures every citizen of work and livelihood by direction of the economy. Where the citizen cannot be referred to suitable employment, provision is made for his needs in respect of maintenance.

Section 16:

Every working person has a right to rest, to paid annual leave, to assistance during sickness and old age.

Section 18:

1. The conditions of employment must be such as to safeguard the health, cultural claims and family life of the working population.
2. The remuneration for work must correspond to the results and secure a decent level of existence for the workers and their dependents.

***Costa Rica** : Section 57:*

Every worker shall be entitled to a minimum wage (fixed

periodically) for the normal working day, such as to assure his well being and a decent mode of existence. Equal wages shall in every case be paid for equal work. Where conditions as regards efficiency are identical.

All matters respecting the fixing of minimum wages shall be dealt with by a technical body appointed by the law.

The ordinary hours for day work shall not exceed eight in the day and 48 in the week. The ordinary hours for night shall not exceed six in the day and 36 in the week. The remuneration for overtime shall be 50 percent, more than the stipulated salary or wage, provided that the foregoing provision shall not apply in curtained by the law.

UNO *: Section 21:*

Everyone has the right to work, to just and favourable conditions of work and pay and to protection against unemployment.

Section 22:

1. Everyone has the right to a standard of living, including food, clothing, housing and medical care and to social services adequate for the health and well-being of himself and his family and security in the event of the livelihood in circumstances beyond control.
2. Mother and child have the right to special care and assistance.

Section 24:

Every one has the right to rest and leisure.

Section 23:

Every one has the right to education.

Section 25:

Every one has the right to participate in the cultural life of the community, to enjoy the arts and to share in scientific advancement.

Article 44

The state shall endeavour to secure for the uniform civil code throughout the territory of India.

No corresponding provisions anywhere else.

Article 45

Provision for free and compulsory education for children.

The state shall endeavour to provide, within a period of the years from the commencement of this Constitution, for free and compulsory education for all children until they complete the age of fourteen years.

Corresponding foreign constitutional provisions

Eire : Article 42 states :

The state shall provide for free primary education.

Burma : Article 33 says :

In particular the state shall make provision for free and compulsory primary education.

Article 44 states :

The state shall pay special attention to the young and promote their education.

France :

The preamble in the 1946 Constitution of fourth French Republic states:

"The Establishment of free, secular, public education on all levels is a duty of the state."

Czechoslovakia : Section 12:

(1) All citizens have the right to education.

(2) Elementary education is uniform, compulsory and free.

Germany : Section 39:

1. Every child must be given opportunity to develop thoroughly his physical, mental and moral powers. Attendance at the technical and secondary schools and at institutes of higher learning shall be made possible for all sections of the nation.
2. School shall be free of charge. Learning aids in compulsory schools shall be supplied without payment.

Costa Rica : *Section 78:*

Primary education is compulsory.

Primary, pre-school and secondary education is free and is provided at national expense.

The state shall facilitate the higher studies of persons who lack the necessary funds. The Ministry of Education shall be responsible for the awarding of scholarship and grants-in-aid, through a body appointed by law.

Section 82:

The State shall provide food and clothing for needy pupils in accordance with law.

UNO : Article 23 (1) posits:

> "Elementary and Fundamental education shall be free and compulsory".

Article 46

Promotion of education and economic interests of scheduled castes scheduled tribes and other weaker sections:

The state shall promote with special care the educational and economic interests of the weaker sections of the people, and in particular, of the scheduled castes and the scheduled tribes, and shall protect them from social injustice and all forms of exploitation.

Corresponding provision of Article 46 are as under:

Burma : Article 35 postulates:

The state shall promote with special care the educational and economic interests of the weaker and less advanced sections of the people and shall protect them from social injustice and all forms of exploitation.

Eire : Article 45 clause (4) (1) posits:

The state pledges itself to safeguard with special care the economic interests of the weaker sections of the sport of infirm, the widow, orphan and the aged.

Article 47

Duty of the state to raise the level of nutrition and standard of living and to improve public health.

The state shall regard the raising of the level of nutrition and the standard of living of its people and the improvement of public health as among its primary duties and, in particular, the state shall endeavour to bring about prohibition of the consumption except for medicinal purposes of intoxicating drinks and of drugs which are injurious to health corresponding provision are as under:

Burma : Article 36:

"The state regard the raising of the standard of living of its people and the improvement of public health as among its primary duties."

Article 38:

"The state shall promote the improvement of public health by organizing and controlling health services, hospitals, dispensaries, sanatoria, nursing and convalescent homes and other health institutions."

Article 39:

"The state shall take special care of the physical education of the people in general and of the youth in particular in order to increase the health and working capacity of the people and in order to strengthen the defensive capacity of the state."

Rumania

Vide Article 43 ante of this Book

Article 48

Organization of agricultural and animal husbandry:

The state shall endeavour to organize agriculture and animal husbandry on modern and scientific lines and shall, in particular, take steps for preserving and improving the breeds and prohibiting the slaughter of cows and calves and other mulch and draught cattle.

No corresponding provisions anywhere.

Article 48 A

Protection and improvement of environment and safeguarding of forests and wildlife.

The state shall endeavour to protect and improve the environment and to safeguard the forest and wildlife of the country.

No corresponding provisions anywhere.

Article 49

Protection of monuments and places and objects of national importance.

It shall be the obligation of the state to protect every monument or place or object of artistic or historic interest, (declared by or under law made by parliament) to be national importance from exploitation, disfigurement, destruction, removal, disposal or export as the case may be.

No corresponding provisions anywhere.

Article 50

The state shall take steps to separate the judiciary from executive in public services of the state

No corresponding provisions anywhere.

Article 51

Promotion of international peace and security.

The state shall endeavour to –

(a) Promote international peace and security.
(b) Maintain just and honourable relations between nations;
(c) Foster respect for international law and treaty obligations in the dealings of organized people with one another, and
(d) Encourage settlement of international dispute by arbitration.

Analogic provisions are as under:

French

The French Republic faithful in tradition abides by the rules of international public law. It will not undertake wars of conquest and will never use its arms against the freedom of any people. On condition of reciprocity, France accepts the limitations of sovereignty necessary to the organization and defence of peace.

Eire : Article 29 says:

(1) Ireland affirms its devotion to the ideal of peace and friendly cooperation amongst nations founded on inter-national justice and morality disputes by international arbitration or judicial determination.
(2) Ireland accepts the generally recognized principles of international law as its rule of conduct in its relation with other states.

Article 51 A

Fundamental duties:

It shall be the duty of every citizen of India –

(a) To abide by the Constitution and respect its ideals and institutions, the National Flag and the National Anthem;

(b) To cherish and follow the noble ideals which inspired our national struggle for freedom;

(c) To uphold and protect the sovereignty, unity and integrity of India;

(d) To defend the country and render national service when called upon to do so;

(e) To promote harmony and the spirit of common brotherhood amongst all the people of India transcending religious, linguistic and regional or sectional diversities; to renounce practices derogatory to the dignity of women;

(f) To value and preserve the rich heritage of our composite culture;

(g) To protect and improve the natural environment including forests, takes river and wild life, and to have compassion for living creatures;

(h) To develop the scientific temper, humanism and the spirit of inquiry and reform;

(i) To safeguard public property and to abjure violence;

(j) To strive towards excellence in all spheres of individual and collective activity so that the nation constantly rises to higher levels of endeavour and achievement;

The fundamental duties which were added by the Forty Second Amendment of the Constitution in 1976, in addition to creating and promoting a culture, also strengthened the hands of the legislature in enforcing these duties vis-à-vis the Fundamental Rights. Since the duties are imposed upon the citizen and not upon the state, legislation in necessary for their implementation. For example mandamus cannot be sought against an individual who does not observe his duties under this Article.[1] With respect to the duty under clause (a) of this Article, it has been held that "proper respect is shown to the national Anthem by standing up when the national anthem is sung. It will not be right to say that disrespect is shown by not joining in the singing.[2]

Notes

1. Surya Narain V/S Union of India AIR 1982 S.C. (1)
2. Bi Joi immanel V/S State of Kerla Air 1987 S.C. 748

CHAPTER 4

FUNDAMENTAL RIGHTS AND DUTIES IN CHINA, RUSSIA, PAKISTAN, NEPAL AND BANGLADESH

A view of Fundamental Rights and duties in China, Russia, Pakistan, Nepal and Bangladesh is presented here for specific knowledge of these countries.

Let us first glance at Fundamental Rights and duties in the People's Republic of China; this nation has one of the oldest cultures and civilizations of the world. I am here gathering only the latest available position of Fundamental Rights and duties.

The Constitution of the People's Republic of China was adopted and promulgated for implementation by the proclamation of the National People's Congress on December 4, 1982. Chapter 2 prescribes the Fundamental Rights and duties of the citizens. It shows that these rights are not available to those who are not citizens of China. A list of 24 Articles of the second chapter of the Constitution of citizens are reproduced as under:

Article 33

All persons holding the nationality of the People's Republic of China are citizens of the People's Republic of China.

All citizens of the People's Republic of China are equal before the law.

Every citizen is entitled to the rights and at the same time must perform the duties prescribed by the Constitution and the law.

Article 35

Citizens of the People's Republic of China enjoy freedom of speech, of the assembly, of association, of procession and demonstration.

Article 36

Citizens of the People's Republic of China enjoy freedom of religious belief.

No State organ, public organization or individual may compel citizens to believe in, or not to believe in, any religion; nor may they discriminate against citizens who believe in, or do not believe in, any religion.

The state protects normal religious activities. No one may make use of religion to engage in activities that disrupt public order, impair the health of citizens or interfere with the educational system of the state.

Religious bodies and religious affairs are not subject to any foreign domination.

Article 37

Freedom of the person of citizens of the People's Republic of China is inviolable.

No citizen may be arrested except with the approval or by decision of a people's procurator or by decision of a people's court, and arrests must be made by a public security organ.

Unlawful detention or deprivation or restriction of citizens' freedom of the person by other means is prohibited, and unlawful search of the person of citizens is prohibited.

Article 38

The personal dignity of citizens of the People's Republic of China is inviolable. Insult, libel, false accusation or false incrimination directed against citizens by any means is prohibited.

Article 39

The residences of citizens of the People's Republic of China are inviolable. Unlawful search of, or intrusion into, a citizen's residence is prohibited.

Article 40

Freedom and privacy of correspondence of citizens of the People's Republic of China are protected by law. No organization or individual may, on any ground, infringe upon citizens' freedom and privacy of correspondence, except in cases where, to meet the needs of state security or of criminal investigation, public security or procurator organs are permitted to censor correspondence in accordance with procedures prescribed by law.

Article 41

Citizens of the Republic of China have the right to criticize and make suggestions regarding any state organ or functionary. Citizens have the right to make to relevant state organs complaints or charges against, or exposures of, any state organ or functionary or violation of the law or dereliction of duty; but fabrication or distortion of facts for purposes of libel or false incrimination is prohibited.

The state concerned must deal with complaints, charges or exposures made by citizens in a responsible manner after ascertaining the facts. No one may suppress such complaints, charges and exposures or retaliate against the citizens making them.

Citizens who have suffered losses as a result of infringement of their civic rights by any state organ or functional have the right to compensation in accordance with the law.

Article 42

Citizens of the People's Republic of China have the right as well as the duty to work.

Through various channels the state creates conditions for employment, enhances occupational safety and health, improves working conditions and, on the basis of expanded production, increases remuneration for work and welfare benefits.

Work is a matter of honour for every citizen who is able to work. All working people in state enterprises and in urban and rural economic collectives should approach their work as the masters of the country that they are. The state promotes socialist labour emulation, and commends and rewards model and advanced workers. The state encourages citizens to take part in voluntary labour. The state provides necessary vocational training for citizens before they are employed.

Article 43

Working people in the People's Republic of China have the right to rest.

The state expands facilities for the rest and recuperation of the working people and prescribes working hours and vacations for workers and staff.

Article 44

The state applies the system of retirement for workers and staff of enterprises and institutions and for functionaries of organs of according to law. The livelihood of retired personnel is ensured by the state and society.

Article 45

Citizens of the People's Republic of China have the right to material assistance from the state and society when they are old, ill or disabled. The state develops social insurance, social relief and medical and health services that are required for citizens to enjoy this right.

The state and society ensure the livelihood of disabled members of the armed forces; provide pensions to the families of martyrs and preferential treatment to the families of military personnel.

The state and society help make arrangements for the work, livelihood and education of the blind, deaf-mutes and other handicapped citizens.

Article 46

Citizens of the People's Republic of China have the duty as well as the right to receive education.

The state promotes the all-round development of children and young people, morally, intellectually and physically.

Article 47

Citizens of the People's Republic of China have the freedom to engage in scientific research, literary and artistic creation and other cultural pursuits. The state encourages and assists creative endeavours conducive to the interests of the people that are made by citizens engaged in education, science, technology, literature, art and other cultural work.

Article 48

Women in the People's Republic of China enjoy equal rights with men in all spheres of life, in political, economic, cultural, social and family life.

The state protects the rights and interests of women, applies the principle of equal work to men and women alike and trains and selects cadres from among women.

Article 49

Marriage, the family and mother and child are protected by the state. Both husband and wife have the duty to practice family planning.

Parents have the duty to rear and educate their children who are minors, and children who have come of age have the duty to support and assist their parents.

Violation of the freedom of marriage is prohibited. Maltreatment of old people, women and children is prohibited.

Article 50

The People's Republic of China protects the legitimate rights and interests of Chinese nationals residing abroad and protects the lawful rights and interests of returned overseas Chinese and of family members of Chinese nationals residing abroad.

Article 51

Citizens of the People's Republic of China, in exercising their freedom and rights, may not infringe upon the interests of the state, of society or of the collective, or upon the lawful freedoms and rights of other citizens.

Article 52

It is the duty of citizens of the People's Republic of China to safeguard the unification of the country and the unity of all its nationalities.

Article 53

Citizens of the People's Republic of China must abide by the Constitution and the law, keep state secrets, protect public property, observe labour discipline and public order and respect social ethics.

Article 54

It is the duty of citizens of the People's Republic of China to safeguard the security, honour and interests of the motherland; they must not commit acts detrimental to the security, honour and interests of the motherland.

Article 55

It is the sacred duty of every citizen of the People's Republic of China to defend the motherland and resist aggression.

It is the honourable duty of the People's Republic of China to perform military service and join the militia in accordance with the law.

Article 56

It is the duty of citizens of the People's Republic of China to pay taxes in accordance with the law.

A gist of all these Articles shows that at least on paper and in writing, violations of Fundamental Rights and infringement of human rights are not possible. Equality before law and equal protection of laws, the right to adult franchise, the right to various personal freedoms, freedom of religion, the right to life, liberty and property, individual dignity, privacy, the right and duty to work, rest and livelihood and material assistance to the ill or disabled and old, the right to education, protection to ladies, parents and child, safeguard to citizens of China residing abroad and unification of the country have been, broadly speaking, recognized. Two distinct features of this constitutional provision, from the point of view of human rights, are the recognition of the right to compensation to be paid by state as a result of infringement of their civil rights and prohibition of arrest and detain.

Russia (USSR)

The Constitution of USSR 1977 and Russia 1995 differs in major respect to the old Constitution of 1936,37, Chapter VI and VII of the present Constitution described these rights and duties as follows: -

Citizens of Russia
Equality of Citizens Rights

Article 33

Uniform federal Citizenship shall be established for the Russia. Every citizen of a Union Republic is a citizen of Russia.

The grounds and procedure for acquiring or forfeiting Soviet citizenship are defined by the law on citizenship of the Russia.

When abroad, citizens of the Russia shall enjoy the protection and assistance of the Soviet state.

Article 34

Citizens of the Russia are equal before the law, without distinction of right, Social or property status, race or nationality, sex, education, domicile or other status.

The equal rights of citizens of the Russia shall be guaranteed in all fields of economic, political, social and cultural life.

Article 35

Women and Men shall have equal rights in the Russia.

Exercise of these rights is ensured by according women equal access with men to education and vocational training, equal opportunities in employment, remuneration and promotion and in social and health protection measures for women; by providing conditions enabling mothers to work; by legal protection, and material and moral support for mothers and children, including paid leaves and other benefits for expectant mothers, and gradual reduction of working time for mothers with small children.

Article 36

Citizens of the Russia of different races and nationalities have equal rights.

Exercise of these rights is ensured by policy of all-round development and drawing together of all the nations and nationalities of the Russia, by educating citizens in the spirit of Soviet patriotism and socialist internationalism, and by the possibilities to use their native language and the languages of other peoples of the Russia.

Any direct or indirect limitation of the rights of citizens or establishment of direct or indirect privileges on grounds of race or nationality, enmity or contempt, shall be punishable by law.

Article 37

Foreign Nationals and stateless persons in the Russia shall be guaranteed the rights and freedoms provided by law, including the right to apply to a Court and other state bodies for the protection of their personal, property, family, and other rights.

Foreign nationals and stateless persons, When in the Russia are obliged to respect the constitution of the Russia and observe Soviet laws.

Article 38

The Russia shall grant the right of asylum to foreigners persecuted for defending interests of the working people and the cause of peace, or for participation in the revolutionary and national liberation movement, or for progressive social and political, scientific or other creative activity.

Article 39

Citizens of the Russia enjoy in full the socio-economic, political and personal rights and freedoms proclaimed and guaranteed by the constitution of the Russia and by Soviet laws. The Socialist system shall ensure enlargement of the rights and freedoms of citizens and continuous improvement of their living standards as social, economic and cultural development programs are fulfilled.

Enjoyment by citizens of their rights and freedoms shall not be to the detriment of the interests of society and the state, or infringe the rights of other citizens.

Article 40

Citizens of the Russia shall have the right to work (that is, to guaranteed employment and pay in accordance with the quantity and quality of their work, and not below the state established minimum norms), including the right to choose their trade or profession, type of occupation and work in accordance with their inclinations, abilities, vocational training and education, with due account of the needs of society.

The right shall be ensured by the socialist economic system, steady growth of the productive forces, free vocational training, improvement of skills, training in the new trades or professions, and development of the system of vocational guidance and job placement.

Article 41

Citizens of the Russia shall have the right to rest and leisure.

The right shall be ensured by the introduction of a working hours not exceeding 41 hours, of workers and other employees, a shorter working day in a number of traders and industries and shorted hours for night work; weekly days of rest, extension of the net work of cultural, educational and health building institutions, and the development on a mass scale of sport, physical culture, and tourism; by the provision of neighbor - hood recreational facilities, and of other opportunities for rational use of free time.

The length of collective farmer's working and leisure time shall be established by their collective farms.

Article 42

Citizens of the Russia shall have the right to health protection.

This right shall be ensured by free, qualified medical care provided by state health institutions; by extension of the network of therapeutic and improvement of safety and hygiene in industry; by carrying out broad preventive measures; by measures to improve the environment; by special care for the health of the rising generation, including prohibition of child labour excluding the work done by children as part of the school curriculum and labour education; and by developing research to prevent and reduce the incidence of disease and ensure citizens a long and active life.

Article 43

Citizens of Russia shall have the right to maintenance in old age, in sickness and in the event of complete or partial disability or loss of the breadwinner.

This right shall be guaranteed by social insurance of workers and other employees and collective farmers; by allowance for temporary disability; by the provision by the state or by collective forms of the breadwinner; by providing employment for the partially disabled ; by care for the elderly and the disabled and by other of social security.

Article 44

Citizen of the Russia shall have right to housing.

This right shall be ensured by the development and upkeep of state and socially owned housing; by assistance for cooperative and individual house building; fair distribution, under social control, of the housing that becomes available through fulfillment of the program of building well-appointed dwellings and by low rents and low charges for utility service. Citizens of the Russia shall take good care of the housing allocated to them.

Article 45

Citizens of the Russia have the right to education.

This right shall be ensured by free provision of all forms of education, by the institution of universal, compulsory secondary education for young people, and broad development of vocational, specialized secondary and higher education, in which instruction is oriented towards practical activity and production; by the provision of state scholarships a grants and privileges for students; by attending a school with the teaching in the native language; and by the provision of facilities for self-education.

Article 46

Citizens of the Russia shall have the right to enjoy cultural benefits.

This right shall be ensured by broad access to the cultural treasure of their own land of the world that are preserved in state and of the world that are preserved in state and other public collections; by the development and even distribute broadening scientific research, encouraging invention, and developing literature and the arts. The state shall provide the necessary material conditions for this and support for voluntary societies and unions of workers in the arts, organize introduction of inventions and innovations in the national economy and other spheres of activity.

Article 48

Every citizen of the Russia have right to submit proposals to state bodies and social organizations for improving their activity, and to criticize shortcoming in their work.

Officials are obliged, within established time limits, to examine citizen's proposals and requests, to reply to them, and to take appropriate action.

Persecution for criticism is prohibited. Persons guilty of such persecution shall be called to account.

Article 50

In accordance with the interests of the people and in order to strengthen and develop the socialist system, citizens of the Russia shall be guaranteed freedom of speech, of the press and of assembly, meetings, street processions and demonstrations.

Exercise of these political freedoms shall be ensured by putting public buildings, streets and squares at the disposal of the working people and their organization, by board dissemination of information and by the opportunity to use the press, television and radio.

Article 51

In accordance with the aims of building communism citizens of the Russia have the right to associate in social organizations that promote of their political activity and initiative and satisfaction of their various interests?

Social organization shall be guaranteed condition for successfully performing the functions defined in their rules.

Article 52

Citizens of Russia shall be guaranteed freedom of conscience, the right to profess or not to profess any religion, and to conduct religious worship or atheistic propaganda. Incitement of hostility or hatred on religious grounds is prohibited.

Article 53

The family shall enjoy the protection of the state.

Marriage is based on the free consent of the women and the man; the spouse shall be completely equal in their family relations.

The State show concern for the family by providing and developing a broad system of childcare, institutions, by organizing and improving communal service and public catering, by paying grants on the birth of a child; by providing of family, and other forms of family allowances and assistance.

Article 54

Citizens of the Russia shall be guaranteed inviolability of the person. No one may be arrested except by a court decision or on the warrant of a procurator.

Article 55

Citizens of the Russia shall be guaranteed protection of the home. No one may, without lawful grounds, enter a home against the will of those residing in it.

Article 56

The privacy of citizens, and of their correspondence, telephone conversations, and telegraphic communications shall be protected by law.

Article 57

Respect for the individual and protection of the rights and freedoms of citizens shall be the duty of all state bodies, social organizations, and officials.

Citizens of Russia shall have the right to protection by the courts against encroachments on their honour and reputation, life and health, and personal freedom.

Article 58

Citizens of the Russia shall have the right to lodge a complaint against the actions of officials, state bodies and social bodies. Complaints shall be examined according to the procedure and within the time limit established by law.

Actions by officials that contravene the law or exceed their power, and infringe the rights of citizens, may be appealed against in a court in the manner prescribed by law.

Citizens of the Russia shall have the right to compensation for damage resulting from unlawful actions by state organizations and social organizations, or by officials in the performance of their duties.

Article 59

Citizen's exercise of their right and freedoms is inseparable from the performance of their duties and obligations.

Citizens of the Russia are obliged to observe the constitution of the Russia and Soviet laws, comply with the rules of socialist community life, and uphold the honour and dignity of Soviet citizenship.

Article 60

It shall be the duty of, and a matter of honour for, every able-bodied citizen of the Russia to work conscientiously in his chosen, socially useful occupation, and strictly to observe labour discipline. Evasion of socially useful work is incompatible with the principal of socialist society.

Article 61

Citizen of the Russia are obliged to preserve and protect socialist property. It shall be the duty of citizens of Russia to combat misappropriation and squandering of state and socially - owned property and to make thriftily use of the people's wealth.

Persons encroaching in any way on socialist property shall be punished according to the law.

Article 62

Citizen of the Russia are obliged to safeguard the interests of Soviet state, and to enhance its power and prestige.

Defence of the socialist motherland is the secret duty of every citizen of the Russia.

Betrayal of the motherland is the gravest of crimes against the people.

Article 63

Military service in the armed forces of the Russia is a honorable duty of Soviet citizen.

Article 64

It shall be the duty of every citizen of the Russia to respect the national dignity of their citizens, and to strengthen friendship of the nations and nationalities of the multinational Soviet state.

Article 65

A citizen of Russia is obliged to respect the rights and lawful interests of other personal, to be uncompromising towards anti-social behavior, and to help to, maintain public order.

Article 66

A citizen of the Russia is obliged to concern himself with the upbringing of children, to train them for socially useful work, and to raise them as worthy members of socialist society. Children are obliged to care for their parents and support them.

Article 67

Citizens of the Russia are obliged to protect nature and conserve its riches.

Article 68

Concern for the preservation of historical monuments and other cultural value is a duty and obligation of citizens of the Russia.

Article 69

It shall be the international duty of citizens of the Russia to promote friendship and co-operation with peoples of other lands and help maintain and strengthen world peace.

The above text of the new constitution shows that the Russia treats citizenship matters in connection with the General status of the individual. It does differ from the 1936 constitution, which mentioned citizenship only in connection with the national state structure. The new constitution understands citizenship as a man belonging to a given state, as a stable legal bond between the state and the individual implying that both have corresponding right and duties with respect to one another. The 1977 constitution has considerably extended soviet citizens economic, social and cultural rights. It has added new elements to the rights to labour, rest and ensure material maintenance and education, as contained in the former constitution and has given constitutional sanction to the right to health protection and housing including care for disabled and other form of social security.

The right to enjoy cultural benefits and freedom of scientific, technological and artistic work has been secured for the first time at the constitutional level.

The new constitution has further developed the political rights and freedoms mentioned in the former constitution i.e. those of speech, of the press and of assembly, meetings, street procession and demonstrations and right to associates in social organizations including respect for the individual and concern for protection of citizens personal rights and freedoms. The new constitution, like the former one, record same duties of citizens. It has added one more duty reflecting society's concern for future generations and it is that to protect nature and conserve its riches.

Fundamental Rights and Duties in Pakistan

The following comparative table will show the present position of Fundamental Rights to be enjoyed by public or citizens. An attempt has been made out to show the position of Indian Fundamental Rights to be enjoyed by public or citizens. We may realize the wholesale position of Pakistan ourselves.

	Pakistan	India
A. Rights to Equality.	: Available to citizen only: (Art. 5(1)	Available to none-Citizens also (Art.-14) Art.15 contains this.
B. Prohibition against	: Nil	Discrimination on the ground of Religion, race, Caste, Sex, or place of birth.

	Pakistan	India
c. Equality of opportunity in public Services.	: No provision like art. 16(1) of India but see Pak. Consti, Rights 16 & 17 which provides for prohi-bition on the ground of race, religions, caste, sex residence and place, of birth, art.17(2) corresponds to art.16(3) of India.	: Art.16 (1) covers this see also art.(4)
d. Abolition of untouchability.	: Article 20	: Article 17
e. Seven freedoms in Art. 19 of India	: In more or less similar forms see arts. 7,9,10,11 12,16, to 20	: Article 19
f. Personal Liberty Provisions vary somewhat.	: Article 6	: Article 20 (1)
	Article 5 (2)	Article 21
	Article 6	Article 20 (1)
	NIL	Article 20 (3)
	Article 7(1) & (2)	Article 21(1)&(2)
	Article 7 (4)	Article 22 (4)
	Article 7 (5)	Article 22 (5)
	Article 22 (7)	
g. Right to Property.	Article 15	: Article 31 (Now repealed)

The constitutional rights under the 1956 document are enforceable by writs in Pakistan under arts. 22 and 170 which are analogous to arts 32 and 226 of the Indian constitution. But the Pakistan constitution of 1962 had no such provisions. The usual appeal remedies are contained in arts. 58 and 98 of the 1962 document. Appeal could lie on a point of substantial question of constitutional law. It was only in 1956 that in Pakistan the Government of India act 1935 was replaced by a constitution that herald cited Fundamental Rights to the citizens of Pakistan but this constitution of 1956 was abrogated in 1958, which was the result of the deliberations of a constituent assembly indirectly elected. In 1963 new constitution under the powers derived by a referendum to the elected members of local government Board, came into force and reintroduced an abridged Fundamental Rights with remedies for their infringements. They were called principles of law making.

The constitution of 1963 has been replaced by the new constitution during the regime of general Zia-Ul-Haque President. This constitution has also occupied limited Fundamental Rights only to citizens with consequential remedy in case of violation of these rights through court of law. This constitution, likewise India, is not secular and does not recognize the rights of minorities at all. It is highly surprising that Non-Muslims cannot cast their vote to Muslims candidates similarly Muslims cannot cast their vote to non-Muslims. Non-Muslims cannot contest election except for those seats, which are fixed for them.

Fundamental rights and duties in Nepal

The constitution of Nepal is the latest and modern. It has been enforced in the year 1990. All the Fundamental Rights of India have been incorporated into it. It has also provided about right to nationality. (Section 21), right to privacy. (Section (22), right to press and right to information. (Section 16), Nepal constitution has deviated only in one respect. It has not recognized special or privileged treatment to minorities. They have been treated at par with others.

Nepal constitution has also promised Directive Principles. These are as under: -

(a) For the establishment of welfare state.
(b) Utilization of all economic resources to maintain social justice.
(c) For removal of disparities in society and all round progress of society based on parity, coordination, morality and justice.
(d) Maintainance of law and order and protection of human rights.
(e) To maintain the national integrity & sovereignty. This constitution has also directed to observe following policies in law making: -
    (1) Upliftment of living standard of common man.
    (2) Fortification of national Unity.
    (3) Utilization of natural resources.
    (4) To maintain environmental balances.
    (5) Development of Agriculture Industry.
    (6) Cooperative Development.
    (7) Participation of women's in National progress
    (8) Free Education to children.
    (9) Special protection to Weaker and disabled.

(10) Advancement of Backward classes.
(11) Development of Local self Government system.
(12) Foreign Capital investment.
(13) Special care program for Village development.
(14) Free Legal aid to poor.
(15) Observance of Non-Aligned foreign policy.
(16) Institutional service for maintenance of peace.

There is nothing as such Directive Principles in the American constitution. The constitutional history of America, however, reveals admirably a gradual growth in the scope of duties of state towards welfare of society. It must be remembered that when peoples of U.S.A. framed their constitution they stated in the preamble that' In order to form a more perfect union, establish justice, ensure domestic tranquility provide for the common defence, promote the general welfare and, the blessings of liberty to ourselves and to our posterity, indirectly it can be said to be Directive Principles like India. In England the parliament is the Supreme law making body and no court of justice can question parliament's wisdom or its laws, Magna Crata and Bills of Right were, however, conventionally accepted as incorporating the aspirations of the people. Parliamentary power exercised through administrative agencies has first interpreted as the social needs of the people. Gradually it was recognized as rules of inter-predation tended towards the needs of the citizen. Thus the place of Directive Principles in English history was taken by convention and interpretative sphere of court of justice, which always took a progressive view of matters, in consonance with the social aspirations of the citizen without effecting parliamentary supremacy. These conventions are unwritten they are nevertheless recognized as effective.

The Weimer (German) constitution did declare many socio-economic rights along with other rights like fundamental Rights in India. They have stressed the need for fair distribution of land and dwelling houses to be seen to by state (Article 155) these citizens' rights are provided for the protection and promotion of labour and economic condition. But the whole defect is that neither Fundamental Rights nor these socio-economic rights were made justifiable.

Article 45 of Irish constitution provides the real picture of Directive Principles of state policy. It says "the state shall strive to promote the welfare of the whole of the people by securing and protecting as effectively as it may a social order in which justifiability and charity shall inform all the institutions of national life-such as securing all men and women citizens fair means of making through their occupation, reasonable provision for their domestic needs, and that ownership and control of material resources of the community are industry and is to be encouraged and supplemented by the state. The state is to safeguard the economic interest of the health of workers, men and women and young children, but these provisions were not made cognizable by court under any provisions of the constitution.

BANGLADESH

Let us now consider constitutional status of *Directive Principles and Fundamental Rights in Bangladesh*, which is as follows: -

PART II

Fundamental Principles of State Policy

1. [(1) The principles of absolute trust and faith in the Almighty Allah, nationalism, democracy and socialism meaning economic and social justice, together with the principles derived from them as set out in this Part, shall constitute the Fundamental Principle of State policy.

> [1](1A) Absolute trust and faith in the Almighty Allah shall be the basis of all actions.]
>
> (2) The principle set out in this Part shall be fundamental to the governance of Bangladesh, shall be applied by the State in the making of laws, shall be a guide to the interpretation of the Constitution and of the other laws of Bangladesh, and shall from the basis of the work of the State and of its citizens, but shall not be judicially enforceable.

[2][3. The State shall encourage local Government institution composed or representatives of the areas concerned and in such institutions special representation shall be given, as far as possible, to peasants, workers and women.

4. Steps shall be taken to ensure participation of women in all spheres of national life.]

5. The Republic shall be a democracy. Democracy in which fundamental human rights and human and freedoms and respect for the rights dignity and worth of the human person shall be guaranteed [3]****

6. The people shall own or control the instruments and means of production and distribution, and with this end In view ownership shall assume the following forms –

(a) State ownership, that is ownership by the State on behalf of the people through the creation of an efficient and dynamic nationalized public sector embracing the key sectors of the economy;

(b) Co-operative ownership, that is ownership by co-operatives on behalf of their members within such limits as may be prescribed by law; and

(c) Private ownership, that is ownership by individuals within such limits as may be prescribed by law.

7. It shall be a fundamental responsibility of the State to emancipate the toiling masses-the peasants and workers-and backward sections of the people from all forms of exploitation.

8. It shall be a fundamental responsibility of the State to attain, through planned economic growth, a constant increase of productive forces and a steady improvement in the material and cultural standard of living of the people, with a view to securing to its citizens –

(a) The provision of the basic necessities of life, including food, clothing, shelter, education and medical care;

(b) The right of work, that is the right to guaranteed employment at a reasonable wage having regard to the quantity and quality of work;

(c) The right to reasonable rest, recreation and leisure; and

(d) The right to social security, that is to say to public assistance in cases of undeserved want arising from unemployment, illness or disablement, or suffered by widows or orphans or in old age, or in other such cases.

9. The State shall adopt effective measures to bring about a radical transformation in the rural areas through the promotion of an agriculture revolution, the provision of electrification, the development of cottage and other industries,

and the improvement of education, communication and public health, in those areas, so as progressively to remove the disparity in the standards of living between the urban and rural areas.

10. The State shall adopt effective measure for the purpos e of –

(a) Establishing a uniform, mass-oriented and universal system of education and extending free and compulsory education to all children to such stage as may be determined by law;
(b) Relating education to the needs of society and producing properly trained and motivated citizens to serve those needs;
(c) Removing illiteracy within such time as may be determined by law.

11. (i) The State shall regard the raising of the level of nutrition and the improvement of public health as among its primary duties, and in particular shall adopt effective measures to prevent the consumption, except for medical purposes or for such other purposes as may be prescribes by law, of alcoholic and other intoxicating drinks and of drugs which are injurious to health.

(ii) The State shall adopt effective measure to prevent prostitution and gambling.

12. (i) The State shall endeavour to ensure equality of opportunity to all citizens.

(ii) The State shall adopt effective measures to remove social and economic inequality between man and man and to ensure the equitable distribution of wealth among citizens and of opportunities in order to attain a uniform level of economic development throughout the Republic.

13. (i) Work is a right, a duty and a matter of honour for every citizen who is capable of working, and every one shall be paid for his work on the basis of the Principle according to his abilities to each according to his work.

(ii) The State shall endeavour to create conditions in which, as a general principle, persons shall not be able to enjoy unearned incomes, and in which human labour in every form, intellectual and physical, shall become a fuller expression of creative endeavour and of the human personality.

14. (i) It is the duty of every citizen to observe the Constitution and the laws, to maintain discipline, to Perform public duties and to protect public property

(ii) Every person in the service of the Republic has a duty to strive at all times to serve and people.

15. The State shall ensure the separation of the judiciary from the executive organs of the State.

16. The State shall adopt measures to conserve the cultural traditions and heritage of the people, and so to foster and improve the national language, literature and the arts that all sections of the people can afford the opportunity to contribute towards and to participate in the enrichment of the national culture.

17. The State shall adopt measures for the protection against disfigurement, damage or removal of all monuments, objects or places of special artistic or historic importance or interest.

18. [1](i) The State shall base its international relations on the principles of respect for national sovereignty and equality, non-interference in the internal affairs of countries, peaceful settlement of international disputes, and respect for international law and the principles enunciated in the United Nations Charter, and on the basis of those principles shall –

a. Strive for the renunciation of the use of force in international relations and for general and complete disarmament;
b. Uphold the right of every people freely to determine and build up its own social, economic and political system by ways and means of its own free choice; and
c. Support oppressed peoples throughout the world waging a just struggle against imperialism, colonialism or racialism.

[2][(ii) The State shall endeavour to consolidate, preserve and strengthen fraternal relations among Muslim countries based on Islamic solidarity.]

PART III

FUNDAMENTAL RIGHTS

19. (i) All existing laws inconsistent with the provisions of this part shall, to the extent of such inconsistency, become void on the commencement of this Constitution.

(ii) The State shall not make any law inconsistent with any provisions of this Part, and law so made shall, to the extent of such inconsistency, be void.

[1][(iii) Nothing in this article shall apply to any amendment of this Constitution made under article 142].

20. All citizens are equal before law and are entitled to equal protection

21. (i) The State shall not discriminate against any citizen on grounds only of religion, race, castes, sex or of religion, place of birth. etc.

(ii) Women shall have equal rights with men in all spheres of the State and of public life.

(iii) No citizen shall, on grounds only of religion, race, caste, sex or place of birth be subjected to any disability, liability, restriction or condition with regard to access to any place of public entertainment or resort, or admission to any educational institution.

(iv) Nothing in this article shall prevent the State from making special provision in favour of women or children or for the advancement of any backward section of citizens.

22. (i) There shall be equality of opportunity for all citizens in respect of employment or office in the service of the Republic.

23. (II) No citizen shall, on grounds only of religion, race, caste, sex or place of birth, be ineligible for, or discriminated against in respect of, any employment or office in the service of the Republic.

(III) Nothing in this article shall prevent the state from –

a. Making special provision in favour of any backward section of citizens for the purpose of securing their adequate representation in the service of the Republic;

b. Giving effect to any law which makes provision for reserving appointments relating to any religious or denominational institution to persons of that religion or denomination;

c. Reserving for members of one sex any class of employment or office on the ground that it is considered by its nature to be unsuited to members of the opposite sex.

2[24. No citizen shall, without the prior approval of the President, accept any title, honour, award or decoration from any foreign state.]

25. To enjoy the protection of the law, and to be treated in accordance with law, and only in accordance with law, is the inalienable right of every citizen, wherever he may be, and of every other person for the time being within Bangladesh, and in particular no action detrimental to the life, liberty, body, reputation or property of any person shall be taken except in accordance with law.

26. No person shall be deprived of life or personal liberty save in accordance with law.

[1][27.(i) No person who is arrested shall be detained in custody without being informed, as soon as may be, of the grounds for such arrest, nor shall he be denied the right to consult and be defended by a legal Practitioner of his choice.

(ii) Every person who is arrested and detained in custody shall be produced before the nearest magistrate within a period of twenty-four hours of such arrest, excluding the time necessary for the journey from the place of arrest to the court of the magistrate and no such person shall be detained in custody beyond the said period without the authority of a magistrate.

(iii) Nothing in clauses (1) and (2) shall apply to any person –

(a) Who for the time being is an enemy alien; or

(b) Who is arrested or detained under any law providing for preventive detention.

(iv) No law providing for preventive detention shall authorize the detention of a person for a period exceeding six months unless an Advisory Board consisting of three persons, of whom two shall be persons who are, or have been, or are qualified to be appointed as, Judges of the Supreme Court and the other shall be a person who is a senior officer in the service of the Republic, has, after affording him an opportunity of being heard in person, reported before the expiration of the said period of six months that there is, in its opinion, sufficient cause for such detention.

(v) When any person detained in pursuance of an order shall, as soon as may be, communicate to such person the grounds on which the order has been made, and shall afford him the earliest opportunity of making a representation against the order:

> Provided that the authority making any such order may refuse to disclose facts which such authority considers to be against the public interest to disclose.

(vi) Parliament may by law prescribe the procedure to be followed by an Advisory Board in an inquiry under clause (4).]

28. (1) All forms of forced labour are prohibited and any contravention of this provision shall be an offence punishable in accordance with law.

(2) Nothing in this article shall apply to compulsory labour –

(a) By persons undergoing lawful punishment for a criminal offence; or

(b) Required by any law for public purposes.

29. (1) No person shall be convicted of any offence except for violation of a law in force at the time of the commission of the act charged as an offence, nor be subjected to a penalty greater than, or different from, that which might have been inflicted under the law in force at the time of the commission of the offence.

(2) No person shall be prosecuted and punished for the same offence more than once.

(3) Every person accused of a criminal offence shall have the right to a speedy and public trial by an independent and impartial court or tribunal established by law.

(4) No person accused of any offence shall be compelled to be a witness against himself.

(5) No person shall be subjected to torture or to cruel, inhuman or degrading punishment or treatment.

(6) Nothing in clause (3) or clause (5) shall affect the operation of any existing law, which prescribes any punishment of procedure for trial.

30. Subject to any reasonable restriction imposed by law in the public interest, every citizen shall have the right to move freely throughout Bangladesh, to reside and settle in any place therein and to leave and re-enter Bangladesh.

31. Every citizen shall have the right to assemble and to participate in public meetings and procession peacefully And without arms, subject to any reasonable restriction imposed by law in the interest of public order or public health.

32. Every citizen shall have the right to form association or unions, subject to any reasonable restriction imposed by Law in the interest of morality or public order:

* * * * * * * *

33. (1) Freedom of thought and conscience is guaranteed.

(2) Subject to any reasonable restriction imposed by law in the interest of the security of the state, friendly relation with foreign states, public order decency or morality, or in relation to contempt of court, defamation or incitement to an offence.

(a) The right of every citizen to freedom of speech and expression; and

(b) Freedoms of the press are guaranteed.

34. Subject to any restrictions imposed by law, every citizen possessing such qualifications, if any, as may be prescribed by law in relation to his profession, occupation, trade or Business shall have the right to enter upon any lawful profession or occupation, and to conduct any lawful trade or business.

35. (1) Subject to law, pubic order and morality-

(a) Every citizen has the right to profess, practice or propagate any religion;

(b) Every religious community or denomination has the right to establish, maintain and manage its religious institution.

(2) No person attending any educational institution shall be required to receive religious instruction, or to take part in or to attend any religious ceremony or worship, if that instruction, ceremony or worship relates to a religion other than his own.

36. (1) Subject to any restrictions imposed by law, every citizen shall have the right to acquire, hold, transfer or otherwise dispose of property, and no property shall be compulsorily acquired, nationalized or requisitioned save by authority of law.

[1][(2) A law made under clause (1) shall provide for the acquisition, nationalization or requisition with compensation and shall either fix the amount of compensation or specify the principle on which, and the manner in which, the compensation is to be assessed and paid; but no such law shall be called in question in any court on the ground that any provision in respect of compensation is not adequate.

2. Nothing in this article shall affect the operation of any law made before the commencement of the proclamation (amendment) order, 1977 (Proclamations Order No. 1 of 1977), in so far as it relates to the acquisition, nationalization or acquisition of any property without compensation.

37. Every citizen shall have the right, subject to any reasonable restriction imposed by law in the interest of the security of the State, public order, public morality or public health-

(a) To be secured in his home against entry, search and seizure; and

(b) To be privacy of his correspondence and other means of communication.

[2][38. (1) The right to move the [3][High Court Division] in accordance with [4][clause (1)] of article 102, for the enforcement of the rights conferred by this Part is

(2) Without prejudice to the powers of the [3][High Court Division] under article 102, Parliament may by law empower any other court, within the local limits of its jurisdiction, to exercise all or any of those powers.]

39. Nothing in this Part shall apply to any provision of a disciplinary law relating to members of a disciplined force, being a provision limited to the law. purpose of ensuring the proper discharge of their duties or the Maintenance of discipline in that force.

40. Notwithstanding anything in the foregoing provisions this Part, Parliament may by law making provision for indemnity.

Indemnifying any person in the service of the Republic or any other person in respect of any act done by him in connection with the national liberation struggle or the maintenance or restoration of order in any area in Bangladesh or validate any sentence passed, punishment inflicted, forfeiture ordered, or other act done in any such area.

41. (1) No law providing for any of the following matters shall be deemed to be void on the ground that it is Inconsistent with, or takes away or abridges, any of the rights guaranteed by this Part-

(a) the compulsory acquisition, nationalization or requisition of any property, or the control or management thereof whether temporarily or permanently;

(b) The compulsory amalgamation of bodies carrying on commercial or other undertakings;

(c) The extinction, modification, restriction or regulation of rights of directors, managers, agents and officers of any such bodies, or of the voting rights of persons owning shares or stock (in whatever form) therein;

(d) The extinction, modification, restriction or regulation of rights to search for or win minerals or mineral oil;

(e) The carrying on by the Government or by a corporation owned, controlled or managed by the Government, of any trade, business, industry or service to the exclusion, complete or partial, of other persons; or

(f) The extinction, modification, restriction or regulation of any right to property, any right in respect of a profession, occupation, trade or business or the rights of employers or employees in any statutory public authority or in any commercial or industrial undertaking;

If Parliament in such law (including, in the case of existing law, by amendment) expressly declares that such provision is made to give effect to any of the fundamental principles of state policy set out in Part II of this Constitution.

(2) Notwithstanding anything contained in this Constitution the laws specified in the First Schedule (including any amendment of any such law) shall continue to have full force any effect, and no provision of any such law, nor anything

done or omitted to be done under the authority of such law, shall be deemed void or unlawful on the ground of inconsistency with, or repugnance to, any provision of this Constitution: -

[1][Provided that nothing in this article shall prevent amendment, modification or repeal of any such law.]

[2][(2) Notwithstanding anything contained in this Constitution, no law nor any provision thereof providing for detention, prosecution or punishment of any person, who is a member of any armed or defence or auxiliary forces or who is a prisoner of war, for genocide, crimes against humanity or war crimes and other crimes under international law shall be deemed void or unlawful, or ever to have become void or unlawful, on the ground that such law or provision of any such law is inconsistent with, or repugnant to, any of the provisions of this Constitution.]

[3][47A. (1) The rights guaranteed under article 31, clauses (1) and (3) of article 35 and article 44 shall not apply to any person to whom a law specified in clause (3) of article 47 applies.

(2) Notwithstanding anything contained in this Constitution, no person to whom a law specified in clause (3) of article 47 applies shall have the right to move the Supreme Court for any of the remedies under this Constitution.]

CHAPTER 5
FUNDAMENTAL RIGHTS AND DUTIES AT THE INTERNATIONAL LEVEL

Various kinds of Fundamental Rights and duties at the international level are found under the Universal Declaration of Human Rights and its various covenants under the UN Charter. Let us consider all these provisions.

Universal Declaration of Human Rights

(Article 1)

The International Bill of Human Rights consists of the Universal Declaration of Human Rights, the International Covenant on Economic, Social and Cultural Rights, and the International Covenant on Civil and Political Rights and its two Optional Protocols.

Human rights had already found expression in the Covenant of the League of Nations, which led to, inter alia, the creation of the International Labour Organization. At the 1945 San Francisco Conference, held to draft the Charter of the United Nations, a proposal to embody a Declaration on the essential Rights of Man was put forward but was not examined because it required more detailed consideration than was possible at the time. The Charter clearly speaks of "promoting and encouraging respect for human rights and for fundamental freedoms for all without distinction as to race, sex, language or religion" (Article 1. Para 3). The idea of promulgating an International Bill of Rights was also considered by many as basically implicit in the Charter.

The Preparatory Commission of the United States, which met immediately after the closing session of the San Francisco Conference, recommended that the Economic and Social Council should, at this first session, establish a commission for the promotion of human rights as envisaged in Article 68 of the Charter. Accordingly, the Council established the Commission on Human Rights early in 1946.

At the first session in 1946, the General Assembly considered a draft Declaration of Fundamental Human Rights and Freedoms and transmitted it to the Economic and Social Council "for reference to the Commission on Human Rights for consideration... in preparation of an international bill of rights" [Resolution 43 (I)]. The Commission, at its first session early in 1947, authorized its officers to formulate what it termed a "preliminary draft International Bill of Human Rights." Later the work was taken over by a formal drafting committee, consisting of members of the Commission from eight States, selected with due regard for geographical distribution.

Towards the Universal Declaration

In the beginning, different views were expressed about the form the bill of rights should take. The Drafting Committee decided to prepare two documents: one in the form of a declaration, which would set forth general principles or standards of human rights; the other in the form of a convention, which would define specific rights and their limitations. Accordingly, the Committee transmitted to the Commission on Human Rights draft Articles of an international declaration and an international convention on human rights. At the second session in December 1947, the Commission decided to apply the term "International Bill of Human Rights" to the series of documents in preparation and established three working groups: one on implementation. The Commission revised the draft declaration at this third session in May/June 1948, taking into consideration comments received from governments. It did not have the time, however, to consider the covenant or the question of implementation. The declaration was therefore submitted through the Economic and Social Council to the General Assembly meeting in Paris.

By its Resolution 217 A (III) of 10 December 1948, the General Assembly adopted the Universal Declaration of Human Rights as the first of these projected instruments.

Towards the International Covenants

On the same day that it adopted the Universal Declaration, the General Assembly requested the Commission of Human Rights to prepare, as a matter of priority, a draft covenant on human rights and draft measures of implementation. The Commission examined the text of the draft covenant in 1949 and the following year it revised the first 18 Articles, on the basis of comments received from governments. In 1950, the General Assembly declared that "the enjoyment of civic and political freedoms and of economic, social and cultured rights are interconnected and inter dependent"' [Resolution 421(V), sect. E]. The assembly thus decided to include in the covenant on human rights, economic, social and cultured rights and an explicit recognition of the equality men and women in related rights, as set forth in the Charter. In 1951, the Commission drafted fourteen Articles on economic, social and cultural rights on the basis of proposal made by Government and suggestion by specialized agencies. It also formulated ten Articles on measures for implementation of those rights under which States party to the covenant would submit periodic reports stop. After the long debate and its sixth session in 1951/1952, the General Assembly requested the Commission ``to draft two Covenants on Human Rights, ...one to contain civil and political rights and the other to contain economic, social cultural rights''. [Resolution 543 (VI, Para. 1)]. The assembly specified that the two covenants should contain as many similar provisions as possible. It also decided to include an Article providing that "all peoples shall have the right of self-determination" [Resolution 545 (VI)].

The Commission completed preparation of the two drafts at its ninth session, in 1953 and 1954. The General Assembly reviewed those texts at its ninth session in 1954, and decided to give the drafts the widest possible publicity in order that governments might study them thoroughly and that public opinion might express itself freely. It recommended that its Third Committee start an Article-by-Article discussion of the text at its tenth session in 1955. Although the Article-by-Article discussion began as scheduled, it was not until 1966 that the preparation of the two covenants was completed.

The International Covenant on Economic, Social and Cultural Rights and the International Covenant on Civil and Political Rights were adopted by the General Assembly by its Resolution 2200 A (XXI) of 16 December 1966. The first Optional Protocol to the International Covenant on Civil and Political Rights, adopted by the same resolution, provided international machinery for dealing with communications from individuals claiming to be victims of violations of any rights set forth in the Covenant.

The International Bill of Human Rights

Universal Declaration of HumanRights[A]

Preamble

Whereas recognition of the inherent dignity and of the equal and inalienable rights of all members of the human family is the foundation of freedom, justice and peace in the world.

Whereas disregard and contempt for human rights have resulted in barbarous acts, which have outraged the conscience of mankind, and the advent of a world in which human beings shall enjoy freedom of speech and belief and freedom from fear and want has been proclaimed as the highest aspiration of the common people.

Whereas it is essential, if cannot be compelled to have recourse, as a last resort, to rebellion against tyranny and oppression, that human rights should be protected by the rule of law.

Whereas it is essential to promote the development of friendly relations between nations.

Whereas the peoples of the United Nations have in the Charter reaffirmed their faith in fundamental human rights, in the dignity and worth of the human person and in the equal rights of men and women and have determined to promote social progress and better standards of life in larger freedom.

Whereas Member States have pledged themselves to achieve, in cooperation with the United Nations, the promotion of universal respect for and observance of human rights and fundamental freedoms.

Whereas a common understanding of these rights and freedoms is of the greatest importance for the full realization of this pledge.

Now, therefore, The General Assembly

Proclaims this Universal Declaration of Human Rights as a common standard of achievement for all peoples and all nations, to the ends that every individual and every organ of society, keeping this Declaration constantly in mind, shall strive by teaching and education to promote respect for these rights and freedoms and by progressive measures, national and international, to secure their universal and effective recognition and observance, both among the peoples of Member States themselves and among the peoples of territories under their jurisdiction.

Article 1

All human being are born free and equal in dignity and rights. They are endowed with reason and conscience and should act towards one another in a spirit of brotherhood.

Article 2

Everyone is entitled to all the rights and freedoms set forth in this Declaration, without distinction of any kind, such as race, colour, sex, language, religion, political or other opinion, national or social origin, property, birth or other status.

Furthermore, no distinction shall be made on the basis of the political, jurisdictional or international status of the country or territory to which a person belongs, whether it be independent, trust, non-self-governing or under any limitation of sovereignty.

Article 3

Everyone has the right to life, liberty and security of person.

Article 4

No one shall be held in slavery or servitude; slavery and the slave trade shall be prohibited in all their forms.

Article 5

No one shall be subjected to torture or to cruel, inhuman or degrading treatment or punishment.

Article 6

Everyone has right to recognition everywhere as a person before the law.

Article 7

All are equal before the law and are entitled without any discrimination to equal protection of the law. All are entitled to equal protection against any discrimination to violation of this Declaration and against any incitement to such discrimination.

Article 8

Everyone has right to an effective remedy by the competent national tribunals for acts violating the Fundamental Rights granted him by the Constitution or by law.

Article 9

No one shall be subjected to arbitrary arrest, detention or exile.

Article 10

Everyone is entitled in full quality to a fair and public hearing by an independent and impartial, in the determination of his rights and obligations and of any criminal charge against him.

Article 11

1. Everyone charged with a penal offence has the right to be presumed innocent until proved guilty according to law in a public trial at which he has had all the guarantees necessary for his defence.

2. No one shall be held guilty of any penal offence on account of any act or omission, which did not constitute a penal offence, under national or international law, at the time when it was committed. Nor shall a heavier penalty be imposed than the one that was applicable at the time the penal offence was committed.

Article 12

No one shall be subjected to arbitrary interference with his privacy, family, home or correspondence, or to attacks upon his honour and reputation. Everyone has the right to the protection of the law against such interference or attacks.

Article 13

1. Everyone has the right to freedom of movement and residence within the borders of each State.
2. Everyone has the right to leave any country, including his own, and to return to his country.

Article 14

1. Everyone has the right to seek and to enjoy in other countries asylum from persecution.
2. This right may not be invoked in the case of prosecutions genuinely arising from non-political crimes or from acts contrary to the purpose and principles of the United Nations.

Article 15

1. Everyone has the right to a nationality.
2. No one shall be arbitrarily deprived of his nationality nor denied the right to change nationality.

Article 16

1. Men or women of full age, without any limitation due to race, nationality or religion, have the right to marry and to found a family. They are entitled to equal rights as to marriage, during marriage and its dissolution.
2. Marriage shall be entered into only with the free and full consent of the intending spouses.
3. The family is the natural and fundamental group unit of society and is entitled to protection by society and the State.

Article 17

1. Everyone has the right to own property alone as well as in association with others.
2. No one shall be arbitrarily deprived of his property.

Article 18

Everyone has the right to freedom of thought, conscience and religion; this right includes freedom to change his religion or belief, and freedom, either alone or in community with others and in public or private, to manifest his religion or belief in teaching, practice, worship and observance.

Article 19

Everyone has the right to freedom of opinion and expression; this right includes freedom to hold opinions without interference and to seek, receive and impart information and ideas through any media and regardless of frontiers.

Article 20

1. Everyone has the right to freedom of peaceful assembly and association.
2. No one may be compelled to belong to an association.

Article 21

1. Everyone has the right to take part in the government of his country, directly or through freely chosen representative.
2. Everyone has the right to equal access to public service in his country.
3. The will of the people shall be the basis of the authority of government; this will shall be expressed in periodic and genuine elections, which shall be by universal and equal suffrage and shall be held by secret vote or by equivalent free voting procedures.

Article 22

Everyone, as a member of society, has the right to social security and entitled to realization, through national effort and international cooperation and in accordance with the organization and resources of his dignity and the free development of his personality.

Article 23

1. Everyone has the right to work, to free choice of employment, to just and favourable conditions of work and to protection against unemployment.
2. Everyone, without any discrimination, has the right to equal pay for equal work.
3. Everyone who works has the right to just and favourable remuneration ensuring for himself and his family an existence worthy of human dignity, and supplemented, if necessary, by other means of social protection.
4. Everyone has the right to form and to join trade unions for the protection of his interest.

Article 24

Everyone has the right to rest and leisure, including reasonable limitation of working hours and periodic holidays with pay.

Article 25

1. Everyone has the right to a standard of living adequate for the health and well-being of himself and of his family, including food, clothing, housing and medical care and necessary social services, and the right to security in the event of unemployment, sickness, disability, widowhood, old age or other lack of livelihood in circumstances beyond his control.
2. Motherhood and childhood are entitled to special care and assistance. All children whether born in or out of wedlock, shall enjoy the same social protection.

Article 26

1. Everyone has the right to education. Education shall be free at least in the elementary and fundamental stages. Elementary education shall be compulsory. Technical and professional education shall be made generally available and higher education shall be equally accessible to all on the basis of merit.
2. Education shall be directed to the full development of the human personality and to the strengthening of respect for human rights and fundamental freedoms. It shall promote understanding, tolerance and friendship among all nations, racial or religious groups, and shall further the activities of the United Nations for the maintenance of peace.
3. Parents have a prior right to choose the kind of education that shall be given to their children.

Article 27

1. Everyone has the right freely to participate in the cultural life of the community, to enjoy the arts and to share in scientific advancement and its benefits.
2. Everyone has the right to the protection of the moral and material interests resulting from any scientific, literary or artistic production of which he is the author.

Article 28

Everyone is entitled to a social and international order in which the rights and freedoms set forth in this Declaration can be fully realized.

Article 29

1. Everyone has duties to the community in which alone the free and full development of his personality is possible.
2. In the exercise of his rights and freedoms, everyone shall be subject only to such limitations as are determined by law solely for the purpose of securing due recognition and respect for the rights and freedoms of others and of meeting the just requirements of morality, public order and the general welfare in a democratic society.
3. These rights and freedoms may in no case be exercised contrary to the purpose and principles of the United Nations.

Article 30

Nothing in this Declaration may be interpreted as implying for any state, group or person any right to engage in any activity or to perform any act aimed at the destruction on any of the rights and freedoms set forth herein.

INTERNATIONAL COVENANT ON ECONOMIC, SOCIAL AND CULTURAL RIGHTS[B]

The States party to the present Covenant,

Considering that, in accordance with the principles proclaimed in the Charter of the United Nations, recognition of the inherent dignity and of the equal and inalienable rights of all members o the human family is the foundation of freedom, justice and peace in the world,

Recognizing that these rights derive from the inherent dignity of the human person,

Recognizing that, in accordance with the Universal Declaration of Human Rights, the ideal of free human beings enjoying freedom from fear and want can only be achieved if conditions are created whereby everyone may enjoy his economic, social and cultural rights, as well as his civil and political rights,

Considering the obligation of States under the Charter of the United Nations to promote universal respect for, and observance of, human rights and freedoms,

Realizing that the individual, having duties to other individuals and to the community to which he belongs, is under a responsibility to strive for the promotion and observance of the rights recognized in the present covenant,

Agree upon the following Articles:

PART I

Article 1

1. All peoples have the right of self-determination. By virtue of the right they freely determine their political status and freely pursue their economic, social and cultural development.
2. All peoples may, for their own ends, freely dispose of their natural wealth and resources without prejudice to any obligations arising out of international economic cooperation, based upon the principle of mutual benefit, and international law. In no case may a people be deprived of his own means of subsistence.
3. The States party to the present Covenant, including those having responsibility for the administration of Non-Self-Governing and Trust Territories, shall promote the realizing of the right of self-determination, and shall respect that right, in conformity with the provisions of the Charter of the United States.

PART II

Article 2

1. Each State party to the present Covenant undertakes to take steps, individually and through international assistance and cooperation, especially economic and technical, to the maximum of its available resources, with a view to achieving progressively the full realization of the rights recognized in the present Covenant by all appropriate means, including particularly the adoption of legislative measures.
2. The States party to the present Covenant undertake to guarantee that the rights enunciated in the present Covenant will be exercised without discrimination of any kind as to race, colour, sex, language, religion, political or other opinion, national or social origin, property, birth or other status.
3. Developing countries, with regard to human rights and their national economy, may determine to what extent they would guarantee the economic rights recognized in the present Covenant to non-nationals.

Article 3

The States party to the present Covenant undertake to ensure the equal rights of men and women to the enjoyment of all economic, social and cultural rights set forth in the present Covenant.

Article 4

The States party to the present Covenant recognize that, in the enjoyment of those rights provided by the State in conformity with the present Covenant, the State may subject such rights only to such limits with the nature of these rights and solely for the purpose of promoting the general welfare in a democratic society.

Article 5

1. Nothing in the present Covenant may be interpreted as implying for any State, group or person any right to engage in any activity or to perform for any act aimed at the destructing of any of the rights or freedoms recognized herein, or at their limitation to a greater extent than is provided for in the present Covenant.
2. No restriction upon or derogation from any of the fundamental human rights recognized or existing in any country in virtue of law, conventions, regulations or custom shall be admitted on the pretext that the present Covenant does not recognize such rights or that it recognizes them to a lesser extent.

Part III

Article 6

1. The States party to the present Covenant recognize the right to work, which includes the right of everyone to the opportunity to gain his living by work which he freely chooses or accepts, and will take appropriate steps to safeguard this right.
2. The steps to be taken by States party to the present Covenant to achieve the full realization of this right shall include technical and vocational guidance and training programmes, policies and techniques to achieve steady economic, social and cultural development and full and productive employment under conditions safeguarding fundamental political and economic freedoms to the individual.

Article 7

The State party to the present Covenant recognize the right of everyone to the enjoyment of just and favourable conditions of work which ensure, in particular:

(a) Remuneration which provides all workers, as a minimum with:

i. Fair wages and equal remuneration for work of equal value without distinction of any kind, in particular women being guaranteed conditions of work not inferior to those enjoyed by men, with equal work;

ii. A decent living for themselves and their families in accordance with the provisions of the present Covenant;

(b) Safe and healthy working conditions;

(c) Equal opportunity for everyone to be promoted in his employment to an appropriate higher level, subject to no considerations other than those of seniority and competence;

(d) Rest, leisure and reasonable limitation of working hours and periodic holidays with pay, as well as remuneration for public holidays.

Article 8

1. The States party to the present Covenant undertake to ensure;

(a) The right of everyone to form trade unions and join the trade union of his choice, subject only to the rules of the organization concerned, for the promotion and protection of his economic and social interests. No restrictions may be placed on the exercise of this right other than those prescribed by law and which are necessary in a democratic society in the interests of national security or public order or for the protection of the rights and freedoms of others;

(b) The right of trade unions to establish national federations or confederations and the right of the latter to form or join international trade-union organizations;

(c) The right of trade unions to function freely subject to no limitations other than those prescribed by law and which are necessary in a democratic society in the interests of national security or public order or for the protection of the rights and freedoms of others;

(d) The right to strike provided that it is exercised in conformity with the laws of the particular country.

2. This Article shall not prevent the imposition of lawful restriction of the exercise of these rights by members of the armed forces or of the police or of the administration of the State.

3. Nothing in this Article shall authorize States party to the International Labour Organization Convention of 1948 concerning Freedom of Association and Protection of the Right to Organize to take legislative measures which would prejudice, or apply the law in such a manner as would prejudice, the guarantees provided for in that Convention.

Article 9

The States party to the present Covenant recognize the right of everyone to social security, including social insurance.

Article 10

The States party to the present Covenant recognize that:

1. The widest possible protection and assistance should be accorded to the family, which is the natural and fundamental group unit of society, particularly for its establishment and while it is responsible for the care and education of dependent children. Marriage must be entered into with the free consent of the intending spouses.
2. Special protection should be accorded to mothers during a reasonable period before and after childbirth. During such period working mothers should be accorded paid leave or leave with adequate social security benefits.
3. Special measures of protection and assistance should be taken on behalf of all children and young persons without any discrimination for reasons of parentage or other conditions. Children and young persons should be protected from economic and social exploitation. Their employment in work harmful to their morals or health or dangerous to life or likely to hamper their normal development should be punishable by law. States should also set age limits below which the paid employment of child labour should be prohibited and punishable by law.

Article 11

1. The States party to the present Covenant recognize the right of everyone to an adequate standard of living for himself and his family, including adequate food, clothing and housing, and to the continuous improvement of living conditions. The States party will take appropriate steps to ensure the realization of this right, recognizing to this effect the essential importance of international cooperation based on free consent.
2. The States party to the present Covenant, recognizing the fundamental right of everyone to be free from hunger, shall take, individually and through international cooperation, the measures, including specific programmes, which are needed:
   (a) To improve methods of production, conservation and distribution of food by making full use of technical and scientific knowledge, by disseminating knowledge of the principles of nutrition and by developing or reforming agrarian systems in such a way as to achieve the most efficient development and utilization of natural resources;
   (b) Taking into account the problems of both food-importing and food-exporting countries, to ensure and equitable distribution of world food supplies in relation to need.

Article 12

1. The States party to the present Covenant recognize the right of everyone to the enjoyment of the highest attainable standard of physical and mental health.
2. The steps to be taken by the States party to the present Covenant to achieve the full realization of this right shall include those necessary for:
   (a) The provision for the reduction of the stillbirth rate and of infant mortality and for the healthy development of the child;
   (b) The improvement of all aspects of environmental and industrial hygiene;
   (c) The prevention, treatment and control of epidemic, endemic, occupational and other diseases;
   (d) The creation of conditions which would assure to all medical service and medical attention in the event of sickness.

Article 13

1. The State party to the present Covenant recognize the right of everyone to education. They agree that education shall be directed to the full development of the human personality and the sense of its dignity, and shall strengthen the respect for human rights and fundamental freedoms. They further agree that education shall enable all person to participate effectively in a free society, promote understanding, tolerance and friendship among all nations and all racial, ethnic or religious groups, and further the activities of the United Nations for the maintenance of peace.
2. The States party to the present Covenant recognize that, with a view to achieving the full realization of this right:
   (a) Primary education shall be compulsory and available free to all;
   (b) Secondary education in its different forms, including technical and vocational secondary education, shall be made generally available and accessible to all by every appropriate means, and in particular by the progressive introduction of free education;
   (c) Higher education shall be made equally accessible to all, on the basis of capacity, by every appropriate means, and in particular by the progressive introduction of free education;
   (d) Fundamental education shall be encouraged or intensified as far as possible for those persons who have not received or completed the whole period of their primary education;
   (e) The development of the system of schools at all levels shall be actively pursued, an adequate fellowship system shall be established, and the material conditions of teaching staff shall be continuously improved.
3. The States party to the present Covenant undertake to have respect for the liberty of parents and, when applicable, legal guardians to choose for their children's school, other than those established by the public authorities, which conform to such minimum educational standards as may be laid down or approved by the state and to ensure the religious and moral education of their children in conformity with their own convictions.

4. No part of this Article shall be construed so as to interfere with the liberty of individuals and bodies to establish and direct educational institutions, subject always to the observance of the principles set forth in Paragraph1 of this Article and to the requirement that the education given in such institutions shall conform to such minimum standards as may be laid down by the State.

Article 14

Each State party to the present Covenant which, at the time of becoming a party, has not been able to secure in its metropolitan territory or other territories under its jurisdiction compulsory primary education, free of charge, undertakes, within two years, to work out and adopt a detailed plan of action for the progressive implementation, within a reasonable number of years, to be fixed in the plan, of the principle of compulsory education free of charge for all.

Article 15

1. The States party to the present Covenant recognize the right of everyone:
   (a) To take part in cultural life;
   (b) To enjoy the benefits of scientific progress and its applications;
   (c) To benefit from the protection of the moral and material interests resulting from any scientific, literary or artistic production of which he is the author.
2. The steps to be taken by the States party to the present Covenant to achieve the full realization of this right shall include those necessary for the conservation, the development and the diffusion of science and cultural.
3. The States party to the present Covenant undertake to respect the freedom indispensable for scientific research and creative activity.
4. The States party to the present Covenant recognize the benefits to be derived from the encouragement and development of international contacts and cooperation in the scientific and cultural fields.

Part IV

Article 16

1. The States party to the present Covenant undertake to submit in conformity with this part of the Covenant reports on the measures, which they have adopted, and the progress made in achieving the observance of the rights recognized herein.
2. (a) All reports shall be submitted to the Secretary-General of the United Nations, who shall transmit copies to the Economic and Social Council for consideration in accordance with the provisions of the present Covenant;

   (b) The Secretary-General of United Nations shall also transmit to the specialized agencies copies of the reports, or any relevant parts therefrom, from States party to the present Covenant which are also members of these specialized agencies in so far as these reports, or parts therefrom, relate to any matters which fall within the responsibilities of the said agencies in accordance with their constitutional instruments.

Article 17

1. The States party to the present Covenant shall furnish their reports in stages, in accordance with a programme to be established by the Economic and Social Council within one year of the entry into force of the present Covenant after consultation with the States party and the specialized agencies concerned.
2. Reports may indicate factors and difficulties affecting the degree of fulfilment of obligations under the present Covenant.
3. Where relevant information has previously been furnished to the United Nations or to any specialized agency by any State party to the present Covenant, it will not be necessary to reproduce that information, but a precise reference to the information so furnished will suffice.

Article 18

Pursuant to its responsibilities under the Charter of the United Nations in the field of human rights and fundamental freedoms, the Economic and Social Council may make arrangements with the specialized agencies in respect of their reporting to it on the progress made in achieving the observance of the provisions of the present Covenant falling within the scope of their activities. These reports may include particulars of decisions and recommendations on such implementation adopted by their competent organs.

Article 19

The Economic and Social Council may transmit to the Commission on Human Rights for study and general recommendation or, as appropriate, for information the reports concerning human rights submitted by States in accordance with Articles 16 and 17, and those concerning human rights submitted by the specialized agencies in accordance with Article 18.

Article 20

The States party to the present Covenant and the specialized agencies concerned may submit comments to the Economic and Social Council on any general recommendation under Article 19 or reference to such general recommendation in any report of the Commission on Human Rights or any documentation referred to therein.

Article 21

The Economic and Social Council may submit from time to time to the General Assembly reports with recommendations of a general nature and summary of the information received from the States party to the present Covenant and the specialized agencies on the measures taken and the progress made in achieving general observance of the rights recognized in the present Covenant.

Article 22

The Economic and Social Council may bring to the attention of other organs of the United Nations, their subsidiary organs and specialized agencies concerned with furnishing technical assistance any matters arising out of the reports referred to in this part of the present Covenant which may assist such bodies in deciding, each within its field of competence, on the advisability of international measures likely to contribute to the effective progressive implementation of the present Covenant.

Article 23

The States party to the present Covenant agree that international action for the achievement of the rights recognized in the present Covenant includes such methods as the conclusion of conventions, the adoption of recommendations, the furnishing of technical assistance and the holding of regional meetings and technical meetings for the purpose of consultation and study organized in conjunction with the Government concerned.

Article 24

Nothing in the present Covenant shall be interpreted as impairing the provisions of the Charter of the United Nations and of the constitutions of the specialized agencies that define the respective responsibilities of the various organs of the United Nations and of the specialized agencies in regard to the matters dealt with in the present Covenant.

Article 25

Nothing in the present Covenant shall be interpreted as impairing the inherent right of all peoples to enjoy and utilize fully and freely their natural wealth and resources.

Part V

Article 26

1. The present Covenant is open for signature by any State Member of the United Nations or member of any of its specialized agencies, by any State party to the Statute of the International Court of Justice, and by any other State which has been invited by the General Assembly of the United Nations to become a party to the present Covenant.
2. The present Covenant is subject to ratification. Instruments of ratification shall be deposited with the Secretary-General of the United Nations.
3. The present Covenant shall be open to accession by any State referred to in Para 1 of this Article.
4. Accession shall be effected by the deposit of an instrument of accession with the Secretary-General of the United Nations.
5. The Secretary-General of the United Nations shall inform all States which have signed the present Covenant or acceded to it of the deposit of each instrument of ratification or accession.

Article 27

1. The present Covenant shall enter into force three months after the date of the deposit with the Secretary-General of the United Nations of the thirty-fifth instrument of ratification or instrument of accession.
2. For each State ratifying the present Covenant or acceding to in after the deposit of the thirty-fifth instrument of ratification or instrument of accession, the present Covenant shall enter into force three months after the date of deposit of its own instrument of ratification or instrument of accession.

Article 28

The provisions of the present Covenant shall extend to all parts of federal States without any limitations or exceptions.

Article 29

1. Any State party to the present Covenant may propose an amendment and file it with the Secretary-General of the United Nations. The Secretary-General shall thereupon communicate any proposed amendments to the States party to the present Covenant with a request that they notify him whether they favour a conference of States party for the purpose of considering and voting upon the proposals. In the event that at least one third of the States party favours such a conference, the Secretary-General shall convene the conference under the auspices of the United Nations. Any amendment adopted by a majority of the States party present and voting at the conference shall be submitted to the Secretary-General assembly of the United Nations for approval.
2. Amendments shall come into force when they have been approved by the General Assembly of the United Nations and accepted by a two-thirds majority of the States party to the present Covenant in accordance with their respective constitutional processes.

Article 30

Irrespective of the notifications made under Article 26, Paragraph 5, the Secretary-General of the United Nations shall inform all States referred to in Paragraph 1 of the same Article of the following particulars:

(a) Signatures, ratifications and accessions under Article 26;

(b) The date of the entry into force of the present Covenant under Article 27 and the date of the entry into force of any amendments under Article 29.

Article 31

1. The present Covenant, of which the Chinese, English, French, Russian and Spanish texts are equally authentic, shall be deposited in the archives of the United Nations.
2. The Secretary-General of the United Nations shall transmit certified copies of the present Covenant to all States referred to in Article 26.

INTERNATIONAL COVENANT ON CIVIL AND POLITICAL RIGHTS[c]

The States party to the present Covenant,

Considering that, in accordance with the principles proclaimed in the Charter of the United Nations, recognition of the inherent dignity and of the equal and inalienable rights of all members of the human family is the foundation of freedom, justice and peace in the world.

Recognizing that these rights derive from the inherent dignity of the human person.

Recognizing that, in accordance with the Universal Declaration of Human Rights, the ideal of free human beings enjoying civil and political freedom and freedom from fear and want can only be achieved if conditions are created whereby everyone may enjoy his civil and political rights, as well as his economic, social and cultural rights.

Considering the obligation of States under the Charter of the United Nations to promote universal respect for, and observance of, human rights and freedoms.

Realizing that the individual, having duties to other individuals and to the community to which he belongs, is under a responsibility to strive for the promotion and observance of the rights recognized in the present Covenant,

Agree upon the following Articles:

Part I

Article 1

1. All peoples have the right of self-determination. By virtue of that right they freely determine their political status and freely pursue their economic, social and cultural development.
2. All peoples may, for their own ends, dispose of their natural wealth and resources without prejudice to any obligations arising out of international economic cooperation, based upon the principle of mutual benefit, and international law. In no case may a people be deprived of its own means of subsistence.
3. The States party to the present Covenant, including those having responsibility for the administration of Non-Self-Governing and Trust Territories, shall promote the realization of the right of self-determination, and shall respect that right, in conformity with the provisions of the Charter of the United Nations.

Part II

Article 2

1. Each State party to the present Covenant undertakes to respect and to ensure to all individuals within its territory and subject to its jurisdiction the rights recognized in the present Covenant, without distinction of any kind, such as race, colour, sex, language, religion, political or other opinion, national or social origin, property, birth or other status.
2. Where not already provided for by existing legislative or other measures, each State party to the present Covenant undertakes to take the necessary steps, in accordance with its constitutional processes and with the provisions of the present Covenant, to adopt such legislative or other measures as may be necessary to give effect to the rights recognized in the present Covenant.

3. Each State party to the present Covenant undertakes:
   a. To ensure that any person whose rights or freedoms as herein recognized are violated shall have an effective remedy, notwithstanding that the violation has been committed by persons acting in an official capacity.
   b. To ensure that any person claiming such a remedy shall have his right thereto determined by competent judicial, administrative or legislative authorities, or by any other competent authority provided for by the legal system of the State, and to develop the possibilities of judicial remedy;
   c. To ensure that the competent authorities shall enforce such remedies when granted.

Article 3

The States party to the present Covenant undertake to ensure the equal right of men and women to the enjoyment of all civil and political rights set forth in the present Covenant.

Article 4

1. In time of public emergency which threatens the life of the nation and the existence of which is officially proclaimed, the States party to the present Covenant may take measures derogating from their obligations under the present Covenant to the extent strictly required by the exigency of the situation, provided that such measures are not inconsistent with their other obligations under international law and do not involve discrimination solely on the ground of race, colour, sex, language, religion or social origin.
2. No derogation form Articles 6,7,8,11,15,16 and 18 may be made under this provision.
3. Any State party to the present Covenant availing itself of the right of derogation shall immediately inform the other States party to the present Covenant, through the intermediary of the Secretary General of the United Nations, of the provisions from which it has derogated and of the reasons by which it was actuated. A further communication shall be made, through the same intermediary, on the date on which it terminates such derogation.

Article 5

1. Nothing in the present Covenant may be interpreted as implying for any state, group or person any right to engage in any activity or perform any act aimed at the destruction of any of the rights and freedoms recognized herein or at their limitation to greater extent than is provided for in the present Covenant.
2. There shall be no restriction upon or derogation from many of the fundamental human rights recognized or existing in any State party to the present Covenant pursuant to law, convention, regulations or custom on the pretext that the Covenant does not recognize such rights or that it recognizes them to a lesser extent.

Part III

Article 6

1. Every human being has an inherent right to life. This right shall be protected by law. No one shall be arbitrarily deprived of his life.
2. In countries which have not abolished the death penalty, sentence of death may be imposed only for the most serious crimes in accordance with the law in force at the time of the commission of the crime and not contrary to the provisions of the present Covenant and to the Convention on the Prevention and Punishment of the Crime of Genocide. This penalty can only be carried out pursuant to a final judgment rendered by a competent court.
3. When deprivation of life constitutes the crime of genocide, it is understood that nothing in this Article shall authorize any State party to the present Covenant to derogate in any way form any obligation assumed under the provisions of the Convention on the Prevention and Punishment of the Crime of Genocide.
4. Anyone sentenced to death shall have the right to seek pardon or commutation of the sentence. Amnesty, pardon or commutation of the sentence of death may be granted in all cases.

5. Sentence of death shall not be imposed for crimes committed by persons below eighteen years of age and shall not be carried out on pregnant women.
6. Nothing in this Article shall be invoked to delay or to prevent the abolition of capital punishment by any State party to the present Covenant.

Article 7

No one shall be subjected to torture or to cruel, inhuman or degrading treatment or punishment. In particular, no one shall be subjected without his free consent to medical or scientific experiment.

Article 8

1. No one shall be held in slavery; slavery and the slave trade in all their forms shall be prohibited.
2. No one shall be held in servitude.
3. (a) No one shall be required to perform forced or compulsory labour;

   (b) Paragraph 3 (a) shall not be held to preclude, in countries where imprisonment with hard labour may be imposed as a punishment for a crime, the performance of hard labour in pursuance of a sentence to such punishment by a competent court;

   (c) For the purpose of this Paragraph the term "forced or compulsory labour" shall not include:

   (i) Any work or service, not referred to in sub-paragraph (b), normally required of a person who is under detention in conscientious objection of a lawful order of a court, or of a person during conditional release from such detention;

   (ii) Any service of military character and, in countries where conscientious objection is recognized, any national service required by law of conscientious objectors;

   (iii) Any service of a military character and, in countries where conscientious objection is recognized, any national service required by law of conscientious objectors;

   (iv) Any work or service, which forms part of normal civil obligations.

Article 9

1. Everyone has the right to liberty and security of person. No one shall be subjected to arbitrary arrest or detention. No one shall be deprived of his liberty except on such grounds and in accordance with such procedures as are established by law.
2. Anyone who is arrested shall be informed, at the time of arrest, of the reasons for his arrest and shall be promptly informed of any charges against him.
3. Anyone arrested or detained on a criminal charge shall be brought promptly before the court or other officer authorized by law to exercise judicial power and shall be entitled to trial within a reasonable time or to release. He shall not be detained in custody, but release may be subject to guarantees to appear for trial, at any other stage of the judicial proceedings, and should occasion arise, for execution of the judgment.
4. Anyone who is deprived of his liberty to arrest or detention shall be entitled to take proceedings before a court, in order that that court may decide without delay on the lawfulness of his detention and order his release if the detention is not lawful.
5. Anyone who has been the victim of unlawful arrest or detention shall have enforceable right to compensation.

Article 10

1. All persons deprived of their liberty shall be treated with humanity and with respect for the inherent dignity of the human person.
2. (a) An accused person shall, save in exceptional circumstances, be segregated from convicted persons and shall be subject to separate treatment appropriate to their status as unconvicted persons;

   (b) Accused juvenile persons shall be separated from adults and brought as speedily as possible to adjudication.

3. The penitentiary system shall comprise treatment of prisoners the essential aim of which shall be their reformation and social rehabilitation. Juvenile offenders shall be segregated from adults and be accorded treatment appropriate to their age and legal status.

Article 11

No one shall be imprisoned merely on the ground of inability to fulfil a contractual obligation.

Article 12

1. Everyone lawfully within the territory of a State shall, within that territory, have the right to liberty of movement and freedom to choose his residence.
2. Everyone shall be free to leave any country, including his own.
3. The above-mentioned rights shall not be subject to any restrictions except those, which are provided by law, are necessary to protect national security, public order (ordre public), public health or morals or the rights and freedoms of others, and are consistent with the other rights recognized in the present Covenant.
4. No one shall be arbitrarily deprived of the right to enter his own country.

Article 13

An alien lawfully in the territory of a State party to the present Covenant may be expelled therefrom only in pursuance of a decision reached in accordance with law and shall, except where compelling reasons of national security otherwise require, be allowed to submit the reasons against his expulsion and to have his case reviewed by and be represented for the purpose before, the competent authority or a person or persons especially designated by the competent authority.

Article 14

1. All persons shall be equal before the courts and tribunals. In the determination of any criminal charge against him, or of his rights and obligations in a suit at law, everyone shall be entitled to a fair and public hearing by a competent, independent and impartial tribunal established by law. The press and the public may be excluded from all or part of a trial for reasons of morals, public order (ordre public) or national security in a democratic society, or when the interest of the private lives of the party so requires, or to the extent strictly necessary in the opinion of the court in special circumstances where publicity would prejudice the interests of justice; but any judgment rendered in a criminal case or in a suit at law shall be made public, except where the interest of juvenile persons otherwise requires, of the proceedings concerning matrimonial disputes or the guardianship of children.
2. Everyone charged with a criminal offence shall have the right to be presumed innocent until proved guilty according to law.
3. In the determination of any criminal charge against him, everyone shall be entitled to the following minimum guarantees, in full equality;
   (a) To be informed promptly and in detail in a language which he understands of the nature and cause of the charge against him;
   (b) To have adequate time and facilities for the preparation of his defence and to communicate with counsel of his own choosing;
   (c) To be tried without undue delay;
   (d) To be tried in his presence, to defend himself in person or through legal assistance of his own choosing, to be informed, if he does not have legal assistance, of this right; and to have legal assistance assigned to him, in any case where the interests of justice so require, and without payment by him in any such case if he does not have sufficient means to pay for it;
   (e) To examine, or have examined, the witnesses against him and to obtain the attendance and examination of witnesses on his behalf under the same conditions as the witnesses against him;

(f) To have the free assistance of an interpreter if he cannot understand or speak the language used in court;

(g) Not to be compelled to testify against himself or to confess guilt.

4. In the case of juvenile persons, the procedure shall be such as will take account of their age and desirability of promoting their rehabilitation.
5. Everyone convicted of a crime shall have the right to his conviction and sentence being reviewed by a higher tribunal according to law.
6. When a person has by a final decision been convicted of a criminal offence and when subsequently his conviction has been reversed or he has been pardoned on the ground that a new or newly discovered fact shows conclusively that there has been a miscarriage of justice, the person who has suffered punishment as a result of such conviction shall be compensated according to law, unless it is proved that the non-disclosure of the unknown fact in time is wholly or partly attributable to him.
7. No one shall be liable to be tried or punished again for an offence for which he has already been convicted or acquitted in accordance with the law and penal procedure of each country.

Article 15

1. No one shall be held guilty of any criminal offence on account of any act or omission, which did not constitute a criminal offence, under national or international law, at the time when it was committed. Nor shall a heavier penalty he imposed than the one that was applicable at the time when the criminal offence was committed. If, subsequent to the commission of the offence, provision is made by law for the imposition of a lighter penalty, the offender shall benefit thereby.

2. Nothing in this Article shall prejudice the trial and punishment of any person for any act or omission which, at the time when it was committed, was criminal according to the general principles of law recognized by the community of nations.

Article 16

Everyone shall have the right to recognition everywhere as a person before the law.

Article 17

1. No one shall be subjected to arbitrary or unlawful interference with his privacy, family, home or correspondence, nor to unlawful attacks on his honour and reputation.
2. Everyone has the right to the protection of the law against such interference or attacks.

Article 18

1. Everyone shall have the right to freedom of thought, conscience and religion. This right shall include freedom to have or to adopt a religion or belief of his choice, and freedom, either individually or in community in worship, observance, practice and teaching.
2. No one shall be subject to coercion, which would impair his freedom to have or to adopt a religion or belief of his choice.
3. Freedom to manifest one's beliefs may be subject only, to such limitations as are prescribed by law and are necessary to protect public safety, order, health, or morals or the Fundamental Rights and freedoms of others
4. The States party to the present Covenant undertake to have respect for the liberty of parents and, when applicable, legal guardians to ensure the religious and moral education of their children in conformity with their own convictions.

Article 19

1. Everyone shall have a right to hold opinions without interference.
2. Everyone shall have the right to freedom of expression; this right shall include freedom to seek, receive and impart information and ideas of all kinds, regardless of frontiers, either orally, in writing or in print, in the form of art, or through any other media of his choice.
3. The exercise of the rights provided for in Paragraph 2 of this Article carries with its special duties and responsibilities. It may therefore be subject to certain restrictions, but these shall only be such as are provided by law and are necessary
   (a) For respect of the rights or reputations of others;
   (b) For the protection of national security or public order (order public), or of public health or morals.

Article 20

1. Any propaganda for war shall be prohibited by law.
2. Any advocacy of national, racial or religious hatred that constitutes incitement to discrimination, hostility or violence shall be prohibited by law.

Article 21

The right of peaceful assembly shall be recognized. No restrictions may be placed on the exercise of this right other than those imposed in conformity with the law and which are necessary in a democratic society in the interests of national security or public safety, public order (ordre public), the protection of public health or morals or the protection of the rights and freedoms of others.

Article 22

1. Everyone shall have the right to freedom of association with others, including the right to form and join trade unions for the protection of his interests.

2. No restrictions may be placed on the exercise of this right other than those which are prescribed by law and which are necessary in a democratic society in the interests of national security or public safety, public order (ordre public), the protection of public health or morals or the protection of the rights and freedoms of others. This Article shall not prevent the imposition of lawful restrictions on members of the armed forces and of the police in their exercise of this right.
3. Nothing in this Article shall authorize States party to the International Labour Organization Convention of 1948 concerning Freedom of Association and Protection of the Rights to Organize to take legislative measures which prejudice, or to apply the law in such a manner as to prejudice, the guarantees provided for in that Convention.

Article 23

1. The family is the natural and fundamental group unit of society and is entitled to protection by society and the State.
2. The right of men and women of marriageable age to marry and to found a family shall be recognized.
3. No marriage shall be entered into without the free and full consent of the intending spouses.
4. States party to the present Covenant shall take appropriate steps to ensure equality of rights and responsibilities of spouses as to marriage, during marriage and at its dissolution. In the case of dissolution, provision shall be made for the necessary protection of any children.

Article 24

1. Every child shall have, without any discrimination as to race, colour, sex, language, religion, national or social origin, property or birth, the right to such measures of protection as are required by his status as a minor, on the part of his family, society and the State.

2. Every child shall be registered immediately after birth and shall have a name.
3. Every child has the right to acquire a nationality.

Article 25

Every citizen shall have the right and the opportunity, without any of the distinction mentioned in Article 2 and without unreasonable restriction:

(a) To take part in the conduct of public affairs, directly or through freely chosen representatives;

(b) To vote and to be elected at genuine periodic elections which shall be by universal and equal suffrage and shall be held by secret ballot, guaranteeing the free expression of the will of electors;

(c) To have access, on general terms of equality, to public service in his country.

Article 26

All persons are equal before the laws and are entitled without any discrimination to the equal protection of the law. In this respect, the law shall prohibit any discrimination and guarantee to all persons equal and effective protection against discrimination on any ground such as race, colour, sex, language, religion, political or other opinion, national or social origin, property, birth or other status

Article 27

In those States in which ethnic, religious or linguistic minorities exist, persons belonging to such minorities shall not be denied the right, in community with the other members of their group, to enjoy their own culture, to profess and practice their own religion, or to use their own language.

Article 28

1. There shall be established a Human Rights Committee (here after referred to in the present Covenant as the Committee). It shall consist of eighteen members and shall carry out the functions hereinafter provided.

2. The committee shall be composed of nationals of the States party to the present Covenant who shall be persons of high moral character and recognized competence in the field of human rights, consideration being given to the usefulness of the participation of some persons having legal experience.
3. The members of the committee shall be elected and shall serve in their personal capacity.

Article 29

1. The members of the committee shall be elected by secret ballot from a list of persons possessing the qualifications prescribed in Article 28 and nominated for the purpose by Sates party to the present Covenant.
2. Each State party to the present Covenant may nominate not more than two persons. These persons shall be nationals of the nominating State.
3. A person shall be eligible for renomination.

Article 30

1. The initial election shall be held no later than six months after the date of the entry into force of the present Covenant.
2. At least four months before the date of each election to the Committee, other than an election to fill a vacancy declared in accordance with Article 34, the Secretary-General of the United Nations shall address a written invitation to the States party to the present Covenant to submit their nominations for membership of the committee within three months.
3. The Secretary-General of the United Nations shall prepare a list in alphabetical order of all the persons thus nominated, with an indication of the State party which nominated them, and shall submit it to the States party to the present Covenant no later than one month before the date of each election.

4. Elections of the members of the Committee shall be held at a meeting of the States party to the present Covenant by the Secretary-General of the United Nation at the Headquarters of the United Nations. At that meeting, for which two thirds of the States party to the present Covenant shall constitute a quorum, the persons elected to the committee shall be those nominees who obtain the largest number of votes and an absolute majority of the votes of the representatives of States party present and voting.

Article 31

1. The committee may not include more than one national of the same State.
2. In the election of the Committee, consideration shall be given to equitable geographical distribution of membership and to the representation of the different forms of civilization and of the principal legal systems.

Article 32

1. The members of the Committee shall be elected for a term of four years. They shall be eligible for re-election if re-nominated. However, the terms of nine of the members elected at the first election shall expire at the end of two years; immediately after the first election, the names of these nine members shall be chosen by lot by the Chairman of the meeting referred to in Article 30, Paragraph 4.
2. Elections at the expiry of office shall be held in accordance with the preceding Articles of this part of the present Covenant.

Article 33

1. If, in the unanimous opinion of the other members, a member of the Committee has ceased to carry out his function for any cause other than absence of a temporary character, the Chairman of the Committee

shall notify the Secretary-General of the United Nations, who shall then declare the seat of that member to be vacant.

2. In the event of the death or the resignation of a member of the Committee, the Chairman shall immediately notify the Secretary-General of the United Nations, who shall declare the seat vacant from the date of death or the date on which the resignation takes effect.

Article 34

1. When a vacancy is declared in accordance with Article 33 and if the term of office of the member to be replaced does not expire within six months of the declaration of the vacancy, the secretary-General of the United Nations shall notify each of the States party to the present Covenant, which may within two months submit nominations in accordance with Article 29 for the purpose of filling the vacancy.
2. The Secretary-General of the United Nations shall prepare a list in alphabetical order of the persons thus nominated and shall submit it to the States party to the present Covenant.
3. A member of the Committee elected to fill a vacancy declared in accordance with Article 33 shall hold office for the remainder of the term of the member who vacated the seat on the Committee under the provisions of that Article.

Article 35

The members of the Committee shall, with the approval of the General Assembly of the United Nations, receive emoluments from United Nations resources on such terms and conditions as the General Assembly may decide, having regard to the importance of the Committee's responsibilities.

Article 36

The Secretary-General of the United Nations shall provide the necessary staff and facilities for the effective performance of the functions of the Committee under the present Covenant.

Article 37

1. The Secretary-General of the United Nations shall convene the initial meeting of the Committee at the Headquarters of the United Nations.
2. After the initial meeting, the Committee shall meet at such times as shall be provided in its rules of procedure.
3. The Committee shall normally meet at the Headquarter of the United Nations or at the United Nations Office at Geneva.

Article 38

Every member of the committee shall, before taking up his duties, make a solemn declaration in open committee that he will perform his functions impartially and conscientiously.

Article 39

1. The Committee shall elect its officers for a term of two years. They may be re-elected.
2. The Committee shall establish its own rules of procedure, but these rules shall provide, inter alia, that:
   (a) Twelve members shall constitute a quorum;
   (b) Decisions of the Committee shall be made by a majority vote of the members present.

Article 40

1. The States party to the present Covenant undertake to submit reports on the measures they have adopted which give effect to the rights recognized herein and on the progress made in the enjoyment of those rights:
   (a) Within one year of the entry into force of the present Covenant for the States party concerned;
   (b) Thereafter whenever the Committee so requests.

2. All reports shall be submitted to the Secretary-General of the United Nations, who shall transmit them to the Committee for consideration. Reports shall indicate the factors and difficulties, if any, affecting the implementation to the present Covenant.
3. The Secretary-General of the United Nations may after consultation with the Committee, transmit to the specialized agencies concerned copies of such parts of the reports as any fall within their field of competence.
4. The Committee shall study the reports submitted by the States party to the present Covenant. It shall transmit its reports, and such general comments, as it may consider appropriate, to the States party. The Committee may also transmit to the Economic and Social Council these comments along with the copies of the reports it has received from States party to the present Covenant.
5. The States party to the present Covenant may submit to the Committee observations on any comments that may be made in accordance with Paragraph 4 of this Article.

Article 41

1. A State party to the present Covenant may at any time declare under this Article that it recognizes the competence of the Committee to receive and consider communications to the effect that a State party claims that another State party is not fulfilling its obligations under the present Covenant. Communication under this Article may be received and considered only if submitted by a State party, which has made a declaration recognizing in regard to itself the competence of the Committee. No communication shall be received by the Committee if it concerns a State party which has not made such a declaration. Communication received under this Article shall be dealt with in accordance with the following procedure:

(a) If a State party to the present Covenant considers that another State party is not giving effect to the provisions of the present Covenant, it may, by written communication, bring the matter to the attention of that State party. Within three months after the receipt of the communication, the receiving State shall afford the State which sent the communication an explanation or any other statement in writing clarifying the matter, which would include, to the extent possible and pertinent, reference to domestic procedures and remedies taken, pending, or available in the matter;

(b) If the matter is not adjusted to the satisfaction of both States party concerned within six months after the receipt by the receiving State of the initial communication, either State shall have the right to refer the matter to the Committee, by notice given to the Committee and to the other State;

(c) The Committee shall deal with a matter referred to it only after it has ascertained that all available domestic remedies have been invoked and exhausted in the matter, in conformity with the generally recognized principles of international law. This shall not be the rule where the application of the remedies is unreasonably prolonged;

(d) The Committee shall hold closed meetings when examining communications under this Article;

(e) Subject to the provisions of sub-paragraph (c), the Committee shall make available its good offices to the States party concerned with a view to a friendly solution of the matter on the basis of respect for human rights and fundamental freedoms as recognized in the present Covenant;

(f) In any matter referred to it, the Committee may call upon the States party concerned, referred to in sub-paragraph (b), to supply any relevant information;

(g) The States party concerned, referred to in sub-paragraph (b), shall have the right to be represent when the matter is being considered in the Committee and to make submission orally and/or in writing;

(h) The Committee shall, within twelve months after the date of receipt of notice under sub-paragraph (b), submit a report:

(i) If a solution within the terms of sub-paragraph (e) is reached, the Committee shall confine its report to a brief statement of the facts and of the solution reached;

(ii) If a solution within the terms of sub-paragraph (e) is not reached, the Committee shall confine its report to a brief statement of the facts, the written submissions and record of the oral submission made by the States party concerned shall be attached to the report.

In every matter, the report shall be communicated to the States party concerned.

2. The provisions of this Article shall come into force when ten States party to the present Covenant have made declarations under Paragraph 1 of this Article. Such declarations shall be deposited by the States party with the Secretary-General of the United Nations, who shall transmit copies thereof to the other States party. A declaration may be withdrawn at any time by notification to the Secretary-General. Such a withdrawal shall not prejudice the consideration of any matter which is the subject of a communication already transmit under this Article; no further communication by any State party shall be received after the notification of withdrawal of the declaration has been received by the Secretary-General, unless the State party concerned has made a new declaration.

Article 42

1. (a) If a matter referred to the Committee in accordance with Article 41 is not resolved to the satisfaction of the State party concerned, the Committee may, with the prior consent of the States party concerned, appoint an ad hoc Conciliation Commission (hereinafter referred to as the Commission). The good offices of the Commission shall be made available to the States party concerned with a view to an amicable solution of the matter on the basis of respect for the present Covenant.

(b) The Commission shall consist of five persons acceptable to the States party concerned. If the States party concerned fail to reach agreement within three months on all or part of the composition of the Commission, the members of the Commission concerning whom no agreement has been reached shall be elected by secret ballot by a two-third majority vote of the Committee from among its members.

2. The members of the Commission shall serve in their personal capacity. They shall not be nationals of the States party concerned, or of a state not party to the present Covenant, or of a State party which has not made a declaration under Article 41.
3. The Commission shall elect its own Chairman and adopt its own rules of procedure.
4. The meetings of the Commission shall normally be held at the Headquarters of the United Nations or at the United Nations Office at Geneva. However, they may be held at such other convenient places as the Commission may determine in consultation with the Secretary-General of the United Nations and the States party concerned.
5. The secretariat provided in accordance with Article 36 shall also service the Commissions appointed under this Article.
6. The information received and collected by the Committee shall be made available to the Commission and the Commission may call upon the States party concerned to supply any other relevant information.
7. When the Commission has fully considered the matter, but in any event not later than twelve months after having been seized of the matter, it shall submit to the Chairman of the Committee a report for communication to the States party concerned:
   (a) If the Commission is unable to complete its consideration of the matter within twelve months, it shall confine its report to a brief statement of the status of its consideration of the matter;
   (b) If an amicable solution to the matter on the basis of respect for human rights as recognized in the present Covenant is reached, the Commission shall confine its report to a brief statement of the facts and of the solution reached;
   (c) If a solution within the terms of sub-paragraph (b) is not reached, the Commission's report shall embody its findings on all questions of fact relevant to the issues between the States party concerned, and its views on the possibilities of an amicable solution of the matter. This report shall also contain the written submission and a record of the oral submissions made by the States party concerned;

(d) If the Commission's report is submitted under sub-paragraph (c), the States party concerned shall, within three months of the receipt of the report, notify the Chairman of the Committee whether or not they accept the contents of the report of the Chairman.

8. The provisions of this Article are without prejudice to the responsibilities of the Committee under Article 41.
9. The States party concerned shall share equally all the expenses of the members of the Commission in accordance with estimates to be provided by the Secretary-General of the United Nations.
10. The Secretary-General of the United Nations shall be empowered to pay the expenses of the members of the Commission, if necessary, before reimbursement by the States party concerned, in accordance with Paragraph 9 of this Article.

Article 43

The members of the Committee, and of the ad hoc conciliation commissions which may be appointed under Article 42, shall be entitled to the facilities, privileges and immunities of experts on mission for the United Nations as laid down in the relevant sections of the Convention on the Privileges and Immunities of the United Nations.

Article 44

The provisions for the implementation of the present Covenant shall apply without prejudice to the procedures prescribed in the field of human rights by or under the constituent instruments and the conventions of the United Nations and of the specialized agencies and shall not prevent the States party to the present Covenant from having recourse to other procedures for settling a dispute in accordance with general or special international agreements in force between them.

Article 45

The Committee shall submit to the General Assembly of the United Nations, through economic and social Council, an annual report on its activities.

Part V

Article 46

Nothing in the present Covenant shall be interpreted as impairing the provisions of the Charter of the United Nations and of the constitutions of the specialized agencies which define the respective responsibilities of the various organs of the United Nations and of the specialized agencies in regard to the matters dealt with in present Covenant.

Article 47

Nothing in the present Covenant shall be interpreted as impairing the inherent right of all peoples to enjoy and utilize fully and freely their natural wealth and resources.

Part VI

Article 48

1. The present Covenant is open for signature by any state Member of the United Nations or Member of any of its specialized agencies, by any State party to the Statute of the International Court of Justice, and by any other State which has been invited by the General Assembly of the United Nations to become a party to the present Covenant.
2. The present Covenant is subject to ratification. Instruments of ratification shall be deposited with the Secretary-General of the United Nations.
3. The present Covenant shall be open to accession by any State referred to in Paragraph 1 of this Article.
4. Accession shall be effected by the deposit of an instrument of accession with the Secretary-General of the United Nations.
5. The Secretary-General of the United Nations shall inform all States which have signed this Covenant or acceded to it of the deposit of each instrument of ratification or accession.

Article 49

1. The present Covenant shall enter into force three months after the date of deposit with the Secretary-General of the United Nations of the thirty-fifth instrument of ratification or instrument of accession.
2. For each State ratifying the present Covenant or acceding to it after the deposit of the thirty-fifth instrument of ratification or instrument of accession, the present Covenant shall enter into force three months after the date o deposit of its own instrument of ratification or instrument of accession.

Article 50

The provisions of the present Covenant shall extend to all parts of federal States without any limitations or exceptions.

Article 51

1. Any State party to the present Covenant may propose an amendment and file it with the Secretary-General of the United Nations. The Secretary-General of the United Nations shall thereupon communicate any proposed amendments to the States party to the present Covenant with a request that they notify him whether they favour conference of States party for the purpose of considering and voting upon the proposals. In the event that at least one third of the States party favours such a conference, the Secretary-General shall convene the conference under the auspices of the United Nations. Any amendment adopted by a majority of the States party present and voting at the conference shall be submitted to the General Assembly of the United Nations for approval.
2. Amendments shall come into force when they have been approved by the General Assembly of the United Nations and accepted by a two-thirds majority of the States party to the present Covenant in accordance with their respective constitutional processes.

3. When amendments come into force, they shall be binding on those States party which have accepted them, other States party still being bound by the provisions of the present Covenant and any earlier amendment, which they have accepted.

Article 52

Irrespective of the notifications made under Article 48, Paragraph 5, the Secretary-General of the United Nations shall inform all States referred to in Paragraph 1 of the same Article of the following particulars:

(a) Signatures, ratifications and accessions under Article 48;

(b) The date of the entry into force of the present Covenant under Article 49 and the date of the entry into force of any amendments under Article 51.

Article 53

1. The present Covenant, of which the Chinese, English, French, Russian and Spanish texts are equally authentic, shall be deposited in the archives of the United Nations.
2. The Secretary-General of the United Nations shall transmit certified copies of the present Covenant to all States referred to in Article 48.

OPTIONAL PROTOCOL TO THE INTERNATIONAL COVENANT ON CIVIL AND POLITICAL RIGHTS[d]

The States party to the present Protocol,

Considering that in order further to achieve the purpose of the Covenant on Civil and Political Rights (hereinafter referred to as the Covenant) and the implementation of its provisions it would be appropriate to enable the Human Rights Committee set up in part IV of the Covenant (herein after referred to as the Committee) to receive and consider, as provided in the present Protocol, communications from individual claiming to be victims of violation of any of the rights set forth in the Covenant,

Have agreed as follows:

Article 1

A State party to Covenant that becomes party to the present Protocol recognizes the competence of the Committee to receive and consider communications from individuals subject to its jurisdiction who claimed to be victims of a violation by that Sate party of any of the Rights set forth in the Covenant. No communication shall be received by the Committee if it concerns a State party to the Covenant, which is not a party to the present Protocol.

Article 2

Subject to the provisions of Article 1, individuals who claimed that any of their rights enumerated in the Covenant have been violated and who have exhausted all available domestic remedies may submit a written communication to the Committee for consideration.

Article 3

The Committee shall consider inadmissible any communication under the present Protocol which is anonymous, or which it considers to be an abuse of the right of submission of such communications or to be incompatible with the provisions of the Covenant.

Article 4

1. Subject to the provisions of Article 3, the Committee shall bring any communications submitted to it under the present Protocol to the attention of the Sate party to the present Protocol alleged to be violating any provision of the Covenant.
2. Within six months, the receiving State submit to the Committee written explanations or statements clarifying the matter and the remedy, if any, that may have been taken by that State.

Article 5

1. The Committee shall consider communications received under the present Protocol in the light of all written information made available to it by the individuals by the State party concerned.
2. The Committee shall not consider any communication from an individual unless it has ascertained that:
   a. The same matter is not examined under another procedure of international investigation of settlement;
   b. The individual has exhausted all available domestic remedies.

This shall not be the rule where the application of the remedies is unreasonably prolonged.

3. The Committee shall hold closed meetings when examining communications under the present Protocols.
4. The Committee shall forward its use to the State party concerned and to the individual.

Article 6

The Committee shall include in its annual report under Article 45 of the Covenant a summary of its activities under the present Protocol.

Article 7

Pending the achievements of the objective of resolution 1514(XV) adopted by the general assembly of the United Nations on 14th December1960 concerning the Declaration on the Granting of Independence to Colonial Countries and Pupils, the provisions of the present Protocol shall in no way limit the right of petition granted to these pupils by the Charter of the United Nations and other international conventions and instruments under the United Nations and its specialized agencies.

Article 8

1. The present Protocol is open for signature by any State which has signed the Covenant.

2. The present Protocol is subject to ratification by any State which has ratified or exceeded to the Covenant. Instruments of ratification shall be deposited with the Secretary-General of the United Nations.
3. The present Protocol shall be open to accession by any State which has ratified or acceded to the Covenant.
4. Accession shall be effected by the deposit of an instrument of accession with the Secretary General of United Nations.
5. The Secretary General of United Nation shall inform all States which have signed the present Protocol or acceded to it of the deposit of each instrument of ratification of accession.

Article 9

1. Subject to the entry into force of the Covenant, the present Protocol shall enter into force three months after the date of deposit with the Secretary General of the United Nation of tenth instrument of ratification or instruments of accession.
2. For each State ratifying the present Protocol or acceding to it after the deposit of the tenth instrument of ratification or the instrument of accession, the present Protocol shall enter into force three months after the date of deposit of its own instruments of ratification of instruments of accession.

Article 10

The provisions of the present Protocol shall extend to all parts of federal States without any limitations or exceptions.

Article 11

1. Any State party to the present Protocol may propose an amendment and file it with the Secretary-General of the United Nations. The Secretary-General shall thereupon communicate any proposed amendments to the States party to the present Protocol with a

request that they notify him whether they favour a conference of States party for the purpose of considering and voting upon the proposal. In the event that at least one third of the States party favours such a conference, the Secretary General shall convene the conference under the auspices of the United Nations. Any amendments adopted by a majority of the States party present and voting at the conference shall be submitted to the General Assembly of the United Nations for approval.

2. Amendments shall come into force when they have been approved by the General Assembly of the United Nation and accepted by a two-thirds majority of the States party to the present Protocol in accordance with their respective constitutional processes.
3. When amendments come into force, they shall be binding on those States party which have accepted them, other States party still being bound by the provision of the present Protocol and any earlier amendments which they had accepted.

Article 12

1. Any State party may denounce the present Protocol at any time written notification addressed to the Secretary-General of the United Nations. Denunciation shall take effect three months after the date of receipt of the notification by the Secretary-General.
2. Denunciation shall be without prejudice to the continued application of the provisions of the present Protocol to any communication submitted under Article 2 before the effective date of denunciation.

Article 13

Irrespective of the notifications made under Article 8, Paragraph 5, of the present Protocol, the Secretary-General of the United Nations shall inform all States referred to in Article 48, Paragraph 1, of the Covenant of the following particulars:

(a) Signatures, ratifications and accession under Article 8;
(b) The date of the entry into force of the present Protocol under Article 9 and the date of the entry of any amendments under Article11;
(c) Denunciations under Article 12.

Article 14

1. The present Protocol, of which the Chinese, English, French, Russian and Spanish texts are equally authentic, shall be deposited in the archives of the United Nations.
2. The Secretary-General of the United Nations shall transmit certified copies of the present Protocol to all States referred to in Article 48 of the Covenant.

Second Optional Protocol to the International Covenant on Civil and Political Rights, Aiming at the Abolition of the Death Penalty[e]

The States party to the present Protocol,

Believing that abolition of the death penalty contributes to enhancement of human dignity and progressive development of human rights,

Recalling Article 3 of the Universal Declaration of Human Rights, adopted on 10 December 1948, and Article 6 of the International Covenant on Civil and Political Rights, adopted on 16 December 1966,

Noting that Article 6 of the International Covenant on Civil and Political Rights refers to abolition of the death penalty in terms that strongly suggest that abolition is desirable,

Convinced that all measures of abolition of the death penalty should be considered as progress in the enjoyment of the right to life,

Desirous to undertake here by an international commitment to abolish the death penalty,

Have agreed as follows:

Article 1

1. No one within the jurisdiction of a State party to the present Protocol shall be executed.
2. Each State party shall take all necessary measures to abolish the death penalty within its jurisdiction.

Article 2

1. No reservation is admissible to the present Protocol, except for a reservation made at the time of ratification or accession that provides for the application of the death penalty in time of war pursuant to a conviction for a most serious crime of a military nature committed during wartime.
2. The State party making such a reservation shall at the time of ratification or accession communicate to the Secretary-General of the United Nations the relevant provision of its national legislation applicable during wartime.
3. The State party having made such a reservation shall notify the Secretary-General of the United Nations of any beginning or ending of a state of war applicable to its territory.

Article 3

The State party to the present Protocol shall include in the reports they submit to the Human Rights Committee, in accordance with Article 40 of the Covenant, information on the measures that they have adopted to give effects to the present Protocol.

Article 4

With respect to the States party to the Covenant that have made a declaration under Article 41, the competence of the Human Rights Committee to receive and consider communications when a State party claims that another State party is not fulfilling its obligations shall extend to the provisions of the present Protocol, unless the State party concerned has made a statement to the contrary at the moment of ratification or accession.

Article 5

With respect to the States party to the first Optional Protocol to the International Covenant on Civil and Political Rights adopted on 16 December 1966, the competence of the Human Rights Committee to receive and consider communications from individuals subject to its jurisdiction shall extend to the provisions of the present Protocol, unless the State party concerned has made a statement to the contrary at the moment of ratification or accession.

Article 6

1. The provision of the present Protocol shall apply as additional provisions to the Covenant.
2. Without prejudice to the possibility of a reservation under Article 2 of the present Protocol, the right guaranteed in Article 1, Paragraph 1, of the present Protocol shall not be subject to any derogation under Article 4 of the Covenant.

Article 7

1. The present Protocol is open for signature by any State that has signed the Covenant.
2. The present Protocol is subject to ratification by any State that has ratified the Covenant or acceded to it. Instruments of ratification shall be deposited with the Secretary-General of the United Nations.
3. The present Protocol shall be open to accession by any State that has ratified the Covenant or acceded to it.
4. Accession shall be effected by the deposit of an instrument of accession with the Secretary-General of the United Nations.
5. The Secretary-General of the United Nations shall inform all the States that have signed the present Protocol or acceded to it of the deposit of each instrument of ratification or accession.

Article 8

1. The present Protocol shall enter into force three months after the date of the deposit with the Secretary-General of the United Nations of the tenth instrument of ratification or accession.
2. For each State ratifying the present Protocol or acceding to it after the deposit of the tenth instrument of ratification or accession, the present Protocol shall enter into force three months after the date of the deposit of its own instrument of ratification or accession.

Article 9

The provisions of the present Protocol shall extend to all parts of federal States without any limitations or exceptions.

Article 10

The Secretary-General of the United Nations shall inform all States referred to in Article 48, Paragraph 1, of the Covenant of the following particulars:

(a) Reservations, communications and notifications under Article 2 of the present Protocol;

(b) Statements made under Articles 4 or 5 of the present Protocol;

(c) Signatures, ratifications and accession under Article 7 of the present Protocol;

(d) The date of the entry into force of the present Protocol under Article 8 thereof.

Article 11

1. The present Protocol, of which the Arabic, Chinese, English, French, Russian and Spanish texts are equally authentic, shall be deposited in the archives of the United Nations.
2. The Secretary-General of the United Nations shall transmit certified copies of the present Protocol to all States referred to in Article 48 of the Covenant.

CHAPTER 6

CONCLUSION

Epilogue to the subject

The biggest source of Indianization of fundamental rights, directive principle & duties, In India is preamble to the constitution at the present time.

In the early past the evolution of Indian civilization had the only source of fundamental rights, duties and directives in the vedic concepts of "survee bhawantu sukhinaha" which is first equivalent to the roman concept of sum-Cuigue-tribhere (give every one his due). Our motto and preaching as well as teachings to the world are known. We have not given inconvenience or trouble to any one even subject to trouble or inconvenience to ourselves. Our maxim-respect elders, have sympathy towards children, obey the orders of elders, have mercy over animals and birds, ladies be respected. Sick & infants be treated with mercy, let help to poor society should be respected, do not quarrel with anyone, have equality to all, live and let live, forestry is the life of man, Do not cut trees. This world is one (Vasudhdhav kutumbkum), Bhudhan Movement, obey your teacher etc. are the finest concept of Indian origin which are completely matchless to other societies. The larger concept of have critic with self (nindak niayre rakhaye) of Ramayana is broad one. Let us have critic with us who can critically examine our own position and accordingly he can guide us for future. It is the bigger example of freedom or speech, which is nowhere found. The concept of (SAMBHAV) is the broad spectrum of doctrine of equality. The concept of live and let live is the matching of concept of liberty. The concept of "Satyam Vadh" and "Apriya Satyam Na Vadh" is the finest example of duty to speak the truth only and not to speak bad truth. Duties of king were also defined earlier. People were respected. They always had property with themselves. There is continuous list of several preaching & teaching Shuk-R-Niti, Vidur Niti, Ramayana, Mahabharat, Srimad Bhagwat Geeta and more importantly Vedas and Puranas have set the life of man in an orderly manner. Every aspect of life was well planned and defined. People followed rules of law as past of life. There was no question of right at all but there was always duty to be followed. Everyone was following his duties sincerely consequently there was no problem at all because of it no one felt the need of enforcement of rights.

The gradual change is the nature of people and the society and development of concept of my own in spite of our own. Shifting of welfare of society as a whole or group to the welfare of individual only started to create problem. Then the question of regulation of conduct of man was first felt, that gave rise to observance of duties and enforcement of right and consequently their clarification in society. We are thankful to our own sages and earliest jurist that they made society to follow rules. They directed individuals to do as per norms of society. But it was all without fear of any one only to respect society. Later on peoples attempted to disobey the rules, then came the concepts of *DANDA* or sanction for disobedience of rules and particularly for observance of rules. Individual and society was directed to do as per rules strictly otherwise face the consequences and penalties to be awarded by superiors or kings, to keep the society in order king, or governmental system clarified society and individuals and made norm to be followed. They directed individual to observe these duties and then claim for his enforcement of right. Gradually the present time came where duties and right were treated at par. Now in modern times rights are claimed and enforced first than the observance of duties are thought. The journey of rights and duties from primitive times up to present day had gone a sea change. The changes may be recorded as under: -

I. No right no duty concept = every thing in natural way.
II. No right on duty to be observed = change case focus was only on duty and no concern of rights.
III. Duties to be observed but rights must also be cared to. Consideration should be given to enforcement of rights also. It is the time for observance of duties rather than to rights.
The time for the priority of duties rather than to rights.
IV. There were further changes both rights and duties were started to be treated at par. Both should be treated equally without any more weight age to either of them.
V. The future trend appears to be, which is apparent available presently, that rights should be treated first than duties should be cared. Even our constitution of India is also a fine example of it. Part III deal with fundamental rights then comes part IV directive principles and then comes fundamental duties as part IV-A while it should be in a fashion that fundamental duties should be depicted first then directive principles should be given preference and lastly not only of rights must be normally cared to but should be given due importance for individual and for society also.

We should now turn back again to our present constitution which in its preamble has collected all the best flowers of past and sanely smell of present. I think the preamble it self is a mini-constitution and a wealthy treasuray of Indian cultural thoughts. It is also a sole source of fundamental rights, directive principle and duties also. Further I think of preamble could have been made enforceable yet it is not made enforceable. Its preamble is made impreamble then I do not think that there is any necessity felinity of fundamental rights and duties and what so ever as the preamble is so wide, it include within its ambit every thing every concept of law. It is not wrong to say that the preamble is the sole depository of fundamental rights directive principles and fundamental duties. For the Indianization of rights and duties, we must treat the preamble as an ideal to be achieved for which we have to establish a welfare state in ideal sense. What is ideal state, let us describe it.

A- Welfare State

The objective of the constitution makers was to draft a constitution of socio-economic revolution and they incorporated many provisions in the constitution to make India a Welfare State. A basic aim of a Welfare State was clearly foreshadowed in the Preamble to the constitution, and in virtually all of Part IV containing the Drective principles of State Policy. The Preamble was patterned along the lines of the objectives resolution and it is a "key to open the minds of the constitution-makers"[1]. Justice Hidayatullah said that the preamble resembles the declaration of independence of the United States, but is really more than declaration. It is the soul of the constitution as it lays down the pattern of the society which it states is sovereign socialist, secular, democratic, republic and secures to all its citizens justice, social, economic and political and promotes among them all fraternity assuming the dignity of the individual and the unity of the nation.'[2]

Democracy not only postulates equality but justice also. The essence of justice is the attainment of happiness and good of all as distinguished from the happiness and good of individuals or even the majority of them. Justice in this sense cannot be unless there is a society of equals in status and opportunity. Equality of status and opportunity are not available unless all sections of the people are equally in a position and circumstances to benefit from the social order that prevails. The Constitution of India not only prohibits discrimination on grounds of birth, sex, religion, caste and creed, but also adequately provides for the promotion of the interests of the Backward Classes and areas. It seeks to remove all inequalities created by inequalities in the possession of wealth and opportunity, race, caste and religion by providing just and human condition of work, maternity relief, leisure and cultural opportunity to every individual, prevention of exploitation in labour and industry, free education for all and the like. The ideal of economic justice, the Constitution promises to secure by directing the State policy towards equality of reward for equal work, by the distribution of ownership and control of material resources of the community so as to sub serve the common good and operation of economic system in such a way that it does not result in the concentration of wealth and the means of production to the common detriment.

Jawaharlal Nehru emphasized in a speech in the Constituent Assembly on the imperative needs for India to move into the modern world of science and technology for bringing into existence a social order in which there would be rapid rise in the standards of living with equitable distribution of wealth and equality of opportunity for all to carve out a career for themselves so that all of them may live with dignity and happiness. Since Independent India has been following the path of democratic planning to establish a Welfare State "by compressing the history of centuries into a few decades." The Five Year Plans placed economic development in the framework of social justice. Removal of poverty and attainment of self-reliance were the two major objectives of the Fifth Plan and so are they of the sixth. Special and concerted effort has been paid to the removal of social and legal disabilities imposed under traditional caste and feudal institutions, such social evils like untouchability, bonded labour and dowry, and economic evil like the feudal zamindari system. In order to make equal opportunities to the poor and community services, such as health, education, housing, town planning, community development, etc., have been enacted and various project have been pursued by providing much investment. Particular attention is paid to social security for industrial workers under the Schemes of Employees State Insurance and Employees Provident Fund. The welfare Services for the handicapped and the maladjusted have been provided either directly by the State or grants are given to voluntary welfare institution providing such services. Concerted efforts are being made to end poverty and unemployment and it is the basic commitment of the Government, but it is a slow process and cannot be solved within a specified period of time. It is a ??? glance of Indianization of rights of duties in India.

Fundamental Rights

Demand for Declaration of Rights

Before the enactment of the 1950 Constitution there was no charter of fundamental rights of a justiciable nature, although the demand for such rights and their constitutional guarantees had its deep roots in the nineteenth century. It was implicit in the formation of the Indian National Congress in 1885, which wanted the same rights and privileges for Indians that the British enjoyed in their own country. The promoters of the Indian National Congress emphatically demanded an end to discrimination inherent in a colonial regime. Perhaps, the first implicit demand for fundamental rights appeared in the Constitution of India Bill, 1895. This bill, described by Mrs. Annie Besant as the Home Rule Bill, envisaged to guarantee to all citizens freedom of speech and expression, right to personal liberty, equality to admission to public offices and right to personal liberty, inviolability of one's house, right to property, equality before the law, equality to admission to public offices and right to petition for redress of grievances. Immediately after publication of the National Congress, at its Bombay session in August 1918, demanded that the new constitution of India should contain a "declaration of the right of the people of India as British liberty, inviolability of one's house, right to property, equality before the law, equality to admission to public offices and right to petition for redress of grievances. Immediately after publication of the National Congress, at its Bombay session in August 1918, demanded that the new constitution of India should contain a "declaration of the right of the people of India as British citizens" guaranteeing equality before the law, freedom of speech and press, and protection in respect of liberty, life and property.

Within two years of the publication of The Commonwealth of India Bill came the announcement of the appointment of the Indian Statutory (Simon) Commission, the Forty-third Annual Session of the Congress at Madras in 1927, resolved that the Working Committee be empowered to set up a Committee "to draft a declaration of rights". The Nehru Committee in its report included a comprehensive bill of rights and in recommending their declaration the Committee urged that Ireland is the only country where conditions obtaining before the Treaty are nearest approach to those we have in India. The first concern of the people of India today to secure fundamental rights that had been denied to them". Another reason why India attached importance to the declaration of the fundamental differences in India. "Certain safeguards and guarantees", the committee urged, "are necessary to create and establish a sense of security among those who look upon each other with distrust and suspicion. We could not better secure the full enjoyment of religious and communal rights to all communities than including them among the basic principles of the constitution". The Committee added, "It is obvious that our first care should be to have out fundamental rights guaranteed in a manner which will not permit their withdrawal under any circumstances".

In 1931, the Indian National Congress passed a Resolution on Fundamental Rights. In order to end the exploitation of the masses, the Resolution emphasized, political freedom must include real economic freedom of starving millions. It was further declared that any constitution which might be agreed to on behalf of the Indian National Congress should provide, to enable the Swaraj Government to provide, for certain fundamental rights and duties. But the British Government was in no mood to reconcile itself to this primary demand of the Indians. In fact, such a demand was unsuited to the British genius. The Simon Commission had ridiculed the idea of fundamental rights. "Abstract declaration", the Commission observed, "are useless unless there exists the will and the means to, make them effective''.[4]

The Joint Parliamentary Committee on the Government of India Bill 1934 endorsed the observation of the Simon Commission on the demand for the constitutional guarantee of fundamental rights to subjects of British India. The Committee said, "A cynic might indeed find plausible arguments.... For asserting that the most effective method of ensuring the protection of a fundamental right is to include a declaration of its existence in a constitutional instrument. But there are also strong particle arguments against the proposal, which may be put in the form of dilemma: for either the declaration of rights is of any kind, or its legal will be impose an embarrassing restriction on the power of legislature and to create a grave risk that a large number of laws may be declared invalid by the courts as because of inconsistency with one or other of the rights so declared. There is this further objection, that the States (Princely) have made it abundantly clear that no declaration of fundamental rights is to apply in State territories; and it would be altogether anomalous if such a declaration had legal force in part only of the area of the Federation.... " The Committee. However, conceded that there were some legally recognized principles, which could be included in the new constitution, and, accordingly, the Government of India Act, 1935, conferred certain rights and form of protection on British subjects in India. [4]

Nevertheless, in pre-Independence India there was no chapter of fundamental rights of a justiciable nature, and even such safeguards as were contained in the various statutes could be taken away, abridged or abrogated by the authority enacting the Statute, British Parliament or legislative authority in India, whatever the case was. Moreover, there were certain laws in existence which empowered the competent authorities to set up special courts or tribunals for the trial of certain type of cases which could be tried in camera or by curtailing a person's rights or liberties and all such measures were violative of the basic principles of Fundamental Rights. B.R. Rau thus summed up the position in his report on Human Rights (December 1947); "With a few exceptions human rights in India today (December 31, 1947) are not guaranteed by the Constitution, but embodied in the ordinary law of the law.

The subject of fundamental rights came up for active considerations of the Conciliation Committee, also known as the Sapru Committee, appointed by the All-Parties Conference (1944-45). The Committee was of the opinion that fundamental rights were not only "assurances and guarantees to the minorities but also prescribing a standard of conduct for the legislatures, governments and the courts"[7]. The Committee further said that it was for the constitution-making body to settle the list of fundamental rights and, then, to decide about their division into justiciable and non-justiciable rights and to provide in the case of the former, suitable machinery for their enforcement. A few months more than a year later the Constituent Assembly of India began framing the Fundamental Rights and the Directive Principle and latter non-justiciable. The most striking feature about the treatment of rights in the Sapru Report was the distinction between justiciable and non-justiciable rights.

Constituent Assembly and Fundamental Rights

The Cabinet Mission Plan conceded the demand for the Constituent Assembly as well as the need for a written guarantee of fundamental rights in the Constitution of India. It recommended the appointment of an Advisory Committee on the Rights of Citizens, Minorities the interests affected, which would prepare a list of inclusion in the State, Group or the Union List. By the Objectives Resolution introduced by Jawaharlal Nehru and adopted on January 22, 1947, the Constituent Assembly Solemnly pledged itself to draw up for India's future governance a constitution wherein "shall be guaranteed social, economic and political, equality of status, of opportunity and before the law: freedom of thought, expression, belief, faith, worship, vocation, association and action. Subject to law and public morality." It is also a attempt of Indianization of rights and duties.

The Advisory Committee deliberated on the views of the two sub-Committees and accepted the recommendations for: (1) division of rights into justiciable and non-justiciable rights; that is, rights enforceable by appropriate legal process and rights consisting of directive principles of state policy, which though not enforceable in courts, were nevertheless to be regarded as fundamental in the governance of the country; (2) certain rights being guaranteed to all persons and certain others to citizens only and (3) all such rights being made uniformly applicable to the Union and the units. The Constituent

Assembly adopted all these recommendations and the Constitution of 1950 contains two Chapters-Chapter III enumerating the Fundamental Rights and Chapter IV dealing with the directive Principles of State Policy. The Constitution (Forty-Second Amendment Act, 1976 inserted a new Chapter Part IV A containing fundamental duties which are covered by Article 51A.

Whereas some of the rights conferred by the Constitution are limited to citizens, such as freedom of speech, assembly and cultural and educational rights, in the case of others, as equality before the law, religious freedom, etc., such a limitation does not exist; these are applicable to citizens and aliens alike. The relevant Articles of the Constitution make use of the two terms 'citizens' and 'persons' and they are indicative of the distinction between citizens and aliens. Even in the absence of such a distinction all the rights could not have been available to citizens and aliens alike, but the matter would have remained undecided until the Supreme Court had determined so.

Some of the provisions of Chapter III of the Constitution are of the nature of prohibitions and place constitutional limitations on the authority of the State, for instance, no authority of the State can deny to any person equality before the law or the equal protection of the laws; discrimination against any citizen; and no titles other than a military or academic distinction can be conferred. From the point of view of an individual. Such rights may be termed as negative rights. The remaining provisions of the Chapter on fundamental rights, as such, can be set to contain positive rights of the individuals. In spite of this distinction no clear-cut line of division can be drawn between the two. There is however, one important distinction between them. The provisions, which impose constitutional limitation on the authority of the state, are binding for all intents and purposes and any action, legislative or executive, which contravenes any of this provision, would be void altogether. The provisions relating to individual rights, on the other hand, are subject to the regulation to the state within certain prescribed limits and restrictions so imposed cannot be held to be void unless they travel beyond those limits.

The fundamental rights place limitations on all kinds of authority that has either the power to make laws or have discretion vested in it. The fundamental rights accordingly binding on the Union Government, the state Government and the local body including village, Panchayats, and other authority within the territory of India. Article 12 of the constitution defines the state, inclusively, to mean the Government and Parliament of India and the government and legislature of each of the States and all local or other authorities within territory of India or under the control of the government of India. Ambedkar made this point clear in the constituent assembly. He explained that the object of the fundamental rights was two fold. "First, that every citizen must be in a position to claim those rights. Secondly, they must be binding upon authority.... Upon every authority, which has got either the power to make, law or the power to have discretion vested in it. Therefore, it is quiet clear that if the fundamental rights are to be real, then they must be binding not only upon the Central Government, they must not only be binding upon the provincial government.... They must also be binding upon district local boards, municipalities, even village panchayats has been created by law and which has God certain power to make laws, to make rules, or make by laws".[6]

Absolute or unrestricted rights are not possible. This is the position in Britain, although there are no constitutional guarantees of fundamental rights in that country.[7] In the United States there are no direct restrictions imposed by the First Ten Amendments, which determine the American Bill of Rights. But under the doctrine of Police Power the Supreme Court has recognized the inherent power of the State to impose such restrictions on Fundamental Rights as may be deemed reasonable to protect the common good. The final say, however, rests with the Supreme Court to determine whether such restrictions justify the common good or not. There is no doctrine of the "security of the State" in the United States and no legislation can override any individual right on the ground that the safety of the State is in danger. The Constitution of India, on the other hand, imposes direct limitations on Fundamental Rights. Ambedkar, while introducing the Draft constitution and supporting the restriction clauses, maintained, "what the Draft Constitution has done is that instead of formulating fundamental rights in absolute terms and depending upon our Supreme Court to come to the rescue of Parliament by inventing the doctrine of police power, it permits the State directly to impose limitations upon the fundamental rights.[8] Courts in India cannot, therefore, question the propriety of legislation once it has been established that it is within the competence of the legislature to make such a law or in any law to modify its effect on the ground that it seeks to "unduly restrict personal liberty".[9] Thus the supremacy of law over king or Parliament has been up held in India now, which is in consonance of old Indian maxim that king is also subject to law and justice. He is not above law. It is directly in contrast to English maxim. King can do us wrong.

The constitution of India thus did not recognize the supremacy of the judiciary against the Legislature although the constitution gave to the judiciary the power to review legislation repugnant to the Fundamental Rights. The position before February 1967 was that Parliament would abrogate or abridge Fundamental Rights by amending the Constitution under the provisions of Article 368 and thereby override the unwholesome decision of the Judiciary simple by securing the requisite special majority, which the Congress Party had commanded in Parliament all those years. The first Amendment of the Constitution, in 1951, was necessitated with a view to overriding a series of decisions rendered by the Supreme Court and thus to save the Zamindari Abolition Acts from judicial scrutiny. The Fourth Amendment was enacted to render the question of reasonable compensation for acquisition of estates non justiciable. In 1961 and 1963, the Supreme Court declared that the Kerala and Madras Land Reform Acts, which provided for ceiling on land holdings, were bad. In the wake of these declarations the Seventeenth

Amendment was enacted in 1964 where under 44 laws passed by both the States were included in the Ninth Schedule in order to maintain them valid. A good number of writes petitions challenging the competence of Parliament to enact the Seventeenth Amendment were moved in the Supreme Court. The Supreme Court by a 6-5[10] ruling on February 27,1967 reversed its earlier decisions [11] and declared that Parliament has no power to abridge or take away. Fundamental Rights by Amending the Constitution under Article 368. Chief Justice Subba Rao, speaking for the majority, declared. "The Constitution has given by its scheme a place of permanence to the fundamental freedom. In giving to themselves the Constitution, the people have reserved the fundamental freedom to themselves. Article 13 merely incorporates that reservation. The importance attached to the fundamental freedom is so transcendental that a bill enacted by a unanimous vote of all the members of both Houses (of Parliament) is ineffective to derogate from its guaranteed exercise...." The Court rejected the Government's argument that if the power to amend the Constitution was not all comprehensive, no way would be left to change the structure of the Constitution or to abridge the Fundamental Rights even if the whole country demanded such a change. It was declared that "this visualizes an extremely enforceable and extravagant demand; but even if such a contingency arises, the residuary power of the Parliament may be relied power of the Constituent Assembly for making a new Constitution or radically changing it.[12]

The resultant position was that the amendment of the fundamental rights was not forbidden, but the Supreme Court reserved to itself the power of determining in each specific case whether the amendment in question took away or abridged those rights contained in Part III of the Constitution. Thus, the precariously balanced six to five decisions established the supremacy of the Judiciary so far as Fundamental Rights were involved. The Supreme Court of India, like its counterpart in the United States assumed the role of a super-legislature because what is taken away by the Justices from Parliament is taken away from the people, Justice K.N. Wanchoo, who was with the minority in the Golak Nath case, observed that the Constitution should in order to endure, sub serve the needs of generations which came into being after its adoption. Delivering the Feroze Memorial Lecture, Justice Wanchoo said that the decision taken by the Supreme Court by a majority of one showed "how the problem of interpretation of the Constitution by the court may have far-reaching consequences". He affirmed that the contents of the Constitution may change from time to time as new ideas gain force in the body politic of the country and new concepts of law and justice emerge. He added that it was inevitable that the view of life of individual Judges would have an impact when considering the question of Fundamental Rights but "at the same time it must not be forgotten that the view of the elected legislatures should not be over ridden lightly".[13]

The Constitution (twenty-forth Amendment) Act, 1971, was enacted to get over the difficulty created by the Golak Nath care. The amendment empowered Parliament to abridge or abrogate any of the Fundamental Rights including the right, under Article 32, to move the Supreme Court for the enforcement of Fundamental Rights. The validity of this amendment was questioned in the Supreme Court through a series of writ petitions. In Kesavananda Bharati v. The State of Kerala the Court reversed the Golak Nath case judgment by upholding the validity of the twenty-forth Amendment and thereby restored the supremacy of Parliament in regard to legislation on Fundamental Rights, a position that existed prior to 1967. But the Court also ruled that Parliament couldn't alter the basic structure or framework the Constitution. What exactly did the basic structure mean, the Court said nothing about it.

The Swaran Singh Committee on Constitutional Reforms appointed by the President of Indian National Congress early in 1976, suggested that the primacy of the Directive Principles of State Policy over Fundamental Rights must be proclaimed once for all and no law giving effect to the Directive Principles should be called in question on the ground of infringement of any of the Fundamental Rights. He asserted that the proposed constitutional reforms sought to pave the way to a "revolutionary" socio-economic programme. The Committee also proposed that any amendment of the Constitution under the constituent power of Parliament should not be called in question on any grounds. The final word must, therefore, rest with Parliament.

The Constitution (Forty-second Amendment) Act, 1976, was mainly based on the recommendations of the Swaran Singh Committee Report. The objects of this Act were expressed in the Statement of Objects and reasons appended to the Constitution (Forty-second Amendment) Bill. It, inter alia, said; "A Constitution to be living must be growing. If the impediments to the growth of the Constitution are not removed, the Constitution will suffer virtual atrophy. The question of amending the Constitution for removing the difficulties which have arisen in achieving the objective of socio-economic revolution, which would end poverty and ignorance and disease and inequality of opportunity, has been engaging the active attention of Government and the public for some years now." Accordingly, the scope of Article 31-C was widened so as to cover legislation for implementation of all or any of the Directive Principles enumerated in Part IV of the Constitution and no law could be called in question in any court on the ground of infringement of any of the Fundamental Rights. After Article 31-C a new Article 31-D was inserted for saving of laws in respect of anti-national activities. No law made to prevent of prohibit anti-national activities or the prevention of formation or prohibition of anti-national associations was to be deemed void on the ground that it was inconsistent with, or took away or abridged any of the rights conferred by Articles 14, 19 and 31 of the Constitution.

The supremacy of Parliament, thus, remained unchallenged, though the decision in the Kesavananda Bharati case, reaffirmed in Indira Gandhi v. Raj Narain, still prevailed. The validity of the forty-second Amendment was questioned through various writs and the Supreme Court in the Minerva Mills case struck down in May 1980 Section 4 and 55 of the Amendment incorporated in Articles 31C and 368 (4) (5) of the

Constitution. The Court held that in giving boundless and unchallenged power to Parliament is violative of the basic structure or essential features of the Constitution and, accordingly, void in terms of Kesavananda Bharati judgment of April 24 1973.

Another important feature of the Fundamental Rights is that there is a special constitutional provision (Article 32) for their enforcement. The right to move the Supreme Court for the enforcement of Fundamental Rights is itself a guaranteed right under Article 32. A citizen whose rights have been infringed by any public authority in India can move the Supreme Court by appropriate proceedings for the enforcement of his rights and the Court is empowered to issue directions or orders including writs in the nature of *Habeas Corpus, mandamus,* prohibition, *quo warranto* and *certiorari,* whichever may be appropriate. The State High Courts have also the power of issuing writs under Article 226 and enforce rights in the same manner within the limits of their respective jurisdictions. Thus, the constitutional remedies for the enforcement of Fundamental Rights are made available to every citizen and within his easy reach. But during the operation of emergency, under Article 352, the President may by order suspend the right to move any Court for the enforcement of any rights mentioned in the Presidential order except the rights conferred by Article 20 and 21-protection in respect of conviction for offences, and protection of life and personal liberty.

Fundamental Rights can also be restricted or suspended. Article 33 provides that Parliament may by law determine to what extent any of the rights conferred by Part III shall, in their application to members of the Armed Forces or the Forces charged with the maintenance of public order, be restricted or abrogated so as to ensure the proper discharge of their duties and maintenance of discipline among them. The special feature of the Indian Constitution is that the provisions of Article 33 apply not only to the Armed Forces but also to the ordinary police and the civil employees in the defence establishment as also the office bearers of their Unions. The

Supreme Court held in O.K.A. Nair v. Union of India (1976) that office bearers of the civil employees unions in defence establishments are integral to the Armed Forces as they answer the description of the "members of the Armed Forces" in their contemplation in Article 33. Consequently by virtue of Section 21, Army Act, the Central Government was competent to make rules restricting or curtailing their Fundamental Rights under Article 19(i) (c). Article 34 further empowers Parliament to pass a law indemnifying any person in the service of the Union or of a State or any other person in respect of any act done by him in connections with the maintenance or restoration of order where material law was in force or validate any sentence passed, punishment inflicted, forfeiture ordered or other act done under material law in such area.

Rights relating to freedoms as contained in Article 19 may be suspended during the period when the Proclamation of Emergency is in operation. Article 358 (1), provides that while a Proclamation of Emergency is in operation, "nothing in Article 19 shall restrict the power of the State as defined in Part III to make any law or to take any executive action which the State would but for the provisions contained in that Part (Part III-Fundamental Rights) be competent to make or to take". But any law so made, shall to the extent of in competency, cease to have effect as soon as the Proclamation of Emergency ceases to operate. If the Proclamation of Emergency is in operation only in any part of the territory of India, any such law may be made, or any such action may be taken, under Article 358 (1) in relation to any State or Union Territory in which the Proclamation of Emergency is not in operation, if the security of India or any part thereof is deemed to be threatened by activities in that part of the territory of India in which the Proclamation of Emergency is in operation.

44th Amendment omitted the sub-heading "Right to Property" occurring after Article 30, and Article 31 which guaranteed of his property except by authority of law Omission of right to property from Part III of the Constitution does not affect the right of a citizen to acquire, hold or dispose of property. [14] Nor can it be acquired except by the authority of law. The only difference that its omission from the Chapter on Fundamental Rights makes is that while under the omitted constitutional provision the right to property could be adversely affected only by a constitutional amendment in accordance with the prescribed procedure whereas now the right to property can be modified by a law passed by Parliament in accordance with the procedure adopted for ordinary laws. The sanctity hitherto attached to the right to property as an inalienable right, therefore, disappears by its omission from the Chapter on Fundamental Rights.

There are no natural or unremunerated rights under the Indian Constitution. This is in sharp contrast to the Constitution of the United States. Amendment IX to the American Constitution provides that "enumeration in the Constitution of certain rights shall not be construed to deny or disparage others retained by the people". The Supreme Court, accordingly, held that an Act of the Legislature which is contrary to the first principles of social compact will be *ultra vires.*"[15] What these principles of social compact are, it is for the courts to determine. In this respect the Supreme Court in the United States assumes the role of a super-legislature. The Constitution of India does not permit so. The Supreme Court in India has definitely held that unless there is an express provision in the Constitution with which the Act of a Legislature conflicts, it cannot be held to the void merely on the ground of its being inconsistent with what the court considers to be the spirit of the Constitution.[16] In other word, a right which has not been enumerated and expressly declared to be a Fundamental Right in Part III of the Constitution is not a Fundamental Right. It does not, however, mean that there are no rights apart from those include in the Fundamental Rights. But all such rights are ordinary legal rights and not Fundamental Rights and they cannot be enforced in the Supreme Court under Article 32 or in the State High Courts under Article 226. The legal remedies provided under Article 32 are only applicable to Fundamental Rights. Take, for example, Article 265. It provides that no tax shall be levied or collected except by authority of law. Although this right is a constitutional right, yet it is not a Fundamental

Rights and it cannot be enforced by the Supreme Court under Article 32, as remedies provided under Article 32 are only applicable to Fundamental Rights.

During the last few years the Supreme Court has, through the process of judicial activism, emerged as the custodian of the rights of the deprived and vulnerable sections of society by waiving legal procedures and formalities and have made available to those who had hitherto no access to legal remedies due essentially to their illiteracy and economic inhibitions and had silently suffered all along. The Supreme Court has consequently stepped in to protect the rights of millions of destitute where welfare laws have been implemented in a niggardly manner. Judgments in cases, like the Minerva Mills, Asiad Labour, the National Textiles Workers, Bombay pavement dwellers and quite a few more have sounded in favour of the deprived and, as the Chief Justice of India, has claimed, that in public interest litigation cases the Supreme Court "had struck error in the hearts of the erring-authorities". But that ethos of judicial activism has yet to percolate down from the Supreme Court.

Finally there are the Directive Principles of State Policy as contained in Chapter IV. In considering the question of fixing the Fundamental Rights and incorporating them into the Constitution, the Advisory Committee appointed by the Constituent Assembly,[17] came to the conclusion that the Fundamental Rights should be divided into two parts-the first justiciable rights are put under the heading Directive Principles of State Policy and according to Article 37 they are not enforceable by any court, "but the principle laid down are nevertheless Fundamental in the governance of the country and it shall be the duty of the state to apply these principles in making laws." To be precise, whereas the Fundamental Rights are in effect, injunctions prohibiting Government from doing certain things, the Directive Principles are affirmative instructions to Government to do certain things.

Whatever be the legal nicety between the Fundamental Rights and Directive Principles of State Policy, the Constitution of India is "first and foremost", as Granville Austin says, "a social document. The majority of its provision are either directly aimed at furthering the goals of the social revolution or attempt to foster this revolution by establishing the conditions necessary for its achievement''. The core of the commitment to the social revolution lies in Parts III and IV, in the Fundamental Rights and in the Directive Principles of the State Policy. Both together constitute the conscience of the Constitution. They has their roots in the struggle for independence and were included in the Constitution in the expectation that one day the tree of true liberty and justice, with their concomitant requisites, would bloom in India. The Fundamental Rights and Directive Principles of State Policy connect India's future, present and past 'adding greatly to their significance of inclusion in the Constitution, and giving strength to the pursuit of the social revolution in India.''

The Right to Equality

The right to equality guaranteed in Part III of the Constitution has no social implication. It is essentially negative in character and is intended to remove the social and civil disabilities from which the masses of India had suffered all through these ages. Democracy can only exist and flourish amongst a society of equals and the Indian polity. It guarantees equality of all persons before the law prohibits discrimination on grounds of religion, race, caste, sex or place of birth as between citizens, grants to all equality of opportunity in the matter of public employment, and abolishes untouchability on the one side and titles on the other. Citizens may not be denied admission to educational institutions maintained by the State or receiving aid out of religion, race, caste, or language. Minorities may establish their own schools and government may not discriminate against them in making grants on the grounds of religion, race or language.

Some exceptions are, however, inevitable and the Constitution sets out these exceptions. A legislature may make laws with special provisions for women and children. The Constitution (First Amendments) Act, 1951, further provided that " Nothing in this Article (15) or in clause (2) of Article 29 shall prevent the State from making any special provision for the advancement of any special provisions for the advancement of any socially and educationally backward classes of citizens or for the Scheduled Caste and the Scheduled Tribes. Another exception made is with regard to the equality of opportunity in public employment. Parliament may confine employment under a State or local authority to residents. A State may also provide for the reservation of appointments or posts for members of backward classes, which, in the opinion of the State, are not adequately represented in the services under the State. Offices connected with religious or denominational institutions may be reserved for the adherents of a particular religion or belonging to a particular denomination.

The right to equality, therefore, aims at protecting citizens against discriminatory treatment by the State in the fields of administration and legislation, to advance the uplift of the socially backward classes even to the exception of granting them special privileges for removing other and cruder forms of social inequality. Such social customs and disabilities as enforced segregation of the so-called untouchable at wells, in streets, schools and places of worship are declared illegal. In fact, the Constitution bans all kinds of untouchability specified and unspecified and uplifts more than 50 millions untouchables from their age-old degraded social status. The right to equality, in sum, fosters the social revolution by creating a society egalitarian to the extent that all citizens are to be equally free from coercion or restriction by the State, or by the society privately. Liberty is no longer the privilege of the few, but a social content and right of all, high and low, men and women irrespective of religion, caste and creed.

Abolition of titles as finally embodied in Article 19 of the Constitution was the subject of discussion in the sub-Committee on the Fundamental Rights. The note prepared by K. T. Shah on clauses devoted to titles, honours, distinctions and privileges.[18] Despite objections Alladi Krishnaswami Ayyar's amongst them Shah succeeded in getting the Sub-Committee to accept by a majority vote the draft went of a provision dealing with the conferment and acceptance of titles. But when the draft went to the Advisory Committee it ran to heavy weather, with several influential members expressing themselves against the abolition of titles. Shah, however, was emphatic that the conferring of titles offended against the principle of equality of all citizens so solemnly sought to be enshrined in the Constitution. The entire provision was finally re-drafted by the Committee and Vallabhbhai Patel moving the clause for the consideration of the Constituent Assembly on April 30, 1947, observed that titles were "often being abused for corrupting the public life of the country" and that it was therefore better for their abolition should be provided as fundamental right.

When on November 30,1948, draft article 12 came up for consideration before the Constituent Assembly. T.T. Krishnamachari sought to add the words, "not being a military or academic distinction ", after the word title in clause (1). Krishnamachari's contention was that it was necessary, firstly, because certain types of titles had to be permitted, the Government having, for example, already decided to confer certain military distinctions, secondly, because the State might decide to revive academic titles. Ambedkar accepted the amendment to the clause moved by Krishnamachari and the Constituent Assembly adopted it on December 1948. When on November 30,1948, draft article 12 came up for consideration before the Constituent Assembly. T.T. Krishnamachari sought to add the words, "not being a military or academic distinction ", after the word title in clause (1). Krishnamachari's contention was that it was necessary, firstly, because certain types of titles had to be permitted, the Government having, for example, already decided to confer certain military distinctions, secondly, because the State might decided to revive academic titles. Ambedkar accepted the amendment to the clause moved by Krishnamachari and the Constituent Assembly adopted it in December 1948.

The Right to Freedom

The right to freedom is covered by Article to 22 and embraces the classical liberties of the individual, of these, Article 19 is the most important as it originally guaranteed six fundamental rights, which may be described as six freedom, viz., (a) freedom of speech and expression; (b) freedom of assembly; (c) freedom of association; (d) freedom of movement; (e) freedom of residence and settlement; and (f) freedom of property, and (g) freedom of profession, occupation, trade or business. All these freedoms are the most important ingredients of human happiness and progress, as without them no individual can rise to the full stature of his personality. The Preamble of almost every Constitution epitomizes these freedoms and declares them as its objectives. For instance, the Preamble to the Constitution f the United States, inter alia, declares " to secure the blessings of liberty to ourselves and to our posterity. The Preamble to the Indian Constitution declares that one of its objectives is to secure to all citizens Liberty of thought, expression, belief, faith and worship.

Article 19 may be divided into two parts. The first is the declaration of rights. The second part contains limitations [clauses (2) to (6)] each governing one or more clause of the first part. Consistent with the theory that rights can never be absolute, the Constitution imposes specific limitations on their exercise and enjoyment. This is an improvement on the American Constitution, which leaves the determination of restrictions and adjustment of conflicting interests of the individual and society to the courts. The Constitution of India defines the scope of limitations and authorises the State to restrict the exercise of freedoms guaranteed by Article 19 within the restricting clauses of the same Article. It has been maintained that these limitations are, in fact, a partial codification of the American doctrine of Police Power.

The limitation imposed on the freedom of speech and the rights to property were substantially modified by the Constitution (First Amendment) Act, 1951. The main objects of amending the Constitution can best be explained by the Statement of Objects and Reasons attached to the Amending Bill. The Statement read, "During the last fifteen months of the working of the Constitution, certain difficulties have been brought to light by judicial decisions and pronouncements especially in regard to the Chapter on Fundamental Rights. The citizen's right to freedom of speech and expression guaranteed by Article 19(a) has been held by some courts to be so comprehensive as not to render a person culpable even if he advocates murder and other crimes of violence. In other countries with written Constitutions, freedom of the speech and press is not regarded as debarring the State from punishing or preventing abuse of this freedom. The citizen's right to practice any profession or to carry on any occupation, trade or business conferred by Article 19(1)(g) is subject to reasonable restriction, which the laws of the State may impose 'in the interests of the general public'. While the words cited are comprehensive enough to cover any scheme of nationalization, which the State may undertake, it is desirable to place the matter beyond doubt by a clarificatory addition to Article 19(6).

The scope of the freedom of speech under the original provisions was exceptionally wide. There were only four reservations restricting this right, viz, laws relating to libel, slander and defamation; contempt of court; decency or morality; and security of the State. Thus, "public order" was not one of the purposes for which the freedom of speech could be restricted. Similarly, incitement to an offence was not made one of the subjects to restrict the freedom of speech and not relating to defamation or contempt of court and not involving offences against decency or morality would be ultra virus unless it related to any matter, which undermined the security of or tended to overthrow the State. In Ramesh Thapar v. The State of Madras it was held that the Constitution "has placed in a distinct category those offences against public order which aim at undermining the security of the State or overthrowing it and made their prevention the sole justification of legislative abridgement of the freedom of speech and expression, that is to say, nothing less than endangering the foundations of the State or threatening its overthrow could justify the curtailment of the freedom of speech and expression".

The Amendment of 1951 added three more reservations to the existing list contained in Article 19(2). The new reservations were: friendly relations with foreign States, public order, and incitement to an offence. Article 19(2) read: "Nothing in sub-clause (a) of clause (1) shall effect the operation of any existing law, or prevent the State from making any law, in so far as such law imposes reasonable restrictions on the exercise of the right conferred by the said sub-clause in the interests of the security of the State, friendly relations with foreign States, public order, decency or morality, or in relation to contempt of court, defamation or incitement to an offence". With the inclusion of the three additional reservations the right to freedom of speech was considerably curtailed and the scope of interference appreciably widened, provided the courts could be satisfied about the reasonableness of restrictions. By reasonable restrictions, the Supreme Court meant restrictions, which are not excessive in nature and beyond what is required in the interests of the public. The Supreme Court also held that "the determination by the Legislature of what constitutes a reasonable restriction is not final or conclusive; it is subject to supervision by this court. In the matter of Fundamental Rights the Supreme Court watches and guards the rights guaranteed by the Constitution and in exercising its functions it has the power to set aside the Act of the Legislature if it is in violation of the freedoms guaranteed by the Constitution".[19]

Similarly, sub-clauses (b) and (c) of Article 19(1) confer the freedom to assemble peaceably and to form associations or unions. The freedom to speech is complimentary to the freedom to assemble and the freedom to form associations or unions. The Sixteenth Amendment, however, restricted their scope. Clauses 3 and 4 of Article 19 empower the State to make any law imposing, in the interests of sovereignty and integrity of India or public order or morality reasonable restrictions on the exercise of these freedoms.

Other rights guaranteed by Article 19 may be briefly stated. The right to move freely is the right to movement unchecked and unrestricted anywhere within the territory of the Indian Union, subject to such restrictions as are imposed by any existing law or such as the State may in future impose in the public interest or to safeguard the interests of any Scheduled Tribes. In time of emergency, such as war, every citizen cannot claim as a matter of right access to places considered of military or strategic importance. Similarly, when an epidemic spreads in one part of the country, people may be prohibited by law from entering or leaving the affected areas in the interests of public health. The freedom of movement also does not take away the right which the law gave to the Government to extern any person from any part of the country for a particular period in the interests of maintenance of law and order[20], as also to detain any person for sufficient grounds if the public interest demanded it.[21]

Allied to the right of free movement is the right to reside and settle in any part of the territory of India. This right is limited by reasonable restrictions in the interests of general public or for the protection of the interests of Scheduled Tribes.

Finally, the right to practice any trade or profession is subject to the right of the state to prescribe professional or technical qualifications to enable a citizen to become a lawyer or an engineer. This restriction is natural and necessary. The Constitution (First Amendment) Act, 1951, further empowered the State to reserve to itself the right to carry on any trade, business, industry or service either directly or through State controlled corporations to the complete or partial exclusion of private citizens. This Amendment was necessitated because of the judgment of the Allahabad High Court in Moti Lal v. The Government of Uttar Pradesh. The U.P. Motor Vehicle Act, 1939, was challenged in the court as it conflicted with Article 14 of the Constitution. The Allahabad High Court decided that it could not allow the exemption of transport vehicle owned by the State Government from Section 43(3)(a) of the Motor Vehicle Act which required that all vehicles should be used in accordance with the conditions of permits granted by the Regional or Provincial Authority. The purpose of the Amendment was explained by the Union Law Minister during the course of debate on the Amendment Bill. He said that the State Government would gradually take to nationalization; hence it was necessary that the Constitution should be amended to provide authority for the same. Article 19(6) was, therefore, amended to avoid the adverse implications of this decision as far as State trading was concerned. The reasonableness of any law permitting nationalization of any trade or business cannot be a subject of judicial review.[22]

It will, therefore, be obvious that under the amended Clause (6) of Article 19 the restrictions on the right of carrying on any profession, etc., fall into these classes: (a) reasonable restriction imposed under the general power in the interests of the general public; (b) restrictions in the form of professional or technical qualifications; and (c) any law relating to carrying on trade or business or industry or service by the State or Corporation owned or controlled by the State. Restrictions imposed in the interests of general public give a very wide scope for interference and can include all matters affecting public welfare, such as, public safety, public health, public morals, etc. Reasonable restrictions include "prohibition", having regard to the exceptional circumstances, which involve patent and widespread danger to the community. It may, accordingly, prohibit a citizen from carrying on a particular trade, business or profession.[23] The State may also create a monopoly in relation to any trade which is liable to cause injury to the public,[24] or any trade in commodities essential to the life of the community.[25]

Life and Liberty

The rights guarantees in Article 20, 21 and 22 relate to the individual's personal liberty and collectively come under the sub-heading "Right to Freedom". These rights strengthen the liberties conferred on citizens under Article 19. Article 20 deals with certain Fundamental Rights of a person accused of a crime and embodies the principles of criminal jurisprudence. Clause

(1) of the Article embodies the principle that no one should be made to suffer any punishment for an offence under any law not in force at the time of the commission of an offence. Similarly, no person shall be subject to a penalty greater than that which might have been inflicted under the law in force at the time of the commission of the offense. Clause (2) of the same Article embodies the fundamental principle that no one should be placed in jeopardy twice for the same offence. The principle underlying this clause is the same as underlies the "double jeopardy" clause of the American Constitution, though the words used are different. Clause (3) gives effect to the principle that no one should be compelled to give clause follows the language of the Fifth Amendment of the Constitution of the United States, though the rule laid down in the Indian Constitution is "narrower than the American rule as expanded by interpretation".

The Constitution (Forty-fourth Amendment) Act, 1978, prohibits the suspension, by Presidential Order, during the operation of the Proclamation of Emergency, the right to move the Supreme Court by appropriate proceedings, including the writ of *habeas corpus,* for the enforcement of rights conferred by Article 20- protection in respect of conviction for offences. Nor has the State the power to make any law or take executive action restricting, abridging or abrogating the rights guaranteed under Article 20.

Article 21 guarantees to every person the most essential of all rights, the right to life and personal liberty, which the Article says cannot be taken away except according to procedure established by law. The Constitution permits the continuance of preventive detention, but only in accordance with the laws providing for it. This Article is not intended to be a constitutional limitation upon the powers of the legislatures. The object is simply to serve as a restraint upon the Executive so that it may not proceed against the life or personal liberty of the individual save under the authority of some law and in conformity with the Article 22 of the Constitution.

The provision of Article 21 are analogous to the provisions of the Fifth and fourteenth Amendments of the Constitution of the United States, except that the Constitution of India gave the right to the property a separate treatment and substituted for "due process of law" "procedure established by the law". The phrase "procedure established by law" was borrowed from the Constitution of Japan (1946), which was also "American inspired". Under the Fifth Statement of the Constitution of the United States no person can be deprived of life, liberty or property without due process of law. Under the Fourteenth Amendment no state can deprive any person of life and liberty without due process of law. The "due process" clause has been liberally interpreted in the United States and it means that the laws should be reasonable, proper and just. Anyone suspected of violating the law must be dealt with according to established rules of justice and not arbitrarily. It also means that the acts of the Legislatures and Executives, both at the Center and in the States, should be reasonable and uniformally applied to all people similarly situated. Finally, it means that it is for the courts determine whether action of the Government and its laws are reasonable or not.

Chief justice Kania observed in A. K. Gopalan v. State of Madras that there were four marked points of distinction between the "due process" clause of the Constitution of the United States and "procedure established by law" of the Constitution of India. The first is that in the United States the word liberty is used simpliciter (unconditionally) whereas in India, it is restricted to personal liberty. Second, some protection is given to property in America while the Indian Constitution gives the right to property a separate treatment. In the third place, the word "due" is omitted altogether and the expression "due process of law" is not used deliberately. Lastly, the word "established" is used and is limited to "procedure". Due process of law covers both substantive as well as procedural laws.

The phrase "established by law" means enacted by law and the word "Law" means State made law. No person can; accordingly, claim that the procedure prescribed by law does not conform to the principles of natural justice. Explaining the implications of the phrase "established by law", justice Das observed that Article 21 defines the ambit of the right to life and personal liberty. It is not an absolute right but is a qualified right- "a right circumscribed by the possibility or risk of being lost according to the procedure established by law.[26] It is for Parliament to enact a law changing the procedure and once it is changed that procedure becomes the procedure established by law. When a person is deprived of liberty otherwise than procedure established according to law, it is only then the courts will interfere. It is not for the courts to determine whether the law is reasonable or not.[27]

During the operation of Proclamation of Emergency the right to move the Supreme Court by appropriate proceedings for the enforcement of the right to the protection of life and liberty conferred by Article 21 cannot be suspended. By interesting this provision the Constitution (Forty-forth Amendment) Act, 1978, nullified the effects of the Supreme Court decision during the emergency in what came to be known as the *Habeas Corpus case* (A.D.M. Jabalpur v. S.S. Shukla 1976 (supp.) SCR, 172). In this case the court ruled that in view of the Presidential Order under Article 359 of the Constitution suspending the enforcement of Fundamental Rights no person had any locus *standi* to move any writ petition for *habeas corpus* or any other writ, or order or direction to challenge the legality of an order of detention on the ground that the order was not under or in compliance with the statute or was illegal or was vitiated by mala fides, factual or legal or was based on extraneous considerations. Justice H.R. Khanna had dissented from the majority opinion of the court.

Article 22 of the Constitution gives certain constitutional right to arrested persons and also lays down certain fundamental rules with regard to preventive detention. It may, however, be noted that provisions relating to the preventive detention are peculiar inasmuch as the Constitution of India permits resort to preventive detention even in peace time. In other democratic countries preventive detention is usually method resorted to in emergencies like war. Prevention detention in India for reasons connected with the security of the State, or the maintenance of public order, or maintenance of supplies and services essential for the community, is on the Concurrent List, but preventive detention for reasons connected with defence, foreign affairs or the security of India is within the exclusive competence of Parliament.

The first two clauses of Article 22 deal with detention under the ordinary law and prescribe the procedure when a person is arrested. It ensures: (i) the right to be informed of the grounds of arrest, (ii) right to consult and to be defended by a legal practitioner of his choice, (iii) right to be produced before a magistrate within twenty-four hours, and (iv) freedom from detention beyond the specified period of twenty-four hours except by order of the magistrate.

The remaining clause of this Article relate to preventive detention. Detention can be of two types: punitive and preventive. A preventive detention is intended to detain a person, without trial and without any charge of commission of an offence. It is a measure to intercept a person as a matter of precaution before the actually commits an offence. No offence is proved nor any charge is formulated, but there is a strong suspicion or reasonable probability that the individual commits or is likely to commit acts prejudicial to the welfare of the society, the security of the State and the stability of the Government established by law. It is not a criminal conviction, which can only be warranted by legal evidence. The person under detention (detenu) is not given immediately on his arrest reasons for such arrest and detention. Neither he has any right to consult a lawyer, nor is he to be produced before a magistrate within twenty-four hours. Provisions of clauses (1) and (2) of Article 22 do not apply to a person arrested or detained under any law providing for prevention detention as also to any person who for the time being is an enemy alien.

Preventive detention legislation contemplates executive action for holding a person in custody for indefinite period without trial. The specific heads of prejudicial activities for which preventive detention can be affected are contained in List I, entry 9 and List III, entry 3, of the Seventh Schedule to the Constitution. The sole justification for arrest is the satisfaction of the competent administrative authority or suspicion of reasonable probability of the deteun committing or likely to commit an act, which may either cause harm to society or endanger the security of the State. Such detention is outside the reach of Article 19(1)(d) which guarantees the right to all citizens to move freely throughout the territory of India.

Article 22 clauses (4) to (7), however, provide safeguards against the rigours of preventive detention:

1. Detention cannot last for a period longer than two months, except on the report of the Advisory Board, constituted in accordance with the recommendations of the Chief Justice of the appropriate High Court and consisting of a serving Judge of the appropriate High Court and not less than two other members who shall be serving or retired Judges of any High Court, reporting that there is in its opinions sufficient cause for such detention; [46]
2. The period of detention can in no case exceed beyond the maximum period prescribed by law made by Parliament; [47]
3. The detaining authority shall, as soon as may be, communicate to the detenu the grounds on which the detention has been made and shall afford him the earliest opportunity of making a representation against the order of his detention;
4. The communication conveying the ground of detention shall contain facts, except those that cannot be disclosed for reasons of public interests;
5. Parliament may by law prescribe the procedure to be followed by an Advisory Board.

Preventive detention has, thus, been given a constitutional sanction. Justice Patanjali Sastri observed in A.K. Gopalan v. State of Madras: " this sinister looking feature, so strangely out of place in democratic Constitution which invests personal liberty with the sacrosanctity of a fundamental right, and so incompatible with the promises of its Preamble, is doubtless designed to prevent an abuse of freedom by anti-social and subversive elements which might imperil the national welfare of the infant republic". [28] In Dr. Ram Krishna Bhardwaj v. State of Delhi and others, he observed, "Preventive detention is a serious invasion of personal liberty and such meager safeguards as the Constitution has provided against the improper exercise of the power must be jealously watched". [29] Quashing the detention of Inderjit alias Billa under the Preventive of Black-marketing and Maintenance of Supplies of Essential Commodities Act, Justice A.P. Sen and Baharul Islam observed, "It cannot be denied that preventive detention is an anachronism in a democratic society like ours". They also observed that detention of individuals without trial for any length of time, however short, was wholly inconsistent with the basic ideals of a parliamentary system of Government. By a four to one majority of the Constitution bench the Supreme Court held the National Security Act, was constitutionally valid, but hedged it with a number of safeguards so as to inhibit the executive using it arbitrarily and indiscriminately. The Court inter alia, wanted that concept like the "defence of India"; the "security of India" and "relations with foreign powers" should be defined as narrowly as possible so as to minimize the scope for offences attracting detention. The Court adjudged detention without trial to be "an evil to be suffered".

In the United States of America, there is no provision for preventive detention in peacetime. The Sixth Amendment to the Constitution guarantees the right to a speedy and public trial for all accused persons involved in criminal prosecutions they should be provided with a copy of the indictment well before the trial begins, and to provide with counsels at public expense if the accused are unable to secure their own attorneys. Provision for the preventive detention in emergency has been made by the Internal Security Act, 1950, and, consequently, it is a part of the law of the United States and not of the Constitution. The Emergency Detention Act, 1950, authorizes the President to bring into operation by a proclamation of an internal security emergency on being satisfied that such a proclamation was necessary for the preservation of the Constitution and maintenance of the safety and security of the United States.

In Great Britain preventive detention by Regulations was made under the Defence of the Realm Act, 1914, and again by the Regulations made under the Emergency Powers (Defence) Act, 1939. It is, therefore, a wartime measure. In Liversidge v. Anderson it was observed, "however precious, the personal liberty of the subject may be, to some extent, sacrificed by legal enactment, namely, final national success in war or escape from national plunder on enslavement''.

Preventive detention was introduced in Northern Ireland on August 9, 1971. The British Government appointed a committee headed by Lord Gardiner "to consider in the context of civil liberties and human rights, measures to deal with terrorism''. Gardiner Committee Report observed, "after long and anxious consideration, we are of the opinion that detention cannot remain as a long-term policy. In the short term, it may be an effective means of containing violence, but the prolonged effects of the use of detention are ultimately intimately to community life, fan a widespread sense of grievance and injustice and obstruct those elements in Northern Ireland society which could lead to reconciliation. Detention can only be tolerated in a democratic society in the most extreme circumstances; it must be used with the utmost restraint and retained only as long as it is strictly necessary. We would like to be able to recommended that the time has come to abolish detention; but the present level of violence, the risks of increased violence, and the difficulty of predicting events even a few months ahead make it impossible for us to put forward precise recommendation on the timing''.

The right to liberty is the very essence of a free society and it must be safeguarded at all times. The European Court of Human Rights has ruled that detention without trial is violative of the European Convention on Human Rights, except "in time of war or other public emergency threatening the life of the nation", and even then to the extent "strictly required by the exigencies of the situation", as the Convention says. The International Covenant on Civil and Political Rights, which India supported in the General Assembly, are almost identically worded. "To brush aside internationally recognized norms", remarks Noorani, "as irrelevant to our 'special condition' is to indulge in special pleading of the most specious variety".

Right against Exploitation

Article 23 and 24 come under the sub-heading right against exploitation. Article 23 categorically prohibits all the traffic in human beings and *beggar* (compulsory labour with or without payment) and other similar forms of forced labour. Traffic in human beings is evidently a very wide expression and would embrace not only the prohibition of slavery and bonded labour but also traffic in women for immoral or other purposes. Contravention of this prohibition has been made an offence punishable in accordance with law. The Constitution-makers had in mind the widespread evil custom of forced labour without remuneration or just a nominal remuneration verging on pittance prevalent in the country since ages.

The right against exploitation was mentioned in the drafts prepared by B. R. Ambedkar, K.M. Munshi and K.T. Shah. While Ambedkar's draft simply provided that subjecting a person to forced labour or to involuntary servitude would be an offence, the draft article suggested by Munshi contained more elaborate provisions for the abolition of all forms of slavery, traffic in human beings, and compulsory labour. Munshi's draft also contained a provision prohibiting child labour in all forms. K.T. Shah's draft expressly forbade slavery of any kind, as well as recognition of any right amounting to property in human beings; prohibited forced labour or *beggar*, and it declared that all human beings in the Union of India would be free and that all labourers attached to land would be remunerated by wages at prescribed or agreed rates. It also recognized the right of the Government to conscript by law the manpower of the country for purposes of national defence, social service or for meeting of a sudden emergency.

Clause 2 of Article 23 provides for the power of the State to impose compulsory service for public purposes. The expression public purpose has nowhere been defined. Alladi Krishnaswami maintained in the Constituent Assembly that Munshi's amendments would not preclude military conscription. In spite of the anti-servitude and anti-slavery clause in the American Constitution, he added, the United

States Supreme Court had held that there was nothing to prevent military conscription so far as the very existence of the State depended upon military force. On the same ground Alladi Krishnaswami Ayyar said, the words "beggar and similar forms of forced labour" could not possibly be interpreted as excluding conscription.

H.V. Kamath suggested in the Constituent Assembly that for the words "service for public purposes" in clause (2) the words "for social or national purposes" be substituted. He felt that national service or social service had a wider and higher and a more comprehensive connotation than public service.[30] Replying to Kamath, Ambedkar said that the words "social and national" were not necessary since the word "public" was wide enough to cover both. The expression "public purposes", accordingly, includes of individuals is directly and vitally concerned.[51] Compulsory service for public purposes necessarily includes military service as it is a service for a public purpose to maintain the Sovereignty and integrity of the country. In Dulal Samanta v. District Magistrate, Howrah, the Calcutta High Court held that the "conscription for police or military service is neither *beggar* nor traffic in human beings and is, therefore, not hit by Article 23".[32] In Atma Ram v. State of Bihar it was held that the provision in the Bihar Finance Act, 1950, making it obligatory on owners of motor vehicles to collect rent and taxes imposed on freights was within the exception of Article 23(2) which allowed the State to impose compulsory service for public purposes.[33]

Article 24 provides that no child below the age of fourteen years shall be employed to work in any factory or mine or engaged in any others hazardous employment. Here the Indian Constitution goes ahead of the American Constitution wherein there is no express prohibition against the employment of children in any factory or mine or in other hazardous occupations.

Right to Freedom of Religion

The guarantee of religious freedom was contained in the draft articles formulated by K.M. Munshi, and B.R. Ambedkar. The clause in Munshi's draft provided that all citizens would be equally entitled to freedom of conscience and the right freely to profess and practice religion. The right was not unrestricted for it had to be exercised in a manner compatible with public order, morality and health. Economic, financial or political activities associated with religious worship were not to be deemed as being included in the right to profess or practice religion. Two other safeguards were also provided. No person was to be compelled to pay taxes the proceeds of which would be specifically appropriated for the payment of religious requirements of any community of which he was not a member, and religious instruction was not be compulsory, for a member of a community which did not profess that religion. Similar provisions were also included in Ambedkar's draft which in addition provided for freedom to preach and to convert; and further that every religious association would be free to regulate and administer its affairs within the limits of the laws applicable to all.

Both Munshi and Ambedkar had included in their drafts certain other proposals relating to freedom of religion, which received some attention initially but were later dropped at once stage or another. Notable among these was a clause by Ambedkar expressly enjoining the State not to " recognize any religion as a State religion''. There were also two provisions in Munshi's draft, one of which said that minors would not be free to change their religious persuasion without the permission of their parents or guardians, while the other prohibited conversion from one religion to another brought about by coercion, undue influence or the offering of material inducement.

The Sub-Committee on Fundamental Rights discussed the clause relating to freedom of religion and recognized at the instance of a Sikh member, Harnam Singh, "the right to wear and carry Kripans'' as part of the practice of Sikh religion. After a good deal of discussion and minor adjustments at various stages the Drafting Committee incorporated them in Draft Article 19 to 22 which were discussed by the Constituent Assembly on December 3, 6 and 7, 1948. A number of amendments moved by Ambedkar and Mrs. Durgabai and the draft articles adopted, as so amended.

The Preamble to the Constitution express a resolve of the people to constitute India into a Sovereign Socialist Secular Democratic Republic in order to ensure among other things, "Liberty of thought, expression, belief, faith and worship". The secular principle, thus, accepted by the people of India was made fundamental and enshrined in Part III of the Constitution as contained in Articles 25 to 28. These rights have a wide scope and include both the personal and social aspects of religion and are equally enjoyed by all persons living in India, citizens and aliens. The Constitution guarantees to all persons freedom of conscience, and to profess, practices and propagate any religion subject to the prescribed limitations of public order, morality and health and other provisions of Part III. The Constitution, as such, does not only guarantee the freedom of religious faith and belief but it protects also acts done in pursuance of religions and this is made clear by the use of the expression "practice of religion". All rituals, ceremonies, observances and modes of worship which are considered as integral part of a religion are permitted to be practiced unhindered provided they do not offend any of the prescribed limitations.

But religious freedom and freedom of conscience do not diminish in any manner the regularity power of the State given to it by the provisions of the Constitution. Religious freedom stands harmoniously with other Fundamental Rights. Religious institutions being on the Concurrent List, the right of freedom to religion does not accordingly, prevent the State Legislatures to enact any law regulating or restricting any economic, financial, political or other secular activity of a religious body, nor render invalid laws throwing open public religious institutions formerly reserved for a section of the adherents of any one of the Hindu, Sikh, Jain, or Buddhist religions, to all adherents of that religion. Similarly, religious freedom is no bar to social welfare and reformatory legislation. For example, progressive legislation relating to marriage, divorce and inheritance cannot be challenged on the ground of being violative of religious freedom. Temple entry of the Scheduled Castes is an important social reform and it has individual's personal and denominational aspects. Religious freedom does not mean denial of similar freedom to any one who professes and practices the same faith and belief.

All religious denomination are guaranteed autonomy, the right to establish institutions, and the right to acquire and deal with property, but only subject to public order, health and morality. No one can be compelled to pay taxes for the propagation and maintenance of any religion and religious instruction is not to be given in schools and colleges wholly maintained out of government revenues. But religions instruction may be imparted in private institutions receiving a grant from public is given religious in structure or made to attend religious worship in a building attached to the institution without his consent, or, if he is a minor, his guardian's consent.

Cultural and Fundamental Rights

Apart from individual's right and freedom the Constitution recognizes and guarantees certain non-political rights of the religious, cultural and linguistic minorities, groups or sections of the people. Article 29 guarantees to every minority or section of the people to preserve its language, script and culture notwithstanding the provisions of Article 343 under which the official language of the Union shall be Hindi in Devnagri script. Clause (2) of the same Article provides that no citizen may be denied admission to State and State-aided educational institutional on the grounds only of religion, race, caste or language. Article 30 guarantees to all minorities whether based on religion or language the right to establish and administer their educational institutions and the State shall not discriminate against them in making grants on grounds of religion, race or language.

There is implicit in the right conferred by Article 30(1), the right to impart instruction in their own institutions, to the children of their own community in their own language. To deny it is tantamount to depriving it of the right conferred by Article 29(1), which guarantees to conserve language or script of a minority community and the right to establish and administer educational institutions of their choice under Article 30(1). Article 30 came for discussion in Kerala Education Bill 1957. Since this Bill, who was reserved for the consideration of the President, imposed serious limitations on the right of the minorities aided and recognized by the Kerala Government, the President referred some of the provisions of the Bill to the Supreme Court for its advisory opinion. The court expressed the opinion that a minority community "can effectively conserve its language, script or culture by and through educational institutions and, therefore, the right to establish and maintain educational institutions of its own choice is a necessary concomitant to the right to conserve its distinctive language, script and culture that is what is conferred on all minorities by Article 30(1)...." There is no constitutional right, the Court remarked, to receive State aid. "If the State does not grant aid, it cannot impose such conditions (e.g., that the State will acquire the institution or will take over the management if certain things are not done) as will deprive it of its right under Article 30(1). The State cannot take over the management of schools established by minorities communities on the plea that it (State) seeks to do so or introduce free and compulsory education as required by Directive Principles". The object can be fulfilled through the State-owned or State-aided institution, the court said.[34]

A special Constitution Bench of the Supreme Court declared on April 26, 197\49, as amended in 1972, governing the affiliation of minority colleges, transforming them into constituent colleges of the University, regulating the appointment and service conditions of the staff and providing for arbitration of disputes, violated the fundamental right of the minorities to administer educational institutions of their choice.[35] The Supreme Court, thus, reaffirmed the rights enshrined in Article 29 and 30. "There can be no surrender of constitutional protection of the right of minorities to popular will masquerading as the common pattern of education", Justice Mathew. This ruling by the Court followed two writ petitions filed by the Ahmedabad St. Xavier College Society and others.

The Constitution (Forty-forth Amendment) Act, 1978, inserted a new clause 30(1A) after Article 30 which ordained that in making any law providing for the compulsory acquisition of any property of an educational institution established and administrated by a minority, the State shall ensure that the amount fixed by or determined by such law for the acquisition of such property "is much as would not restrict or abrogate'' the right guaranteed in Article 30-Right of minorities to establish and administer educational institutions. Whereas the amendment conceded to the State the power to acquire property of an educational institution established and administered by a minority, it is obligatory for the State to ensure that the amount fixed for compensation of that property is adequate so that it may enable that minority to establish and administer a similar institution at an other location.

Right to Property

The consensus reached between the Government and the Opposition parties on April 20, 1978 on deleting the right to property from Chapter III on Fundamental Rights and giving it a statutory status was reflected in the Constitution (Forty-fourth Amendment) Act, 1978, by inserting a new Chapter IV with the heading Right to Property and incorporating Article 300-A which ordains that 'No person shall be deprived of his property save by authority of law''. Section 5 of the Amendment omitted the sub-heading "Right to Property'' occurring after Article 30. Article 31A and Article 31C were suitably amended as to omit all references to the right to property. Similarly, Section 2 omitted Sub-clause (f) in Article 19 (1) that read "to acquire, hold and dispose of property''.

This change does not in any way affect the right of a citizen to hold, acquire or dispose of property except that while under the omitted provision the right to property could be adversely affected only by a constitutional amendment and in accordance with the procedure prescribed under Article 368, under Article 300-A the right to property can be modified by a law passed by Parliament in accordance with the procedure adopted for enactment of an ordinary law. But it does not affect the sanctity or property as an inalienable basic right.

But the Constitution retains Articles 31A and 31B-saving of laws providing for acquisition of estates, etc, and validation of certain Acts and Regulations. The effects of both these Articles are very wide and were intended to validate the acquisition of zamindaries on the abolition of Permanent Settlement without interference from Courts. Article 31A provides that no law, past or future, affecting rights of any proprietor or intermediate holder of any estate or taking over the management of property by the State for a limited period either in the public interest or in order to secure the proper management of the property, or the extinction or modification of any rights of managing agents, Secretaries or treasures, managing directors or managers of corporations or any voting rights of share holders, or extinction or modification of rights under mining leases and other similar agreements regarding any mineral or mineral oil or the permanent termination or cancellation of any such agreement, lease or license shall be deemed void on the ground that it is inconsistent with, or takes away or abridges any of the rights by Article 14 or Article 19. If any law is made by the Legislature of a State, the provisions of Article 31A shall not apply unless it had been reserved for the consideration of the President and received his assent.

The Constitution (Seventeenth Amendment) Act 1964, inserted another proviso to Article 31A. It provided that any law making any provision for the acquisition by the State of any estate and where any land comprised therein is held by a person under his personal cultivation, it shall not be lawful for the State to acquire any portion of such land as is within the ceiling limit or any building or structure standing therein unless the law relating to the acquisition of such land or structure, provides for payments of compensation at a rate which shall not be less than the market value of such a property.

Article 31B was inserted to save the Acts and Religions specified in the Ninth Schedule of the Constitution notwithstanding any decision of a Court or tribunal that any of these Acts, Regulations or provisions is void on the ground that it takes away or abridges or is inconsistent with any of the Fundamental Rights as contained in Part III of the Constitution. This Article, however, reserves the power of the competent Legislature to repeal or amend any of the Acts or Regulations included in the Ninth Schedule.

Article 31C inserted by the Twenty-fifth Amendment provided that no law passed to give effect to the Directive Principles of State Policy in Article 39 Clauses (b) and (c) would be deemed to be void on the ground that it was inconsistent with, took away or abridged any of the Rights conferred by Article 14, Article 19 or Article 31; and no law containing a declaration that it was for giving effect to such policy would be called in question in any Court that it did not give effect to such policy. When such a law was made by the State Legislature, the provisions of Article 31C would not apply unless such law having been reserved for the consideration of the President had received his assent.

In *Keshavananda Bharati* case the Supreme Court allowed the Directive Principles of the State Policy as contained in Article 39 Clause (b) and (c) to override the Fundamental Rights. But the Court also held that any law declared by Parliament to give effect to these Directive Principles would be subject to judicial review in order to determine whether the law did in fact achieve that objective. To nullify this effect of the Supreme Court's ruling, the Constitution (Forty-second Amendment) Act, 1976, amended Article 31C and established the primacy of the Directive Principles. The Supreme Court struck down in the Minerva Mills case the provision in Article 31C-"and no law containing a declaration that it is for giving effect to such policy shall be called in question in any court on the ground that it does not give effect to such policy"-as it changed the basic structure of the Constitution in terms of Keshavananda Bharati.

Right to Constitutional Remedies

The idea of providing in the Constitution effective for the enforcement of the fundamental rights was present in the minds of the Constitution-makers from the very beginning. When the Sub-Committee on Fundamental Rights assembled for the first time on February 27, 1947, Alladi Krishnaswami Ayyar pointed that the citizens' rights embodied in the constitution should consist of guarantees enforceable in courts of law and that it was no use to simply lay down precepts which remained unenforceable or ineffective. As to the precise means by which these rights were to be guaranteed K.M. Munshi was emphatically of the view that the Constitution should provide for writs to be issued by the Courts. B.R. Ambedkar supported Munshi's suggestion.

In his note on Fundamental Rights Munshi pointed out that fundamental rights in the United States and civil liberties in Britain had been preserved by reason of two factors: (a) an independent judiciary, and (b) the prerogative writs of *habeas corpus, mandamus, prohibition, certiorari and quo warranto.* In India, he added, only the High Courts of Madras, Bombay and Calcutta were vested with the power of issuing writs and this power extended only to their respective city areas where these courts exercised original jurisdiction, with the result that except in those three cities the machinery for enforcing civil rights was a slow process and consequently the public conscience was not keenly alive to the assertion of rights against the executive. If writs were not provided for in the new Constitution, he explained, fundamental rights would be of no value because the constitutionality of the Act, if questioned, would take years to be finally decided. "The object of the fundamental law", he added, "will be frustrated if people have to serve sentences, pay fines or deny themselves the privileges given by the Constitution for a long time under an invalid law...without prompt machinery of enforcement, the Union and State Governments might conceivably lapse into a programme inimical to freedom. The existence of a legal right in the individual to intervene in order to make the legal right effective''.

Accordingly, in K.M. Munshi's note, referred to above, the right to Constitutional remedies was incorporated as a fundamental right. It meant that the courts within the Union could be moved for the issue of four writs, namely, (a) the writ of person (*habeas corpus*) to secure the release of any person from unlawful and unjustifiable deprivation of the right of liberty, (b) the writ of enforcement (mandamus) to secure the performance of any specific act by a unit, officer, or a corporation in the discharge of a definite public duty, obligation or requirement with which it was specially charged by the Constitution or by any law, (c) the writ of prohibition, prohibiting any court (other than the Supreme Court) or tribunal from continuing proceedings in contravention of the Constitution or in excess of jurisdiction vested in it by law and (d) the writ of direction (certiorari) for directing a judge (other than the judge of Supreme Court) or a person or a body vested with judicial functions to transmit the record of proceedings pending before him or it and involving a question of a right or a duty for the purpose of quashing the proceedings or referring them to the appropriate tribunal. These writs, however, could not be invoked during the existence of a state of war, armed rebellion or a grave emergency.

Munshi's views were generally shared by other members of the Sub-Committee on Fundamental Rights. The corresponding provisions in Ambedkar's draft only differed from Munshi's proposals in that it vested the authority to issue prerogative writs in the Supreme Court, while Munshi had vested in all courts in the Union of India, and included an additional writ, quo warranto (the writ to be issued for the purpose of determining the right of a person in office to hold on to that office) which Munshi's note lacked. Ambedkar was also in favour of the prerogative writs to be included in the Constitution as writs ensured speedy and effective means of guaranteeing fundamental rights.

At the meeting of the Fundamental Rights Sub-Committee on March 29, 1947 Alladi Krishnaswami Ayyar made a somewhat different proposal. He maintained that *habeas corpus* should be treated differently from other writs. If a complaint was made about the unlawful detention of a person, every High Court and Supreme Court and the judges of these courts should forthwith enquire into it. They could order the detained person to be produced, and could also order his release, unless satisfied that his detention was legally valid. In addition, he suggested that such other remedies and writs would be available to any one whose fundamental rights had been infringed or abrogated as might be provided in the Constitution and the laws of the Union. The Supreme Court and all other courts were to have such jurisdiction as the Constitution and the law might confer on them. The majority opinion in the Sub-Committee was, however, that all the writs should be specified.

In spite of unanimity that writs were to be included in the Constitution and the guaranteeing of their enforcement, differences persisted among members of the Sub-Committee on the jurisdiction of issuing writs and the suspension of rights during emergency. Alladi Krishnaswami Ayyar wanted it to be made clear that the power to be conferred on the Supreme Court would not prevent similar powers being vested in other courts as well. Elaborating this suggestion at the meeting of the Sub-Committee on April 15, 1947, he emphasized the necessity to have a uniform interpretation of the fundamental rights and therefore to give to the Supreme Court an overall jurisdiction in the matter of their interpretation. On practical grounds he thought that there should also be lower courts with the necessary jurisdiction to which aggrieved parties could go. He also wrote a dissenting minutes.

Alladi Krishanaswami Ayyar reiterated his point of view in the Advisory Committee meeting held on April 22, 1947. Eventually, the Chairman of the Advisory Committee requested Munshi, Ambedkar and Ayyar to revise the clause under reference suitably in the light of the views of expressed in the Committee. In the redraft suggested by them sub-clause

(1) was modified to read; (2) Without prejudice to the powers that may be vested in this behalf in other courts, the Supreme Court shall have power to issue directions in the nature of the writs of *habeas corpus, mandamus, prohibition, quowarranto* and *certiorari* appropriate to the right guaranteed in this part of the Constitution. With these amendments it appeared as clause 22 of the Advisory Committee Report.

When the clause was taken up for consideration in the Constituent Assembly on May 22, 1947, K. Santhanam moved an amendment seeking to make it clear that in sub-clause (3) the emergency situation when the privilege of writs could be suspended be defined as one "declared to be such by the Government of the Union or of the unit concerned". He also pointed out that the clause "the right to move the Supreme Court is hereby guaranteed" did not make it clear whether the Supreme Court was to have exclusive original jurisdiction in such matters or whether its power were to be appellate and that the clause was vague on the point whether the authority which could vest jurisdiction in other courts would be Parliament or the Legislatures of the units. Santhanam's own view was that all original jurisdiction should be vested in the High Courts so that they might become the lynch pin for the enforcement of the fundamental rights. He also maintained that the authority conferring powers on other courts should be Parliament and not the Legislatures of the units.

Vallabhbhai Patel accepted Santhanam's amendment. Replying to the points raised by him, Patel said that the clause was intended to provide for a judicial remedy and had nothing to do with the exclusion or appropriation of the jurisdiction of High Courts or any others Courts. All these matters would be considered at the time of deciding the judicial set-up in the Constitution. On this assurance the clause as modified by Santhanam's amendment was adopted.

The ad hoc Committee on the Supreme Court, which, inter alia, examined the question of writ jurisdiction, expressed itself against vesting it exclusively in the Supreme Court. The citizen, said the Committee, would practically be denied fundamental rights if whenever they were violated he was compelled to go to the Supreme Court, as the only court from which he could obtain redress. The Committee recommended that, where there was no other court with the necessary jurisdiction, the Supreme Court should have original jurisdiction. Where there was some other court the Supreme Court should have appellate jurisdiction including the power of revision.

Draft Article 25 relating to the enforcement of fundamental rights as it emerged out of the Drafting Committee was in general widely acclaimed as the "copingstone of the structure of fundamental rights". The general discussion in the Constituent Assembly hinged round clause (4), which provided that "the rights guaranteed by this article shall not be suspended except as otherwise provided for by this constitution". Clause 4 was linked with article 280 which gave power to the President to declare, in an emergency when the security of India was threatened by war or domestic violence, that the right guaranteed by this article would remain suspended. N.G. Ranga strongly supported the provision. He argued that just as individuals and groups had their rights, society as a whole and groups which were bent upon destroying the society, subverting the social order and dissecting the social organization through violent means. Whenever there was serious danger to the very concept of democracy, to the exercise of democratic functions, to the institutions of democracy, it must be the duty of the State to set aside the fundamental rights in order to safeguard the people. Shibban Lal Saxena also considered the clause to be necessary but he expressed the hope that it would be possible to drop it when the State became stable. Rohini Kumar Choudhary expressed the opinion that it should be deleted or it might be modified in such a manner that the article would not be suspended except under the most unavoidable circumstances. Otherwise, he said, it would have the evil effect of allowing even such forbidden practices as untouchability and traffic in human beings to be carried on with impunity when the article was suspended.

Ambedkar replying to debate rejected the suggestion for the deletion of clause (4) as it seemed to him to be an "extravagant demand". In times of emergency, he observed, the superior right of the State to protect itself will be in danger of losing his very existence. The suspension of rights in clause (4) could only take place in times of emergency and was a common feature in all Constitutions. Allaying Tajamul Hussain fears that all fundamental rights might be suspended during the emergency, he said that when a proclamation of emergency was issued, the only rights that would be suspended would be those contained in draft article 13 and 2 and not others. Summing up the importance and significance of the article, Ambedkar said, "If was asked to name any particular article in the Constitution as the most important- an article without which this Constitution would be a nullity- I could not refer to any other article except this one. It is the very soul of the Constitution and the very heart of it". The article was passed when put to vote. Subsequently, at the revision stage, it was renumbered article 32 of the Constitution.

Article 32 guarantees to every citizen the right to move the Supreme Court by appropriate proceedings for the enforcement of the Fundamental Rights. And for that purpose Supreme Court is given general power to safeguard the Fundamental Rights as well as the power to issue the directions or orders or writs in the nature of *habeas corpus, mandamus, prohibition, quowarranto and certiorari* whichever may be appropriate, for the enforcement of any of the Fundamental Rights. A right without a remedies provided in Article 30 are the heart and soul of the Constitution. Before 1978, enforcement of rights, as mentioned in the Presidential Order, could be suspended, under Article 359, when a Proclamation of Emergency was in operation. The Presidential Order could also suspend the enforcement of article 20 and 21. The Forty Fourth Amendment amended Article 359 to the extent that enforcement of rights guarantees under Article 20 and 21 cannot be suspended even during the operation of emergency.

Application of Rights to armed forced

On of the point that came up at an early stage for consideration was the extent to which Fundamental Rights would apply to members of the armed forces. By virtue of their nature of service and position, they had necessarily to be subjected to a code of conduct and discipline not entirely constituent with the exercise of fundamental rights, as they would apply to the ordinary citizen. This fact was realized at the preliminary stages in the discussion of Sub-Committee on Fundamental Rights. Munshi had provided in his draft that the Union Legislature would by law be entitled to determine to what extent any of the fundamental rights should be restricted or abrogated for the members of the armed force or forces charged with the maintenance of public order to ensure the fulfillment of their duties and maintenance of discipline. controversy by the sub-Committee and adopted was non-controversial it was adopted by the Constituent Assembly on December 9,1948, with a minor verbal change suggested by Ambedkar.

Article 33 of the Constitution, accordingly provides that Parliament may by law determine to what extent any of the rights conferred by the Chapter on Fundamental Rights shall, in force charged with the maintenance of public order, be restricted or abrogated so as to ensure the proper discharge of their duties and the maintenance of discipline among them.

Indemnity to public servants

At the revision stage, the Drafting Committee introduced a new Article 34 providing for indemnity to public servants and others for any action taken by them for maintenance or restoration of order in any area where martial law was in force: Justifying the need for such a provision, the Drafting Committee observed that the fundamental rights as contained in Part III of the Constitution might prevent validation by the Legislature for acts done during the period when martial law was in force and also prevent the indemnifying of persons in the service of the Union or the State or other persons in respect of action taken by them during such period.

In the Constituent Assembly when the changes made by the Drafting Committee at the revision stage were considered on November 14,1949, a number of amendments to the new article 34 were proposed by members. Of these the one moved by Shibben Lal Saxena sought deletion of the article on the ground that it might encourage officers working in a martial law area to commit excesses in the hope of indemnification by an Act of Parliament. Kamath favoured the omission of any reference to martial law in the Constitution on the plea that there were sufficient provisions in the Constitution for the maintenance of public order, peace and tranquility in the country. He, however, contended that if omission of article was not agreed to, he made three amendments which in effect sought that the provision for the indemnification of persons for acts done during martial law should be restricted to persons in the service of the Union and the indemnification should not cover any order person s proposed in article 34.

Replying to the debate Ambedkar drew the attention of members to article 20 which provided that no person should be convicted for any offence except the violation of a law in force at the time of the commission of the act charged as an offence, and to article 21, which provided that no person would be deprived of his life or personal liberty, except according to procedure establish by law. He explained that when martial law was introduced-usually when there was a riot, insurrection or rebellion or threat of overthrow of authority-the officer in charge of martial law declared that certain acts would offences against his authority, and prescribed his own procedure for the trial of persons who offended against acts notified by him as offences. An act so notified by the military commander would not be an offence against a law in force because the commander was not the law-making authority; nor would the procedure laid down by him be according to the law. If article 34 were not included in the Constitution, the administration of martial law would not be possible. Referring to Kamath's amendments. Ambedkar said that when martial law was in force, it was the duty of not merely of the military commander and his entourage, but the duty of every individual citizen of the State to take the responsibility on his own shoulders and come to the help of the authority for restoring order. It was, therefore, necessary that indemnification was not restricted to persons in the service of the Union or of State but extended to every person who came forward "to the rescue of the State to establish peace."

The Assembly rejected the amendments moved by Saxena and Kamath and adopted article 34 in the form in which it was proposed by the Drafting Committee. Article 34 of the Constitution, to which article 34 proposed by Drafting Committee corresponds, provides that Parliament may by law, notwithstanding the provisions in Part III relating to the Fundamental Rights, indemnify any person in the service of Union or of a State or any other person in respect of any act done by him in connection with the maintenance or restoration of order in any area within the territory of India where martial law was in force or validate any sentence passed, punishment inflicted, forfeiture ordered or other act done under martial law in that area.

Legislation to give effect to Rights

Article 35 empowers Parliament to make laws with respect to any matter under clause 3 of Article 16 (requirements), clause (3) of Article 32 (empowering any other court to exercise jurisdiction with respect to enforcement of Rights), Article 33 (modification of Rights in their application to Armed forces), and Article 34 (restrictions on rights while martial law is in force in any area). Parliament has also the power to prescribe by law punishment for those acts, which are declared to be offences under Part III relating to Fundamental Rights in case of their violation. Clause (b) of Article 35 provides that in case of Acts already in existence, which provide punishment for breach of fundamental rights, unless and until Parliament makes another provision, such laws would continue in operation.

When draft article 27, corresponding to Article 35 of the Constituent Assembly was put up for consideration, Ambedkar explained the scheme of the draft on which there was hardly any discussion. He said, "the first principle is whenever this

Constitution prescribes that a law shall be made for giving effect to any fundamental right or where a law is to be made for making an action punishable, which interferes with rights, that right shall be exercised only by Parliament, notwithstanding the fact that having regard to the list which deals with the distribution of power, such law may fall within the purview of the State Legislature. The object of this is that fundamental rights, both as to their nature and as to the punishment involved in the infringement thereof shall be uniform throughout India... Ambedkar added that it was only in specific matters that Parliament was being given penal authority and it was therefore considered desirable to specify the relevant articles, which were to be dealt with exclusively by Parliament.

Nature of Fundamental Rights

Rights not Sacrosanct

The Fundamental Rights were intended to serve three important purposes, namely, (i) to prevent the executive from acting arbitrarily; (ii) to ensure some amount of security and protection to various types of minorities; and (iii) to promote and foster social revolution by establishing the conditions necessary for achieving justice, social, economic and political. But the Supreme Court, some eminent jurists and teachers in Political Science as well as quite a few prominent public men considered the rights contained in the Chapter on Fundamental Rights (Part III) as immutable and transcendental. In a series of judgments the Supreme Court described them as "paramount"[36] "sacrosanct"[37] "rights reserved by the people", [38] "inalienable and inviolable", [39] and "transcendental", [40] The immutability and permanence of the Fundamental Rights were sought to be established first on the reasoning that these rights are rooted in the doctrine of natural law and were, therefore, 'natural rights' as expressed in the traditional parlance, and, secondly, on the ground that they have been given a place of permanence by the Constitution within its scheme.[41]

But the Fundamental Rights, contained in Part III of the Constitution, are neither rooted in the doctrine of natural law nor are they based on the theory of 'reserved rights'. They are conferred rights and embody the social values are not static, the Fundamental Rights are subjects to change and modification in order to fulfill the aspirations of man in the context of his changed conditions and the environment in which he lives. Even the Supreme Court admitted in the Gopalan case that the provisions of Part III of the Constitution strikes a balance between a written guarantee of individual rights and the collective interests of the community.[42] Justice J.M. Shelat of the Supreme Court observed in a lecture delivered on December 18, 1966, that a study of the provisions of Part III "will at once show that while laying down the various Fundamental Rights of the citizen, they also effectuate a reconciliation between them and the general needs and welfare of the society and the nation. By so doing, Part III leaves the door ajar for the functional working of the Constitution in future." The provisions of Part III themselves provide, Justice Shelat explained, "that these Fundamental Rights must yield to reasonable restrictions, the imposition of which may become necessary to satisfy the changing necessities and situations which might arise from time to time.[43]

It was, therefore, not the intention of the father-farmers to render the rights sacrosanct otherwise they would not have ventured to strike a balance or effectuate reconciliation between them and the needs and welfare of society. Rights are dynamic realities and they have never been intended to be impediment to progress, development and advancement. They are conferred in fulfillment of the aims of the new social and economic order envisaged in the Directive Principles of the State Policy set out in Part iv of the Constitution. But not manner in which the Forty-second Amendment had done by not even leaving a hazy line of demarcation between the Fundamental Rights and the Directive Principles and, thus, riding roughshod over the intentions of the Constitution-makers. The Amendment was, in fact, designed to personify the absolute authority of the Executive by removing all limitations on the amending power of Parliament and depriving the Courts of their jurisdiction to call in question any amendment of the Constitution. Speaking for himself and

Justice Gupta, Untwalia and Kailasam in the Minerva Mills case, Chief Justice Chandrachaud observed, "our Constitution is founded on a nice balance of power among the three wings of the State, namely, the Executive, the Legislative and the Judiciary. It is the function of the Judges, may their duty, to pronounce on the validity of laws. If Courts are totally deprived of that power, the Fundamental Rights conferred upon the people will become mere adornments because rights without remedies are as writs in water".

Directive Principle of State Policy and Fundamental Duties

If the Preamble is the key to the understanding of the Constitution or to open the mind of its makers, the Directive Principles of State Policy, as enshrined in Part IV, are its beautiful ideal. It is here that the Constitution-makers poured their mind by setting forth the humanitarian socialist principles, which epitomized the hopes and aspirations of the people and declared them as fundamental in the governance of the country. They are affirmative instructions for the ultimate sovereign to the State authorities, which are the creature of the Constitution established by them, to secure to all citizens justice, social, economic and political; liberty of thought, expression, belief, faith and worship; equality of status and opportunity; and to promote among them all fraternity assuring the dignity of the individual and the unity and integrity of the nation.

It is the duty of all the authorities of the State to direct their activities in such a manner so as to secure the high ideas set forth in the Preamble and copiously analyzed and enriched in Part IV of the Constitution. The Directive Principle of State Policy are an amalgam of diverse subjects embracing the life of the nation and include principles which are general statements of social policy, principles of administrative policy, social-economic rights, and a statement of the international policy of the country. B.R. Ambedkar told the Constituent Assembly that every Government, Central, State and local "shall be on the anvil, both in the daily affairs and at the end of a certain period when the voters and the electorate will be given an opportunity to assess the work done by the Government... While we have established political democracy it is also the desire that we should lay down as our ideal economic democracy... There is various ways in which people believe that economic democracy can be brought about; we have deliberately not introduced in the language that we have used in the directive principles something, which is fixed or rigid. We have left enough room for the people of different ways of thinking, with regards to the reaching of the ideal of economic democracy. Our object in framing the Constitution is two fold: (i) to lay down the form of political democracy, and (ii) to lay down that our ideal is economic democracy, and also to prescribe that every Government, whatever is in power, shall strive to bring about economic democracy...."

The idea of making a constitutional declaration of social and economic policy is the recognition of the ideal of a service State in place of regulatory State, which found expression in the 1931 Karachi resolution of the Indian National Congress. The Karachi resolution held that in order to end the exploitation of the masses, political freedom should include economic freedom. Most of the members of the Constituent Assembly, and specially the select group in the Fundamental Rights Sub-Committee, were quite familiar with the political thinking at that time, the practice that the United States of America had of late adopted and the manner in which the Federal and State Governments had begun playing an ever-increasing role in the nation's social and economic life. They had also closely watched the fact that most of the new Constitutions that came into being after World War I, particularly of Germany and East European countries, had recognized that one of the chief functions of the State must be to foster and secure the social well-being of citizens and the economic prosperity of the nation. The Irish Constitution, too, had greatly impressed the wide range of members of the Constituent Assembly. The long-standing affinity of the Indian National Congress with the Irish Nationalist Movement made the example of the Constitutional declaration expressed in the Irish Directive Principles of

State Policy especially attractive to the Congress Assembly Members, particularly the socialist-wing within its fold. But the weightiest support came from B.N. Rau, the Constitutional Advisor to the Constituent Assembly, Alladi Krishanaswami Ayyar, and B.R. Ambedkar & K.T. Shah. Of the four, B.N. Rau was the most influential. He emulated in his Constitutional Presidents the Irish example of distinguishing between justiciable and non-justiciable right. His Precedents, during the actual drafting of the Directive Principles, supplied the members of the Sub-Committee on the Fundamental Rights with at least five of the original twelve provisions and the preamble of the Principles.

Directive Principles and Fundamental Rights

The proposal relating to the incorporation of non-justiciable rights in the constitution initially did not find favour with some members of the Sub-Committee on Fundamental Rights. At the first meeting of the Sub-Committee held on Feb 27, 1947, Alladi Krishanaswami Ayyar saw no use in laying down in the constitution precepts, which would remain, enforceable or ineffective. A similar view was expressed by Munshi and Ambedkar. But the most outspoken critic of the proposal was K.M. Munshi who observe in a note submitted to the Sub-Committee, that most of the general declaration found in the national constitution and international documents had proved ineffective to check the growing power of the modern State. On the contrary, they created an unwarranted impression of progress and freedom. He cited the Weimar Constitution in support of his point of view.

A general feeling against giving constitutional expression to "mere precepts" was also discernible, though indirectly, in sum of he drafts on Fundamental Rights submitted to the Sub-Committee in which not only all sorts of rights, political, economic and social, but also precepts of policy were listed under the title "Fundamental Rights". For example, those enumerated in Munshi's draft among others, were; the right to work, a living wage, condition of work necessary to ensure a decent standard of life, and the right of every citizen to have free primary education with a corresponding "legally incumbent" duty on every unit (state) to introduce free and compulsory primary education. Similarly, Ambedkar's draft contend an elaborate clause design to established socialism in important field of economic life by the law of the Constitution itself, so that the implementation of the plan would not be left to the will of the legislature.

The opposition to the proposal to include non-justiciable rights in the Constitution, however, did not last long. Alladi Krishnaswami Ayyar supported it in a note submitted to the Sub-Committee on Fundamental Rights on March 14,1947 in which he stressed the necessity of distinguishing between justiciable rights and rights which were "merely intended as a guide and directing objectives of State policy."[9] With the precepts set out in the State policy (as they were then called), which were the offspring of the Objectives Resolution, few if any members of the Constituent Assembly disagreed. Almost the only critical voices were those of members who believe that the provisions of the principles should be justiciable if they were to be adequate to their task. Gradually, most other members of the Sub-Committee also veered round to the view that it was not practicable to categorize declaration of economic and social policies as justiciable rights. On March 27,1947 the Sub-Committee came to conclusion that the clauses related to the right to work to secure a living wage and others of a like nature, could not be incorporated in the chapter on the Fundamental Rights. Three days later, the Sub-Committee, having tentatively completed the formulation of justiciable Fundamental Rights, directed its attention to formulation of the directive principles of social policy and adopted a number of clauses. Some more directives were added the next day when it was also decided to add at its beginning preamble to define the position to be accorded to these principle. The preamble read, "the principle of social policy set forth in this part are intended for the general guidance of the appropriate legislature and government in India (hereinafter called collectively as the States). The application of these principles in legislation and administration shall be care of the state and shall not be cognizable by any court."

With a few verbal changes the preamble formed part of the draft report of the Sub-Committee, in addition to the eleven clauses relating to the basic principles of the state policy that it contained. Explaining the nature of the recommendation, the Sub-Committee stated in its drafts report that those rights, which could be normally enforced by legal action, had been listed as "justiciable rights" and other rights either normally capable of, or suitable of enforcement by legal action, had been categorized as "non-justiciable rights". As regards the "non-justiciable rights" the Sub-Committee made it clear that these rights were "intended to be directions for the general guidance of the State and were not cognizable by any court."

But sub members of Sub-Committee Rajkumari Amrit Kaur and Mrs. Hansa Mehata were still not satisfied. They thought that principle of social policy though were not enforceable, were nevertheless fundamental in character inasmuch as they were vital to the well-being and ordered progress of the State. They, accordingly, urged that suitable provision should be incorporated in the chapter enjoining the State to take as soon as possible the necessary action on fulfillment of these directives. K.T. Shah suggested that the principles included in the so-called non-justiciable category should not be treated as mere directions of policy for general guidance; they must be regarded as the objectives of national activity and it must be the endeavour of every unit (State) as well as the Union to give effect to them.

In view of the opinions so expressed the Sub-Committee, in finalizing its report as its meeting on April 15,1947, decided to place emphasis on the fundamental character of these principles. Accordingly, it was decided to redraft the opening clause to read. "The principles of policy in this Part are intended for the guidance of the state. While these principles shall not be cognizable by any court, they are nevertheless fundamental in the governance of the country and their application in the making of laws shall be the duty of the State." Even this change did not fully satisfy some members, particularly K.T. Shah and M.R. Masani. K.T. Shah again expressed his fear that the whole scheme of directives might be reduced to a `needless fraud,'' an excellent window-dressing without any stock behind that dressing.'' M.R. Masani, Mrs. Hansa Mehta and Rajkumari Amrit Kaur held that one of the factors keeping India back from advancing to nationhood was the existence of personal laws based on religion. They suggested, therefore, the transfer of the clause regarding a uniform civil code to the part dealing with justiciable rights. The Minorities Sub-Committee commented on the clause proposing a uniform civil code for citizens and its transfer to the category of justiciable rights, and agreed that a uniform civil code was eminently desirable, but felt that the application of such a code should be made on an entirely voluntary basis.

When the Advisory Committee considered the Reports of the Sub-Committee on Fundamental Rights and Minorities, it fully endorsed the general principles, which laid stress on the fundamental nature of the directives, but made a few change.. It deleted two clauses those relating to freedom of marriage and the promotion of internal peace and security by the elimination of every cause of communal discord-while the clause imposing on the State a duty to provide free and compulsory primary education within a period of ten years from the commencement of the Constitution, which earlier had been included as directive principle. With these amendments the list of the "fundamental principles of governance'' was incorporated in the Committee's supplementary report submitted to the Constituent Assembly on August 25, 1947.

In the general discussion that followed doubts were again expressed about the effectiveness of the directives in the form they were sought to be made part of the Constitution. A common criticism offered was that since there did not exist any provision for their implementation which might be obligatory on the Union and State Governments, their incorporation in the Constitution hardly served any useful purpose or gave any satisfaction to the aspirations of the people for their fulfillment. Another criticism was that the principle were borrowed from other countries and that the Advisory Committee had wholesale adopted the provisions of the Irish Constitution without giving much thought to their usefulness and that did not adequately cater to the genius of the people of India.

In the Draft Constitution prepared by B.N. Rau all the provisions regarding Fundamental Rights and Directive Principles were included in Part III, divided into three chapters. The first chapter contained general provisions, the second Fundamental Rights and the third "Directive Principles of State Policy." The provision emphasizing the fundamental nature of the directives in the governance of the country was included in the first chapter of general provisions, fundamental rights in the second, and the third "Directive Principles of State Policy". The Directive Principles formulated by the Advisory Committee were themselves incorporated in the third chapter.

Subsequently, B.N. Rau went on tour of the United States, Canada, Ireland and the United Kingdom. He discussed at Dublin the position of the working of the directive principles vis-à-vis fundamental rights, from where the idea of directive principle had caught the imagination of the Constitution-makers of Independent India. Rau was of the opinion that some of the fundamental rights guaranteed in the Constitution of Ireland were proving very inconvenient, particularly the one relating to property. This came under consideration in the Irish Supreme Court in connection with the Sinn Fein Funds Act, which related to certain trust moneys lying in deposit in court. Certain other cases had led to the feeling that the fundamental rights had been expressed in too broad terms.

In the light of h discussion in Dublin and with Justice Frankfurter of the United States Supreme Court, B.N. Rau suggested the following new paragraph to be added to clause 10: "No law which may be made by the State in the discharge of its duty under the first paragraph of this section and no law which may have been made by the State in pursuance of the principles of policy now set forth in chapter III of this part shall be void on the ground that it contravenes the provision of Section 9, or is inconsistent with the provision of chapter II of this part." Explaining the object of this and consequential amendments, Rau observed, "The object of these amendment is to make it clear that in a conflict between the rights conferred by chapter II, which are for most part rights of the individuals, and the principles of policy set forth in chapter III, which are intended for the welfare of the State as whole, the general welfare should prevail over the individual right. Otherwise, it would be meaningless to say, as clause 10 does say, that these principles of policy are fundamental and that it is the duty of the State to give effect to them in its laws. In the Constitution of the United States of America there are no express directive principles of State policy, but the courts have developed what is equivalent thereto, namely, the doctrine of the 'policy power' which has been defined as the power 'to prescribe regulations to promote the health, peace, morals-education and the good order of the people, and to legislate so as to increase the industry of the State, develop its resources, and add to its wealth and prosperity'. In the exercise of this power the State may make laws for the general welfare, which would otherwise be inconsistent with the American Bill of Rights. The courts in India might have been able to develop a similar doctrine but for the language of clause 9 of the Draft Constitution. Hence the amendments proposed."

Meanwhile the Drafting Committee was going ahead with its work and at its meeting on October 30 and November 1, 1947, it decided to place all the directive principles in a separate part and to transfer claim 10, which dealt with the fundamental nature of the principles, to this new part. The committee also made certain modifications in some of the clauses enunciating the directives, but all such modifications did not involve any change in their substance. With some other minor changes, the Drafting Committee incorporated in the Draft Constitution of February 1948, all the recommendations of the Advisory Committee in its Supplementary Report without considering the suggestion made by B. N. Rau for strengthening the Constitutional status of the directive principles. If these suggestion could have been accepted then there could have been no conflict before both and no legal before could have started.

When the draft Constitution was circulated for eliciting comments and opinions, the same old two points of criticism, that the directives were unenforceable and that they had been borrowed from external sources, were reiterated. Some other proposals for inclusion in the list of the directives were also suggested. The Drafting Committee itself proposed the addition of a new article prescribing that the State should secure the separation of the judiciary from the executive within three years from the commencement of the Constitution.

Introducing the Draft Constitution in the Constituent Assembly on November 4,1948, Ambedkar said that though the directive principles had no legal force behind them, he was not prepared to admit that they had no "sort of binding force", nor was he prepared to concede that they were "useless" simply because they had no binding force in law. He added, "The inclusion of such instructions in a constitution such as is proposed instructions in a constitution such as is proposed in the Draft becomes justiciable for another reason. The Draft Constitution as framed only provides a machinery for the government of the country. It is not a contrivance to install any particular party in power as has been done in some countries. Who should be in power is left to be determined by the people, as it must be, if the system is to satisfy the people, as it must be, if the system is to satisfy the tests of democracy. But whoever captures power will not be free to do what he likes with it. In the exercise of it, he will have to respect these Instruments of Instructions, which are called Directives Principles. He cannot ignore them. He may not have to answer for their breach in a court of law. But he will certainly have to answer for them before the electorate at election time. What great value these directive principles possess will be realized better when the forces of right contrive to capture power."

Dealing with the criticism that the Constitution was not the place for moral precepts or sermons, B.N. Rau observed in an article published in the Hindu, Madras, "It will be remembered that under previous enactments relating to the Government of India, there used to be Instruments of Instructions from the Sovereign to the Governor. General and the Governors and these Instructions used to contain injunctions which, though unenforceable in the courts, served a useful purpose. For example, one of them specially charged and required the Governor 'to take care that due provision shall be made for the advancement and social welfare of those classes who on account of the smallness of their number or their lack of educational or material advantages or from any other cause specially rely upon our protection.' This may be compared with the article in the draft of the new constitution, which requires that the State shall promote with special care the educational and economic interests of the weaker sections of the people. The former was an instruction from the legal sovereign to the Governors appointed by him; the latter may be looked upon as a similar instruction from the ultimate sovereign, namely, the people of India speaking through their representatives in the Constituent Assembly, to authorities to be set up by or under the Constitution."

The consideration of the draft articles commenced on November 19,1948. in the discussion the title of Part IV "Directive Principles of State Policy" and of draft article 29 dealing with the nature of the directives, a suggestion was made for the replacement of the word "Fundamental" on the ground that though the directives were unjusticiable, they were nevertheless fundamental. It was pointed out by H.V. Kamath, that the Advisory Committee had given them the title "Fundamental Principles of Governance" and the Chairman of the Advisory Committee, Vallabhbhai Patel, had stated that though not cognizable in any court of law, they "should be regarded as fundamental in the governance of the country." But Kamath's suggestion to replace the word "Directive for "Fundamental" was opposed by Ambedkar on the ground that the object that these principles be treated as fundamental was already achieved by the wording of article 29. He observed that it was necessary to retain the word "Directive" to emphasize that in enacting this part of the Constitution the Constituent Assembly was giving certain directions to the future legislatures and executives. If the word "Directive" were omitted, the intension of the members of the Assembly in enacting this Part would fail in its purpose. The directives were meant to be fundamental principles which should necessarily be made the basis of all executive and legislative action that might be taken in future in the governance of the country. The Assembly rejected the amendment and adopted the title "Directive Principles of State Policy.

The Fundamental Rights are justiciable and Article 32 of the Constitution guarantees to all citizens the right to move the Supreme Court for their enforcement in case of violation or their abridgment by any authority of the State. It means that the Fundamental Rights are mandatory whereas the Directive Principles are declaratory, as they have expressly been excluded from the purview of courts. If any authority of the State does not take any positive action in promoting the objects set forth in the Chapter on the Directive Principles no action can be taken against that authority in a court of law. But the courts are bound to declare as void any law or executive action if it violated or infringed any of the provisions of the Chapter on Fundamental Rights. In case of conflict between the two, the Fundamental Rights shall prevail.

Conflicts between the Directive Principles and the Fundamental Rights may arise due to several reasons and one of the important reasons is the presence of Clause 2 of Article 13 which stipulates that "The State shall not make any law which takes away or abridges the rights conferred by this Part (Part III Fundamental Rights) and any law made in contravention of this clause shall, to the extent of contravention, be void." It meant, till the enactment of the twenty-forth Amendment and finally the Forty-second Amendment, the State could not while implementing Directive Principles, make laws in contravention of the Fundamental Rights. Nor could a citizen invoke the sanction of the Directive Principles in support of his claims under the Fundamental Rights. Jawaharlal Nehru was not oblivious of conflicts to arise between the Directive Principles and the Fundamental Rights. Speaking on the Constitution (First Amendment) Bill, 1951, the pointed out how such a conflict could arise. He observed, "The Directive Principles of State

Policy represent a dynamic move towards a certain objective. The Fundamental Rights represent something static, to preserve certain rights which exist. Both again are rights. But somehow and sometime it might so happen that, that dynamic movement and that static stand still do not quite fit into each other.

The Judiciary resolves such conflicts. The Supreme Court till recently took a firm stand that the Directive Principles could not override the Fundamental Rights and they must conform to and run subsidiary to the latter. The State of Madras v. Champakam Dorairajan was the first case decided by the Supreme Court in this respect. Briefly stated, the petitioner challenged the Madras Communal Government Orders, which regulated admission to colleges on the basis of arbitrary ratio as violating Article 15(1) and Article 29(2). The Government of Madras contained in Article 46 which imposed a duty on the State to promote the educational and economic interests of the weaker sections of the society, and, in particular, of the Scheduled Castes and Scheduled Tribes. The High Court of Madras held that Article 46 could not override the provisions contained in Article 13(1) and Article 29(2) or justify any law or act of the State contravening their provisions. The Supreme Court upholding the decision of the Madras High Court ruled that the Chapter on Fundamental Rights "is sacrosanct and not liable to be abridged by any legislative or executive act or order except to the extent provided in the appropriate Articles in Part III. The Directive Principles of State Policy have to conform to and run as subsidiary to the Chapter on Fundamental Rights."[44]

In an analogous case State of Madras v. C.R. Srinivasan the Supreme Court held the that Directive Principles being non-justiciable could not override a Fundamental Rights and, accordingly, the Madras Communal Government Order was inconsistent with the Fundamental Rights of the petitioner. As a result of these judgments and as also the one in B. Venkataraman v. The State of Madras, the Constitution (First Amendment) Act, 1951, was enacted and a new Clause 4 was inserted in Article 15. It provided, "nothing in this Article or in Clause (2) of Article 29 shall prevent the State from making any special provision for the advancement of any socially and educationally backward class of citizens or for the Scheduled Castes and the Scheduled Tribes."[45] Despite this amendment the Courts continued to emphasize the subordinate character of the Directive Principles.

But a change in the attitude of the Supreme Court was discerned in the State of Bihar v. Rameshwar Singh and Bijoy Cotton Mills Ltd. V. The State of Ajmer.[46] In the first case the validity of the Zamindari Abolition Act was questioned on the ground that it violated the guaranteed Fundamental Right to property. Justice M.C. Mahajan speaking for the Court upheld the validity of the Zamindari Abolition Act on the reasoning that the implementation of the Directive Principles set out in Article 39 was such a public purpose. He observed, "Now it is obvious that concentration of big blocks of land in the hands of a few individuals is contrary to the principle on which the Constitution of India is based. The purpose of this acquisition contemplated by the impugned Act therefore is to do away with the concentration of big blocks of the land in the hands of few individuals and to so distribute the ownership and control which come in the hands of the State as to sub serve the common good as best as possible." It was held that the zamindari abolition law, which intended to do away with the concentration of large tracts of land in the hands of a few individuals and benefit large number of tenants must be deemed to be for the public purpose. In Bijoy Cotton Mills Ltd. V. The State of Ajmer the Court did not subscribe to the view that the Minimum Wages Act unreasonably restricted the right of the employers. In a unanimous judgment delivered by Justice Mukerjee, the Court ruled that "securing of living wages to labourers, which ensure not only bare physical subsistence but also maintenance of health and decency, is conducive to the general interest of the public. This one of the Directive Principles of State Policy embodied in Article 43 of our Constitution" and, therefore, a reasonable restriction on the employers right to carry on business could be imposed by the State.

In M.H. Qureshi v. The State of Bihar[47] the Supreme Court was called upon to give its decision on the validity of Bihar, Uttar Pradesh and Madhya Pradesh laws, which banned the slaughter of certain animals including cows. Chief Justice S.R. Das, who delivered the opinion of the Court, held that the State cannot make any law, which takes away or abridges the rights conferred by Chapter III of the Constitution, which enshrines the Fundamental Rights. "The directive principles cannot override this categorical restriction imposed on the legislative power of the State. A harmonious interpretation has to be placed upon the Constitution and so interpreted it means that the State should certainly implement the directive principles but it must not to do so in such a way that its laws take away or abridge the Fundamental Rights for otherwise the protective provisions of Chapter III will be "a mere rope of sand". This decision was almost reminiscent of Champakam Dorairajan case, although the Court introduced the doctrine of harmonious interpretation or construction as a technique of interpretation.

In re on the Kerala Education Bill, 1957", the Supreme Court was called upon to give its opinion, inter alia, on the relationship between the Fundamental Rights and the Directive Principles. Chief Justice S.R. Das, speaking for the Court held that "although this legislation may have been undertaken by the State of Kerala in the discharge of the obligation imposed on it by the directive principles it must nevertheless sub serve and not override the Fundamental Rights. The Directive Principles have to conform to and run subsidiary to the Chapter on Fundamental Rights. Nevertheless, in determining the scope and ambit of the Fundamental Rights relied on by or on behalf of any person or body, the Court may not entirely ignore these directive principles of State Policy, laid down in Part IV of the Constitution but should adopte the principle of harmonious construction and should attempt to give effect to both as much as possible."[48] This opinion related the views expressed in the Cow Slaughter case without introducing of the doctrine of harmonious construction.

But there was a change in judicial thinking and the first indication of it was noticed in the statement of Justice Mudholkar in Sajjan Singh v. State of Rajasthan.[49] In this case the argument before the Supreme Court was that if the Fundamental Rights were not made subject to the amending process of the Constitution there was a danger that the much needed dynamic change or development in the Indian society would be hampered. Though he did not dismiss the argument advanced as of no consequence, he expressed the opinion that even if the Fundamental Rights were taken as unchangeable, the much-needed dynamism could be achieved by properly interpreting the Fundamental Rights in the light of the Directive Principles. He observed that the Directive Principles "are also fundamental in the governance of the country and the provisions of Part III of the Constitution must be interpreted harmoniously with these principles." Two important points may be noted in the opinion expressed by Justice Mudholkar, although he also envisaged the application of the doctrine of harmonious construction. He takes cognizance of the fundamental nature of the Directive Principles and in case of conflict between the Fundamental Rights and Directive Principles suggests resolving it by interpreting the former in the light of the latter. His approach in resolving the conflict is to ensure dynamism in the socio-economic structure in the Indian society. To interpret the Fundamental Rights in the light of the Directive Principles is "definitely to give new meaning, new content and new dimension to the former so that not only the latter could be implemented fully and effectively but the former could find themselves in tune with the changed conditions and the new social order brought about by implementation of the directive principles."[50]

The majority opinion in the Golak Nath case rejected the Government argument that if Parliament was not given the power to amend the Constitution it would be difficult to implement the Directive Principles and there would be a revolution in the country. The Court declined to take a decision on this hypothetical situation and held: "if it is the duty of the Parliament to enforce the Directive Principles it is equally its duty to do so without infringing the Fundamental Rights. The Constitution-makers thought it could be done and we also think that the Directive Principles could reasonably be enforced with the self-regulatory machinery provided by Part III of the Constitution." Proceeding further, Chief Justice K. Subba Rao said, "Nor can we appreciate the argument that all the agrarian reforms which Parliament in power wants to effectuate cannot be brought about without amending the Fundamental Rights." It was in this context that the Chief Justice observed, "The Fundamental Rights and the Directive Principles of State Policy enshrined in the Constitution formed an 'integrated scheme' and elastic enough to respond to the changing needs of the society." [51]

The doctrine of 'integrated scheme' enunciated by Chief Justice Subba Rao admits two important results. In the first place, since Part III and Part IV of the Constitution from an integrated scheme they, undoubtedly, stand on a footing of equality and, therefore, the theory of subordination enunciated by the Supreme Court in Champakam Dorairajan case and reiterated in the Cow Slaughter case and the Kerala Education Bill, stands completely repudiated. Secondly, the doctrine of integrated scheme establishes the elasticity of the Fundamental Rights and Fundamental Rights, as such, must respond to the changing needs of the society reflecting the aspirations of the people. The Directive Principles of State Policy are the conscience of the Constitution and the reservoir of the people's aspiration. Fundamental Rights can, therefore, never be static. They change in their content with the changing needs of the society and justify their dynamism. It is, accordingly, clear that the doctrine of 'integrated scheme' and the theory of "elasticity" of Fundamental Rights establish that Fundamental Rights must be interpreted in the light of the Directive Principles so that the State may be able to carry out its socio-economic obligations imposed on it by the Preamble and Part IV of the Constitution. The Constitutional duty of the State is spelt out in Article 38, which is the keystone of the Directive Principles. It is the star by which the Government is required to chart its course.

If the provisions contained in Part III cause hindrance in the discharge of a constitutional duty, as cast upon it by Article 37, the Government must strive to remove those hindrance and both the Twenty-forth and Twenty-fifth Amendments of the Constitution sought to do it. The Constitution (Twenty-forth Amendment) Act, 1971, set up a mechanism for amending the Constitution and thereby removed the hindrance that the Golak Nath case had created. It also amended Article 13 by inserting a new clause (4) which provides that "Nothing in this Article shall apply to any amendment of this Constitution made under Article 368." The Constitution (Twenty-fifth Amendment) Act, 1971, deleted the word "compensation" occurring in Article 31 (2) and substituted it by the word "amount". It also inserted sub-article (2B) in the same Article thereby nullifying the effect of the judgment in the Bank Nationalization case. Another new Article 31-C was inserted providing that no law seeking to enforce the Directive Principles of State Policy in Clause (b) [33] and (c) [34] of Article 39 shall be held invalid on the ground that it involves any of the Fundamental Rights conferred by Article 14, 19 or 31. Moreover, declaration in the law that it intended to achieve the purposes in the clauses (b) and (c) of Article 39 would render such law immune from challenge in any court. The amendment also provided that no law containing such a declaration could be called in question on the ground that it did not in point of fact promote Directive Principles of State Policy. The State Legislatures were empowered to enact such laws as ordained by Article 31C with the proviso that such laws after passing from the State consideration of the President.

Explaining the import of contents of the Twenty-fifth Amendment, V.P. Krishna Ayyer (afterwards a Judge of the Supreme Court) remarked that it introduces the new Article 31C, whereby a marriage between the most vital Directive Principles and the most potent Fundamental Rights has been effected. A harmony has been established by this provision that no law made to give effect to the Directive Principles specified in Clauses (b) and (c) of Article 39 shall be deemed to be void on the ground that it takes away any of the Fundamental Rights guaranteed by Article 14, 19 and 31."[35] The Supreme Court in the Kesavananda Bharti case upheld Article 31C recognizing the competence of the Legislature of enacting laws to give effect to the Directive Principles in Clauses (b) and (c) of Article 39, but struck down the provision that "no law containing a declaration that it is for giving effect to such policy shall be called in question in any court on the ground that it does not give effect to such policy." The court also rules that though by Article 368 Parliament is given powers to amend the Constitution, that power cannot be exercised so as to alter the basic structure or framework of the Constitution.

To nullify the effects of the Kesavananda Bharti case the Constitution (Forty-second Amendment) Act, 1976, amended Article 31C by providing that no law giving effect to the policy of the State towards securing all or any of the Directive Principles laid down in Part IV shall be deemed to be void on the ground that it is inconsistent with, or takes away or abridges any of the right conferred by Article 14, 19 and 31. As a measure of abundant caution Article 368 was also amended by inserting Clause (4) and (5) debarring the courts from questioning the validity of amendments made and bestowing upon Parliament powers without any limitation to amend any provision of the Constitution.

The validity of the Forty-second Amendment was questioned in the Minerva Mill case. On May 9, 1980 the Supreme Court applied the ruling in Kesavananda Bharti case and held unanimously that Section 55 of the Forty-second Amendment was void. It also held by a majority of 4[36] to 1 that Section 4 of the Act amending Article 31C which exempts from challenge any law which enforces any of the Directive Principles on the ground that it violates Article 14 or Article 19 is also void because it "damages the basic essential features of the Constitution and destroys its basic structure." Justice Bhagwati in his dissenting judgment held that the amended Article 31C, "far from being damages the basic structure of the Constitution strengthens and reinforces it by giving fundamental importance to the rights of the members of the community as against the rights of a few individuals and furthering the objective of the Constitution to build an egalitarian social order where there will be social and economic justice for all, everyone including the low visibility of humanity in the country will be able to exercise Fundamental Rights and the dignity of the individual and the worth of the human person which are cherished values will not remain merely the exclusive privileges of a few but become a living reality for the man." But the majority opinion claimed that "the principle enunciated in Part IV are not the proclaimed monopoly of democracies alone. They are common to all polities, democratic or authoritarian. Every State is goal-oriented and claims to strive for securing the welfare of the people. The distinction between the different forms of Government consists in that in a real democracy the government will endeavour to achieve the objective through the discipline of fundamental freedoms like those conferred by Articles 14 and 19. Those are the most elementary freedoms without which a free democracy is impossible and which must, therefore, be preserved at all cost."

The Minerva Mill case establishes the supremacy of the Fundamental Rights and every legislation or constitutional amendment made in furtherance of the Directive Principles is subjected to the scrutiny of the courts to determine whether it is violative of the Fundamental Rights, particularly Articles 14 and 19. The Congress (I) Government, however, does not believe in the theory of basic structure and does not accept the proposition that there are constraints on the constituent power of Parliament. The Law Minister, Shiv Shankar, said at a meeting of the Consultative Committee of Parliament attached to his Ministry, "while it is certainly not the intention of the Government to effect changes like those which would do away with the secular and democratic character of the Constitution, it does not accept the proposition that there are restraints on the constituent power of amending the Constitution. This suggestion should expressly be curtailed by a constitutional amendment is not acceptable to the Government. This apart from the question whether any such amendment would, in fact, bind future Government."

No less a person than Justice Frankfurter of the United States, whom Rau had consulted, was of the view that the Directive Principles should prevail in case of a conflict with the Fundamental Rights and this should be secured by an express provision in the Constitution. Rau accordingly, suggested to Drafting Committee, but his suggestion did not receive a favouravle response than and "wisely", as A.G. Noorani remarks, the Constitution-framers made Fundamental Rights "justiciable in explicit terms and directive principles non justiciable as explicitly. A chastened B.N. Rau himself came to regard the directives rather like the Instrument of Instructions issued to Governors.

But perusal of debates on the Directive Principles in the Constituent Assembly reveals a few important facts. Firstly, the Directive Principles had been made unenforceable not to render them ineffective or that they should remain like a cheque on a bank payable at the convenience of the bank, as Prof. K.T. Shah believed them to be if not made justiciable within a specified time limit. The intention was, as Ambedkar explained to the Constituent Assembly, that "in future both the legislature and the executive" should not merely pay lip-service to these principles but they should be made "the basis of all legislative and executive function that they may be taking hereafter in the matter of the governance of the country." It was not an attempt, he added, to incorporate in Chapter IV, the positive mandates to the State and prescribe the manner in which those mandates were to be realized. The Directive Principles were intended to impart continuity to the national policies and their flexibility made it possible for the parties of the Right and the Left to strive in their own way to reach the ideals of social and economic democracy whenever they would get an opportunity to form the Government after having received the verdict of the people at the polls, he emphasized.

Secondly, positive emphasis had been laid on the fundamental nature of the Directives so that an express duty may rest on the State to adequately discharge its constitutionel-makers to establish a State which should be a democracy not only in the political area where legislative authority is based on adult franchise and the executive is parliamentary, but also to promote a Welfare State, where social and economic democracy must also prevail. The Directive Principle establishes the conditions necessary for its achievement. Article 36 lays down that the State "shall strive to promote the welfare of the people." Ambedkar explained that the word strive had been purposely used "because their intention was that however adverse the circumstances that stand in the way of Government in giving effect to these principles and however impropitious the time might be they should always strive for the fulfillment of the Principles. Otherwise it would be open to the Government to say that circumstances were not good and the finances were so bad that they could not implement them."[41]

The Constitution-makers, therefore, vested in the people of India the power and the means to compel the Government of the day to implement the Directive Principles or even at a time when it is not financially and administratively possible for it to do. The Constitution establishes a parliamentary system of government. The mechanism of such a system enables the citizens to watch, and scrutinize the acts of the Government and assess the impact of its performance on the body politic of the country and on the well being of common man. At the time of the General Election people measure Government's success or failure in the light of the achievements and the fulfillment of the goals prescribed by the Constitution. To ignore the Directive Principles is to ignore the substance provided in the Constitution, hopes held out to the nation and the very ideals on which the Constitution is built. If the Government irrespective of its party label, pursues a policy which is in accordance with the Principles enunciated in the Constitution and caters to their sense of justice, the electorate will endorse its policy and allow it to continue in office. Otherwise, they will repose their confidence in another party. Parliamentary system accepts alteration in Government and the vigilant public opinion is the sanction behind it. It is for this reason that the Constitution-makers deliberately introduced in the language they have used in the Directive Principles something which is not fixed or rigid. They have left enough room for the people of the different ways of thinking to go to the electorate and persuade them that their policy and programme are the best way of reaching economic democracy; the fullest opportunity for all people to act in the way they want to act.

Finally, the Directive Principles of State Policy, according to the framers of the Constitution, are like the instrument of instructions flowing from the sovereign people to the State directing them to do certain things. These directions are as much binding on the Legislatures and on the Executive as they are on the Judiciary. All these wings of the Government are its components part and they collectively express the will of the State. It is, therefore, the duty of the Judiciary to safeguard the Directive Principles, from the vicissitudes of fortunes of the political parties that come in and go out of office from time to time. As the Directive Principles are intended to impart continue to the national policies, as they represent the deliberate wisdom of the nation through the Constituent Assembly, it is for the Courts to see that this continuity does not become the plaything of party politics and, consequently, retard the progress of their fulfillment. Moreover, many of the Fundamental Rights are subjects to reasonable restrictions in the interests of public. In interpreting these rights, which are justiciable, the Constitution-makers had imposed on the courts a duty to lay down the canons for determining what is "reasonable" and a "public interest" and while doing so due emphasis must be placed on the Directive Principles as the Constitution holds them fundamental in the governance of the country. This path was set in Kameshwar Singh and Bijoy Cotton Mills cases. In both these cases the Supreme Court laid down two rules of construction: (i) that in case of conflict between the right of the individual and laws aiming to implement socio-economic policies in pursuance of the Directive Principles greater weight should be given to the latter; and (ii) that every socio-economic legislation enacted in pursuance of the Directive Principles should be construed as one purporting to "public interest" or as a "reasonable restriction" on the Fundamental Rights. Justice Mudholkar applied the same approach in Sajjan Singh case when he enunciated the doctrine of "dynamism" and the theory of "elastic" Fundamental Rights, as enunciated by Chief Justice K. Subba Rao in the Golak Nath case, implies the same principle or rule of construction. All of them are not only in consonance with the provisions of Article 37 of the Chapter on the Directive Principles of State Policy but in complete conformity with the intentions of the Constitution-makers as well which find their echo in the Preamble to the Constitution.

What Directives have wrought: -

The significance of the Directive Principles was appreciably realized by almost all the members of the Constituent Assembly. They firmly believed that certain social values, especially those related to economic rights, embodied in Part III of the Constitution, were meaningless to large sections of the people if poverty with all its attendant evils of economic and social distress, was to haunt them at every step and account for their inexplicable sufferings. Their primary concern was to usher in a new social order in which justice, social, economic and political, shall inform all institutions of the national life. For the fulfillment of this objective the State has been charged to make effective provision for securing the right to work, to education and to public assistance in case of unemployment, old age, sickness and disablement, and in other cases of undeserved want. These are the minimum requirements of civilized existence and it is the foremost duty of every State, whatever be its label, to ensure that all individuals. The pith of the Directive Principles had a deep impact on a democratic set-up. If democracy is to survive, it must establish and nurture a society resting on social justice. This is the only peaceful and evolutionary method otherwise the answer is revolution. The Constitution-makers adopted the former by playing the role of a constitutional reformer and "attired the aspirations of the people with a constitutional role." The result was the establishment of the socio-economic justice in the Preamble of the Constitution which is to be implemented by the State to achieve the goal.

But the Directive Principles have been skeptically received by some eminent authorities. K. C. Wheare has doubted 'whether there is any gain, on balance, from introducing these paragraphs of generalities into a constitution.'

He is of the view that a Constitution should include only those provisions which can be capable of enforcement and are obligatory on the State. Ivor Jennings has been unduly severer in his criticism. He said, "the ghosts of Sidney and Beatrice Webb stalk through the pages of the text. Part IV of the Constitution expresses Fabian Socialism without the Socialism, for only the 'nationalization of the means of production, distribution and exchange' is missing; but nationalization for the Fabians was a means to an end and not an end itself; the end is quite adequately expressed in the Constitution." Jennings also questioned the reasonable of inserting in a Constitution a collection of political principles which "obviously derive from English experience in the nineteenth century and are deemed to be suitable for India in the middle of the twentieth century." He added that the ideas expressed in Part IV would survive for a generation and some of them may even survive for a longer period. "The question whether they are suitable for the twentieth century. When the Constitution may still be in operation, cannot be answered, but it is quite probable that they will be entirely outmoded."

It cannot, however, be overlooked that the policy of the Government from the beginning of India's republican career has been shaped according to the Directive Principles and every decision of the Planning Commission has been guided or coloured by these Principles. This is more then evident in the social, labour and economic legislation undertaken by the Government and its industrial, agricultural and taxation policies. The taxation Enquiry Commission 1953-54 was asked to examine the tax structure and to suggest measured to reduce the inequalities of income and wealth, analyze their effects on development of productive enterprises and on the inflationary process. The Industrial (Development and Regulation Act) 1954, and the establishment of the Monopolies Inquiry Commission in 1965 were aimed to achieve the objective outlined by the Taxation Inquiry Commission in terms of its reference. The Monopolies Commission made probing inquiries into the causes and extent of concentration of economic power in private hands, the factors responsible for monopolistic tendencies in the national economy and their social consequences. It recommended the Constitution of a permanent body with the duty and responsibility of exercising vigilance, and for taking action to protect the country against dangers of concentrated economic power, consumer, co-operatives etc,'' and recommended that appropriate legislation should be enacted accordingly. The Government acted promptly in accepting and implementing the suggestion of the Monopolies Commission. This is not a complete picture, but it is suggestive of the various steps taken at the Union level in realizing the content of the Directive Principles.

At the State level, legislation to abolish intermediaries and zamindari systems and land reforms was enacted in the early years of 1950 and, today, land, both urban and rural, is subject to ceilings and the surplus land as a result thereof has gone to the weaker sections of the community. In pursuance of the Directive Principles to organize village panchayats and to promote cottage industries in order to ensure decentralized and composite democracy in the form of self-governing village communities, requisite legislation were passed and adequate funds provided. While initiating the debate in Parliament on the economic policy of India, C.D. deshmukh, the then Finance Minister, declared that whereas the development of major industries must continue in national interest, it was necessary to develop small-scale and village industries "with great opportunities for employment and more and more chances of improving the resources of the population.'' Prime Minister Nehru, intervening in the debate, reaffirmed the policy of his Government or bringing about a casteless and stateless society through the peaceful and cooperative method. He asserted that the biggest private sector in the country was "the private sector of the peasant with his small holdings.''

The principle of international peace and security enshrined in Article 51 finds its full expression in the external policy of India. Jawaharlal Nehru's doctrine of dynamic neutrality, India's deep faith in co-existence, her advocacy of Panch Sheel and acceptance of those lofty ideals of peace and mutual tolerance by the major countries of the world is the greatest contribution which Independent India can claim. India has, indeed, saved the world from disaster. Michael Foot wrote, in 1955, "power corrupts and the world owes Independent India an immense debt for helping to save us from the corruption of power on an international scale, which might so easily have led us to disaster."[47] The five Principles[48] (1) mutual respect for each other's territorial integrity and sovereignty; (2) non-aggression; (3) non-interference in each other's internal affairs for any reason, either of an economic, political or ideological character; (4) equality and mutual benefit; and (5) peaceful co-existence-contained in the Panch Sheel-helped to outlaw from the minds of the Heads of the great States the possibility of war, little, of course, knowing that one of the signagtories to the Panch Sheel would become an aggressor. Addressing the Constituent Assembly at mid-night on August 14, 1947, Rajendra Prasad said, "we have only one ambition and that is to make our contribution to the building of peace and freedom for all." India has striven to hold steadfast to this spirit, which inspires the last of the Directives, though herself a victim of four wars. Her recent normalization of diplomatic and trade relations with these neighboring countries reiterates India's dedication to international peace and security.

Classification of the Directive Principles

The first two Articles (36 and 37) of the Chapter on Directive Principles of State Policy are general in character and deal with definitions, legal effects and objectives. The remaining Articles may, for purpose of clarity, be grouped into three distinct categories: (i) those that aim to shape India into a Welfare State; (ii) those that aim to shape India into a Gandhian State; and (iii) those that aim to promote international peace.

Article 38(1) provides that the State shall promote the welfare of the people by securing and protecting as effectively as it may a social order in which justice, social, economic and political, shall inform all the institutions of the national life. Clause (2), inserted by the Forty-fourth Amendment, provides that the State shall, in particular, strive to minimize the inequalities in income, and endeavour to eliminate inequalities in status, facilities and opportunities, not only amongst individuals but also amongst groups of people residing in different areas or engaged in different vocations. Thus, promotion of the welfare of people, both residing in urban and rural areas and engaged in different vocations, is the objective, which the Constitution sets forth, by striving to secure a social order where justice, social, economic and political, shall prevail. Welfare and justice are, accordingly, the twin objective of the Constitution. Article 39, then, proceeds to particularize some of the methods by which the object of general welfare, through justice, can be obtained and the basis of the new social order established. This Article finds adequate support from the provisions of subsequent Articles for bringing about a casteless and classless society. With this end in view the State shall direct its policy in securing: -

(I) a. Adequate means of livelihood for all citizens, men and women equally;

b. Distribution of wealth so as to sub serve the common good;

c. The operation of the economic system which does not result in the concentration of wealth and means of production of the common detriment;

d. Equal pay for equal work for both men and women;

e. Protection of adult and child labour;

f. The Forty-second Amendment altered the original clause in Article 39, which read "protection of child and youth against exploitation and against moral and material abandonment," to emphasize the constructive role of the State with regard to children. It now provides that "children are given opportunities and facilities to develop in a healthy manner and in conditions of freedom and dignity and that childhood and youth are protected against exploitation and against moral and material abandonment."

g. Provision of work and education for all people, relief in case of unemployment, old age, sickness and disablement and in other cases of undeserved want;
h. Just and humane conditions of work and maternity relief;
i. A living wage and decent conditions of work for all workers, agricultural, industrial or otherwise as to ensure to them sufficient leisure and enjoyment of social and cultural opportunities;
j. To secure the participation of workers in the management of undertakings or other organization engaged in any industry. (This provision was inserted by the Forty-second Amendment as Article 43A);
k. Free and compulsory education for all children until they reach the age of fourteen years;
l. Raising the level of nutrition and the standards of living and the improvement of public health;
m. To secure that the operation of the legal system promotes justice, on a basis of equal opportunities, and, in particular, to provide legal aid, by suitable legislation or scheme or in any other way, to ensure that opportunities for securing justice are not denied to any citizen by reason of economic or other disabilities. (This provision was inserted by the Forty-second Amendment as a new Article 39A); and
n. To endeavour to secure for the citizens a uniform civil code throughout the country

(II) Some of the Directive Principles are in accordance with and conform to the Gandhian way of life and fulfill the requirements of Gandhi's conception of the State. These Directive Principles enjoin that:

a. A State shall take steps to organize village panchayats and endow them with such power and authority as may be necessary to enable them to function as units of self-government;
b. The State shall endeavour to promote cottage industries on an individual or cooperative basis in rural areas;

   Both these provisions aim at Sarvodaya or pure socialism as Prof. S.N. Agarwal called it. Sarvodaya is the Gandhian technique of decentralized economy and composite democracy in the form of self-development and self-governing village communities of panchayats.
c. To promote with special care the educational and economic

interests of the weaker sections of the people, and, in particular, of Scheduled Castes and the Scheduled Tribes in order to protect them from social injustice and all forms of exploitation;

d. To bring about prohibition of the consumption, except for medicinal purposes, of intoxicating drinks and of drugs which are injurious to health;

e. To take steps to organize agriculture and animal husbandry or modern and scientific lines and, in particular take steps for preserving and improving the breeds, and prohibiting the slaughter of cows and claves and other mulch and draught cattle;

f. To protect and improve the environment and safeguard the forests and wild life of the country (This provision has been inserted by the Forty-second Amendment as Article 48-A);

g. To protect, preserve and maintain places of national and historical importance; and

h. To take steps to separate the judiciary from the executive; and to secure for citizens a uniform civil code throughout the country.

(III) In the international field India shall strive:

a. To promote international peace and security;

b. To maintain just and honourable relations between nations;

c. To foster respect for international law and treaty obligations; and

d. To encourage settlement of international disputes by arbitration.

Fundamental Duties

Need for inclusion in the Constitution

Incorporation of a charter of Fundamental Duties in the Constitution is one of the important features of the Constitution (Forty-second Amendment) Act, 1976. The Swaran Singh Committee on constitutional reforms, appointed by the Congress President, was asked in a resolution of the All-India Congress Committee, passed at its meeting in New Delhi on May 29, 1976, to formulate proposals to fill what was widely considered a historical Lacuna to India's charter of rights. Within the Congress the sentiment was fairly strong that the Constitution-makers went, in the first flush of Independence, to great lengths to articulate the citizen's fundamental rights in the Constitution but overlooked the need to prescribe the corresponding fundamental duties and obligations. The political crisis that strained the Indian democratic system in the late sixties and more recently in 1974 and 1975 was one of the compelling reasons to necessitate the inclusion of what the Constitution-makers had in their wisdom omitted, although there was some suggestion at the time when the Constitution was drafted that this important aspect should not be ignored.

Nor in the issue of enumerating the citizen's fundamental duties to society and State in a Constitution totally without a precedent. Nearly fifty countries, as Vinod Sethi enumerated, have incorporated duties in their Constitutions, and Japan is one of them whose basic document was consulted by the makers of the Indian Constitution. The Japanese Constitution spells out explicitly some of the citizens countervailing duties in the same breath as his Fundamental Rights. "Rights and Duties of the people" are enshrined in Chapter III of the Constitution.

The Swaran Singh Committee proposed an 8-point code of 'fundamental duties', which, after due process of public consultation, were proposed to be enshrined in the Constitution. The proposed duties were:

(1) To respect and abide by the Constitution and the laws.
(2) To uphold the sovereignty of the Nation and to function in such a way as to sustain and strengthen its unity and integrity.
(3) To respect the democratic institutions enshrined in the Constitution, and not to do anything which may impair their dignity or authority.
(4) To defend the country and to render national service including military service when called upon to do so.
(5) To abjure communalism in any form.
(6) To render assistance and co-operation to the State in the implementation of the Directive Principles of State Policy, and to promote the common good of the people so as to sub serve the interests of social and economic justice.
(7) To abjure violence; to protect and safe-guard public property and not to do anything which may cause damage and destruction to such property.
(8) To pay taxes according to law.

Duties Analyzed

The Constitution (Forty-second Amendment) Act, 1976, inserted a new Chapter Part IV-A and listed in Article 51-A the following ten duties: -

(a) To abide by the Constitution and respect its deals and institutions, the National Flag and the National Anthem;
(b) To cherish and follow the noble ideals which inspired our national struggle for freedom;
(c) To uphold and protect the sovereignty, unity and integrity of India;
(d) To defend the country and render national service when called upon to do so;
(e) To promote harmony and the spirit of common brotherhood amongst all the people of India transcending religious, linguistic and regional or sectional diversities, to renounce practices derogatory to the dignity of women;
(f) To value and preserve the rich heritage of our composite culture;
(g) To protect and improve the natural environment including forests, lakes, rivers and wild life, and to have compassion for living creatures;
(h) To develop, the scientific temper, humanism and the spirit of inquiry and reform;
(i) To safeguard public property and to abjure violence; and
(j) To strive towards excellence in all spheres of individual and collective activity so that the nation constantly rises to higher levels of edeavour and achievement."

The Fundamental Duties inscribed in the Constitution are mixed bag of expectations and exhortations. Quite a good number of these items are those, which are enforceable today even without their being specifically incorporated in the Constitution. In this category fall the items to abide the Constitution, respect the National Flag and the National Anthem, to defend the country and render national service when called upon to do so and safeguard public property. To uphold and protect the sovereignty, unity and integrity of India draws which the Constitution's Sixteenth or anti-secessionist amendment itself stems.

The three most important items in the list of fundamental Duties are those requiring the citizens to respect the ideals of the Constitution and the institutions it establishes, to promote harmony and the spirit of common brotherhood amongst all the people of India professing different religions, speaking different languages, practicing different customs and inhabiting different parts of the country, and to safeguard the public property and to abjure violence. These are clearly intended to meet certain specific political threats that democracy in India has to contend with.

The Indian charter of Fundamental Duties is unique to include the duty to develop the scientific temper, humanism and the spirit of inquiry and reform. It has been incorporated to eradicate superstitions in which India is deeply soaked and to remove the bane of religious fanaticism, regional chauvinism and linguistic frenzy, which have ever plagued India and retarded her unification into a cohesive society. The duty to renounce practices derogatory to the dignity of women and to preserve the rich heritage of India's composite culture are two other moral codes to ennoble the society. These are, in fact, homilies to be taught in schools and colleges, rather than to be incorporated in the Constitution as Fundamental Duties. In all it may be concluded that fundamental rights directive principles & fundamental duties are integrated and complimentary to each other. These are branches of broad spectrum of preamble for the Indianization of rights & duties under constitution and also means to achieve the objectives of preamble. Such kinds of right and duties and directives are found in other nations of world either directly or indirectly but it is not sure that these are whether found for complete enforcement or observance or not. We Indian are fortunate enough that literally we have all such rights, duties and directives for observance as well as for enforcement also.We have attempted to Indianize the fundamental rights, Directive Principle & fundamental duties. The attempt is still not complete. We have still to do a lot. The real Indianization is possible only when the dream of Ram Rajya as contempleted by great saint Mahatma Gandhi is fulfilled the real dream of Mahatma Gandhi was that there shall be no diseriminations in society. Every one shall be happy. There shall be no poverty.

There shall be equality in all respect in society and easily society is free from all kinds of problems & vicas. Let us further try to achieve these aims by the complete Indianization of fundamental rights, Directive principle & duties for the proper implementation of great Indian of preamble.

Notes

1 S.C. (1960) 3 S.C.R. 250, 281.

2 Hidayaullah, M, democracy in India and the judicial process, p-61

3 Report of the Indian Statutory (Simon) Commission, Vol.II, para 36.

4 To Sections 275 and 297 to 300 of the Government of India Act, 1935.

5 Constitutional Problems of the Sapru Committee (1945), pp.256-57.

6 Constituent Assembly Debates, Vol. III, p.110. Statutory corporations carrying on business of public importance are authorities within the meaning of Article 12 and their employees can claim protection of Articles 16 and 14 against the corporations. The Supreme Court in Som Rekhi v. Bharat Petroleum affirmed, (1980), that a writ can be issued against a Government company. Mr. Justice V.R. Krishna Iyer declared that Bharat Petroleum was an "alter ego" of the Central Government and a "double of Bharat Sarkar."

7 Liversidge v. Anderson (1942).

8 Constituent Assembly Debates,.

9 Lakhinarayan v. Prov. Of Bihar (1949). Also refer to Gopalan v. State of Madras.

10 Golak Nath and Others v. State of Punjab, A.I.R., 1967, Supreme Court 1943.

11 Shankar Prasad Singh Deo and other v. Union of India and Others, A.I.R., 1951, Supreme Court 458; and Sajjan Singh v. The State of Rajasthan, A.I.R.,1965, Supreme Court 845.

12 Address to the Students' Representative Council of the University Law College, Nagpur, September23, 1967. The Hindustan Times, New Delhi, September 26, K. Subba Rao reiterated the stand taken by him in Golak Nath case.

13 Feroze Memorial Lecture, New Delhi, September 12, 1967. The Hindustan Times, New Delhi, September 14, 1967

14 Article 300A inserted by the Constitution (Forty-fourth Amendment) Act, 1978, S.34

15 Caldeo vs. Bull

16 A.K. Gopalan v. State of Madras

17 Vide resolution of the Constituent Assembly of January 24, 1947.

18 B. Shiva Rao (Ed.), The Framing of India's Constitution, Select Documents, Vol. II, 2(ii), p. 49.

19 Chintaman Rao v. The State of Madhya Pradesh, A.I.R. 1954 S.C., 118.

20 N.B. Khare v. State of Delhi, 1980

21 A.K. Gopalan v. State of U.P., A.I.R., 1954

22 Saghir Ahmed v. Sate of U.P., A.I.R., 1954 S.C. 224; Ramchandra Palai v. State of Orissa, A.I.R. 1956 S.C. 298.

23 Cammr.Narendra v. Union of India, A.I.R. 1960 2S.C. 375.

24 Cooreji v. Escise Commissioner, A.I.R. 1954 S.C. 220.

25 P.T. Society v. R.T.A., A.I.R. 1960 S.C. 801.

26 AIR 1950 S.C., p. 114.

27 Ram Singh v. State of Delhi, (1951) S.C.R., 451.

28 A.I.R. 1950 S.C. 319.

29 A.I.R. 1953 S.C. 318.

30 Constituent Assembly Debates, Vol. VII, pp, 809-10.

31 State of Bihar v. Kameshwar Singh, A.I.R. 1952, 252.

32 A.I.R. 1958 Cal. 365.

33 A.I.R. 1954 Pat. 359.

34 A.I.R. 1958, S.C. 956.

35 A.I.R. 1974, S.C. 1389

36 A.N. Gopalan v. State of Madras (1950) S.C.J. (1950) S.C.R. 88, p. 198.
37 State of Madras v. Champakam Darairajan (1951) S.C.J. 313 (1951) S.C.R. 825.
38 M.S.M. Sharma v. Shri Krishna Sinha (1959) S.C.J. 925(1959) I.S.C.R. (Supp.) 806.
39 Ujjam Bai v. State of U.P. (1963) I.S.C.R. 778; A.I.R. 1963 S.C. 1621. (1967) 2 S.C.J. 486 pp. 498-99
40 Golak Nath and others v. State of Punjab.
41 Refer to Shetty, K.P. Krishna Fundamental Rights and Socio-Economic Justice in India, p. 19.
42 A.K. Gopalan v. State of Madras.
43 Rajendra Prasad Endowment Lectures, The Spirit of the Constitution (Bharatiya Vidya Mandir, 1967) p. 31.
44 A.I.R. 1951 S.C. 226.
45 A.I.R. 1952 S.C. 52.
46 (1955) I.S.C.R. 752.
47 S.C.R. 629 (1959) 629.
48 A.I.R. 1958 S.C. 956.
49 A.I.R. 1965 S.C. 845.
50 Shetty, B.P. Krishna, Fundamental Rights and Socio-Economic Justice in the Indian Constitution, p. 103.
51 Golak Nath v. State of Punjab (1967) 2 S.C.J. 486.

INDEX